W9-BWB-521

GIRL MANS UP

GIRL MANS UP

M-E GIRARD

HARPER TEEN
An Imprint of HarperCollins Publishers

HarperTeen
is an imprint of HarperCollins Publishers.

Girl Mans Up
Copyright © 2016 by M-E Girard
All rights reserved. Printed in the United States of America.
No part of this book may be used or reproduced in any manner
whatsoever without written permission except in the case of
brief quotations embodied in critical articles and reviews.
For information address HarperCollins Children's Books,
a division of HarperCollins Publishers,
195 Broadway, New York, NY 10007.
www.epicreads.com

ISBN 978-0-06-240417-6

17 18 19 20   PC/RRDH   10 9 8 7 6 5 4 3
❖
First Edition

FOR MELISSA, MY REAL-LIFE PEN.

ONE

THERE ARE FOUR OF US DUDES SITTING HERE right now, and I kick all of their butts when it comes to video games—and I'm not even a dude in the first place. Maybe I'm being a little cocky here, but it's true. My brother says I'm a little psycho, loading my gun and rushing for the middle of the battle, and yeah, sometimes I end up getting my butt kicked. But usually he's there, covering me with his sniper skills, so we both come out on top.

"She's cheating," Garrett says to no one in particular.

"Oh sure, I'm cheating," I tell him, keeping my eyes on Colby's forty-six-inch TV screen. "Obviously I must be cheating."

"You put in the codes, or you're using the glitch, but that's still cheating," he says, then to Colby, "Am I right?"

"Yeah, you're right," Colby says from somewhere behind me, probably sprawled on his bed. "Except, she's not cheating."

"She legit plays that game all weekend with her brother," Tristan says.

"And dude," I tell Garrett, who's somewhere on the floor to my left, "they released the update for that glitch last month. You can't bust open the factory door anymore."

"All right, fine. So you were taught well," Garrett says.

"I taught myself well."

Garrett laughs and I roll my eyes at the TV. He's such a douche, but he can't even try to knock me down in the video games department. I'm on the couch at the foot of Colby's bed, Tristan next to me. When I first got here, I thought it was just going to be Colby, Tristan, and me hanging out. But Garrett's sweaty butt was parked in front of the TV trying to complete this ambush mission in *War Zone 3*, and he was ready to whip the controller at the TV because he stupidly put it on the highest difficulty. So he dared me to do better, and I did. Twenty minutes later, I'm still playing and they're all watching me.

"You watched me take over for you," I tell Garrett. "Did you see me enter any codes? No."

"Penelope, I wasn't watching you the whole time. I was distracted by the Doritos, and we all know girls are pretty shady."

Colby lets out a chuckle, which almost pisses me off, but Garrett's always saying stupid things about Tristan and me to make Colby laugh. Like last month, when he was going off about how I should've picked the girl character in *Slashko*, when meanwhile it's not even a question that none of them would ever pick her—even for her better default weapons. I pick the guy characters because they never make girl characters that look like me. They make them hot, half-naked, and full of makeup—which is nice to look at, but it's not me.

"All right now, calm down, Penelope. Is this your time of the month? Because I don't—"

2

"Suck it, Garrett," Colby tells him before I can throw something back myself. "Period jokes? That's lame."

"All right, all right," Garrett says. There's silence for maybe twenty seconds and then Garrett's at it again. "So, Colby. Would you say that Penelope is better than you at this game?"

"Well, she's definitely better than *you*," Colby says, and I grin like, *In your face, Garrett.* I hear Colby roll off his bed. "This is boring. Let's go out."

He walks right over to the console and shuts it off on me, but I don't say anything because we all know when Colby's done, we're all done.

"What about the mall?" Tristan says. "I still have a gift card from my birthday. The new Masters of Crimson book just came out."

"A book? Seriously?" Garrett turns to Colby. "This guy with his stupid skinny jeans and his books, and that one over there who's sort of a girl, I don't know, I can't tell anymore. Colby, man, it's the first day of grade eleven tomorrow—we should be starting fresh, am I right?"

"Dude, I've known these guys longer than I've known you, so you can suck it," Colby says, stepping into his sneakers. Tristan and I glance at each other, probably both thinking about how much better it was last year, before Garrett moved to Castlehill. Colby checks himself out in the mirror and re-gels his blond hair before throwing on his leather jacket. "Are we going, or not?"

The guys get up and head for their shoes, while I take the controller to the shelf the console's sitting on. When Tristan and Garrett step out into the backyard, I glance at Colby. "I hate that guy."

"He's all right," Colby says. "You just have to man up a little."

"He's a douche."

"He gets us good weed. Plus, he fights."

I say nothing to that because he's got me there. Tristan can't punch, and I'm a girl so even if I knew how to punch, no one would take me on anyway. It's not like I'm some tiny little thing either. I weigh more than these guys do, and I'm built solid like my brother. When we were younger, it was different. It's not like fighting is fun, but at least back then—usually when older jerks would mess with Tristan—I could get in there and break things up, or push someone back. Now no one wants to be the guy who fought with a girl, because only pussies fight with girls. Even with girls like me.

The three of us—Colby, Tristan, and me—can get into some pretty stupid stuff, but it's nothing like what Garrett likes to do for fun. All the dumb stuff we've been up to these days is because of him, so most of the time I tell Colby my mom won't let me go out without even asking her so I won't have to be part of it. They throw eggs at houses, they shoplift, and they sell parsley to grade-nine kids who are too dumb to realize it's fake, then they buy real weed for us with the money. That last part's kind of funny, but still.

"Pen, you coming?" Colby asks.

"Nah," I say. "I'm gonna go home. I'll see you tomorrow on the bus."

"Get over it, dude," Colby says. "Let's just go."

"It's cool, I got a couple of YouTube videos to catch up on. You guys go and—"

"Stop trying to bail. I need you to get something for me," he says, hitching his chin with a serious glare.

I know what that means. It means I get to talk to a pretty girl today.

AT THE MALL, WE walk by all the girly clothing and jewelry stores until Colby starts throwing glances inside one store in particular. Everyone else is getting bored with the aimless wandering.

"I need a smoke," Garrett says.

"You guys go," Colby says. "Me and Pen have something to do."

"What," Garrett says, "kiss?"

It's like he can't go five minutes without saying something stupid.

"You wanna try saying that again?" Colby says, stepping right up to him, and even though Colby's not as tall, Garrett backs off, reaching for his cigarettes and shrugging like nothing's a big deal. Garrett has the face of a UFC fighter, like a big cauliflower. Colby's the good-looking one with the screw-off attitude, which means all the guys know him and all the girls want him, so he gets to call the shots. It's probably also why he gets to be friends with a skinny-jeans-wearing, space-book-reading kid like Tristan, and a boyish, video-game-playing girl like me—and no one tries to mess with him for it.

"You coming, geek?" Garrett says to Tristan.

"Nah. I gotta check out the bookstore," he says, because he's like me and won't hang out with Garrett unless Colby's there, too. He nods at me before wandering off by himself.

"You guys suck! Why am I wasting my time here?" Garrett slips a cigarette between his lips. "I'm gonna go meet up with Ike and them at the skate shop. Colby, text me when you're done, all right?"

"All right, dude," Colby says, while Garrett takes off. Then to me, "Time to work your magic. Redhead, green shirt, big tits. Right over there."

"Come on—I don't wanna go in there," I say. The whole store is pink and sparkly. It's all dangly earrings, flashy pieces of fabric, and hair thingies.

"You can get away with stepping foot in there more than I can," he says. "Go buy something for your hair."

"Like what? A rubber band?" I point to my same old ponytail stuffed in the hole of my baseball cap. "Why don't I just wait until she comes out?"

"You feel like hanging out here for the next hour? Because I don't. Just go buy something for your mom," he says.

I head over, avoiding the looks the girl at the counter throws me. I'm wearing a black T-shirt, faded jeans, and skater shoes. And sometimes I sort of look more like some Portuguese dude with long hair than some Portuguese girl. I so don't belong in here. But I've got a job to do.

I plant myself on the other side of the scarf stand where the girl is standing. She looks pretty focused, picking through whatever's on the shelf in front of her. The first thing I pluck out is this round, pink piece of fabric that's kind of see-through and stuck together with a big plastic buttony thing. There's a clearance sticker on it.

"Uh, excuse me," I say, and the girl looks over. "Can you tell me what the hell this is?"

She gives me an awkward smile. "It's a summer scarf . . . ?"

"Why would anyone wear a scarf in the summer? It's hot."

"Because they're nice."

"Oh. Well, it's September right now—does that matter?"

"Um . . . not really, I guess. But it doesn't really go with, um, that," she says, pointing to my upper body.

This girl so has no idea how to talk to me. I'm used to people staring at me, trying to figure out what my deal is. Ever since I started swiping clothes from my brother Johnny's closet, people have been reacting differently to me. I used to wear jeans and plain T-shirts and I've always hung around guys, so people just figured I was a tomboy, but now it's like it goes beyond that, and I'm sure it's not just because Johnny's clothes are name brand and sweet as hell. I don't really know what people think I am, or what they think I'm not.

I hate dragging this out when the girl wants me to go away, but I try again. "So, what school do you go to?"

"Why?"

"Just curious."

Now I bet she thinks I'm hitting on her, and even though I sort of thought she was good-looking before, the looks she keeps giving me make me rethink my opinion of her.

Colby pokes his head inside, acting all annoyed. "You done?" Then he pretends to notice the girl for the first time, flashing his pale-blue gaze at her and nodding. "What's up?"

"Hey," she says.

He walks off, pretending to wait for me right out front, where this girl can have an unobstructed view of him through the wall of glass we're standing near. I'm not into dudes but even I can understand why girls can't help themselves. He kind of looks like that blond guy from that show where the two brothers hunt monsters and drive around in that sweet-looking old car.

"Who's that?" she asks.

"My buddy Colby," I say.

"Oh." Then she's flashing me a much friendlier face. "So what school do you guys go to?"

"St. Peter's."

"Cool. I go to Castlehill High."

"Oh yeah?" I pretend to look at the scarf thing again before stuffing it back where it was. "Well, do you, uh, want to come to the food court with us? We're just going for ice cream."

She takes another glance at Colby, and he looks over our way at the same time. He grins. Then she's doing it, too. The deal is done.

Colby sends me over to hook them in, because he says girls are less standoffish when I'm the one who breaks the ice because I'm a girl too, which means I'm probably nice, and I'm probably *not* best friends with a jerk just trying to get laid. Colby always says if we all want to be tight and have loyalty, we each have to be useful. Tristan does a lot of Colby's homework and group projects, Garrett gets weed and fights, and I'm the wingman when it comes to girls. I'm just supposed to point the girl in Colby's direction, and the rest takes care of itself. He's the one who wants the girl, except he makes it so that she's the one who chases after him. It's kind of genius, because then he can do whatever he wants and she basically asked for it.

I know the whole thing might seem sort of pathetic, but considering what Colby gives back in return, it's not a bad job at all to have. Besides, I get to talk to all kinds of good-looking girls, and I figure maybe someday, when I finally man up, one of these girls could end up liking me instead. Maybe.

TWO

I BET I'VE PICTURED MYSELF DATING EVERY GIRL at this school at some time or another. I've been at St. Peter's Catholic High for two years and three days: that's a lot of days of staring at the same girls. Lately, I've been stuck on this one. Blake has a boy's name, crazy blond hair, and a lot of black makeup. Last week, I heard her talking about signature melee weapons for *Rusted*, this new Xbox game coming out soon. Ever since then, I can't stop staring at her, at the back of her head, at that long hair, imagining what it would be like to have a girl

9

put on shiny lip stuff just for me. And the first words out of her mouth wouldn't be "Are you a girl or a boy?" or "You're friends with that guy Colby, right?"

Colby snaps his fingers in front of my face. My eyes blur on the back of Blake's head before I turn to the left, where Colby sits, drumming a pencil against his open binder. "What?"

"You checking out my next girl?" he says, pointing at Blake with his pencil.

"But . . . what about the one from the mall last night?"

"Cut her loose. Besides, Blake's looking damn good this year. Way better than that girl."

He just lifted his leg and pissed on Blake, even though there's never any true competition—I mean, Colby's *That Guy*, while I'm not even anything specific. This is usually how it goes. Up ahead, Blake is laughing while she's leaning to the side, twisting her friend Robyn's long red hair into some huge round thing that looks like an orange cinnamon bun tacked on to the back of her head.

"What about Robyn? She's looking pretty good," I say.

Colby makes a face. "Maybe you need glasses?"

I give a shrug, looking at the two of them talking. Robyn's okay-looking, but next to Blake—there's no comparing. I already knew that.

At least I'll get to talk to Blake . . . even if it's for him.

Mrs. Wexler holds a stack of papers and waits for stragglers to take their seats. Meanwhile, she talks about this school anniversary photography project thing and passes around forms to sign up. Colby and I laugh while we fill out a form with Tristan's name. Finally, he zooms into class, all uncoordinated, which is probably due to the stupidly long bangs that cover his eyes. We don't tell him about the form and hand it in when Mrs. Wexler makes the rounds again. He collapses into the seat ahead of Colby and me and turns our way. He makes a funny face.

"You guys are being weird. What'd you do?" Tristan asks.

"Nothing. Relax, dude. You're so paranoid," Colby says.

Tristan looks at me, but all I give him is a shrug. He sighs and goes, "What's going on this weekend?"

Colby's not paying attention anymore. I go over the options in my head: Colby's backyard, video games in Colby's room, standing outside the pizza place, going in and buying pizza, or hanging at the mall.

"Castlehill legit sucks," Tristan says. "Nothing cool ever happens here. We need to be living in Toronto."

"What do you know about Toronto?" Colby asks.

Tristan shrugs and looks at me.

"People get murdered a lot in Toronto," I say. "My mom watches the news and tells me about it."

Tristan says, "We need a car."

"I'm working on it," Colby says.

"Last time I asked my dad about taking the driving test, he said maybe when I'm twenty-eight," I say.

"That's bull. Why?" Tristan asks.

I shrug, but I know why. Johnny says it's a Portuguese thing, but I just think it's a stupid thing. Johnny can drive because he's a guy; I can't drive because I'm a girl. Just like Johnny's been allowed to bring girls home since he was fifteen, and me

11

having a date isn't even something that's a possibility at my house. It never even gets brought up. I'm lucky I'm allowed out after the sun goes down now.

"Settle down. *Veuillez tout ranger, gardant seulement un stylo à encre ou un crayon*," Mrs. Wexler shouts through the noise. "*Taisez-vous!*" The rumbling only gets louder and soon we all cough on purpose because it drives her nuts. She pulls off her glasses with a sigh and pinches the bridge of her nose. "Class, I'm three seconds away from giving everyone a zero on this quiz."

People quiet down—even though she deserves it for having a quiz on the first day.

"Hey, I'm gonna need you to hook that up." Colby hitches his chin toward Blake. "You need to work your magic. Still trying to figure out when she's working, and we're gonna go there. I'll let you know."

"How do you know where—"

"Penelope! Eyes at the front," Mrs. Wexler says, startling me into looking up. "*Les yeux*, you get what I'm saying?"

I don't mean to full-on glare at her, but it's *Pen* and she knows it. She's only been my teacher for three different classes in the last two years. Now everyone turns to look at me.

"Blake, Jackson, Kally, and Tristan," Mrs. Wexler says. Colby and I start laughing when Tristan's head pops up all confused. "I'm going to hand your applications to Mr. Middleton, but remember there's a meeting at lunch next Monday for those interested."

Tristan nods, then he turns to us. "What the shizz, guys? What is she talking about?"

"You're becoming a school photographer," Colby says.

"No way. Come on, guys."

Tristan and I have known each other since grade one, and we started hanging out because neither of us was cool enough to hang out with the cool guys, but we didn't want to hang around girls either. Colby came along, and things got a lot better for Tristan and me, but still, Tristan's sort of a goof so he's an easy target.

After Colby and I are done laughing at Tristan's face, I lean over my desk and smack Tristan's arm. "We're just messing around. Go tell Mrs. Wexler you changed your mind after class."

The quiz gets passed around, and it's three pages long so most of us can't help but grumble. Thirty minutes later, I've given up. As if I'm going to work my butt off learning French when I can barely learn enough Portuguese to make sense to anyone besides my parents.

LATER THAT MORNING, I'M sitting on a toilet seat and it's kind of warm, which means I'm sitting on someone else's butt imprint. That's what I'm thinking about when the door to the girls' bathroom slams open and my piss stream cuts off instantly. There's sniffling, a stall door next to me shutting, then more sniffling. A toilet paper dispenser thunders as it spins, which gives me enough noise cover to let the last of my pee escape. I flush, wash my hands, and head for the exit. Before I can open the door, there's all this retching and gagging.

"Uh, do you need a teacher?" I call.

Stuff splashes into water. Wow.

"Do you . . ." I take another step. "Do you need something?"

"No. I'm okay." Olivia comes out, looking all blotchy. She's a short and pretty Asian girl. I worked my magic on her this summer for Colby, and she went for it. But, like all the others, she didn't last long.

"Oh, I didn't realize it was you," I say. "You're sick?"

"My breakfast just wasn't sitting right." She heaves a breath while wiping her lower eyelids with a thumb.

"But you're crying . . ."

"I just cry when I get sick. It's not real."

"Oh." It looks real to me.

"Can you please keep this to yourself?" she says.

"Who would I tell? Colby?" The way she stares back, it makes me wonder. "Why would he care?"

They had their thing for maybe a week, and then he never talked about her again. She wasn't even his type.

"He wouldn't. I just . . . don't want people to know I barfed in the bathroom."

I throw her a look, but before I can ask anything else, she sweeps past me.

AT LUNCH, I WAIT for Colby by the side doors so we can go out for a smoke. He hands me one because I really only smoke when he's around. We head for the sidewalk where we won't get in trouble for being on school property.

"That Mr. Marsh is full of it. He goes off about the pope declaring himself prisoner of the Vatican," Colby says. "Like

14

how can the dude be a prisoner in his own house? Makes no sense. So I tell Marsh that, and he says I'm being a stubborn hooligan on purpose. I wish these teachers would just teach, instead of acting like know-it-all pricks."

"That's weird," I say. "So the pope was, like, on house arrest? Did he have handcuffs and—"

Just then Olivia steps out of the side doors, heading for a red sports car with tinted windows waiting at the curb. She glances up when Colby and I watch her. He has his tough face on, but that's the look he defaults to most of the time.

"Guess some dude's picking her up," I say.

"Nah. That's her mom's car."

"Oh." While the car pulls away, Colby stares at it. "She was sick earlier."

He turns to me. "How do you know she was sick?"

"I just saw her in the bathroom. She wasn't feeling well."

"You're talking to her?" he says, now totally focused on me. "What did she say to you?"

"I went to take a piss, then she came in and I heard her puke. So I asked if she was all right." When he pulls out his phone, I watch his face. "*Is* she all right?"

"How the hell should I know?" he says, putting the phone back. "Why do you even care? What did she say?"

"I thought you guys hadn't talked since the beginning of August."

"Answer the question, dude."

"Nothing. All she said was that her breakfast didn't sit right or something."

He smokes deep and gazes at the sidewalk. "Listen, it probably won't come to that, but let's say she starts talking shit about me—there's nothing I could do, because she's a girl . . . but you could, right?"

"Huh?"

"You could just tell her to leave me alone, watch her mouth."

He's never asked me to step in like that before. "What happened? I thought you cut her loose."

"I did. But she was different," he says. Different good, different bad—I can't tell. Not that it matters right now because he's working his jaw the way he does when things start getting to him. "If she's got a problem, then it's hers to deal with."

"What kind of problem?"

"I'm just asking you to have my back," he says. The slow nod I give him must not be enough. "That's your job, isn't it? Just like when Garrett and the others talk shit about you, I deal with it. I don't ask questions, I tell them to suck it. And those douches at the movies last spring—I took care of it. Even when they came back to my house and keyed my dad's car, me and Garrett went back there and dealt with it."

"You're right," I say. "I'll deal with it if it comes to that. All I was doing is asking what happened."

"The problem is I shouldn't even have to give you a reason," he says, with this tone like I should know better. "You should just trust me. That's loyalty."

"I know." He's right. He always sticks up for me without my having to ask him to. "I have your back, okay? It's not like I even know that girl. We only all hung out like, twice, and she barely spoke to me."

His shoulders relax as he sighs. "I'm just pissed off because I wish I never saw her at the mall that day. She wasn't worth it."

"It's all right, dude," I say.

He nods, then taps my shoulder. "Don't get too close to her. She's clingy as hell."

If there's one thing I know about, it's loyalty. Colby's had mine since the day we met, when we were nine years old, and he came over to play street hockey with me and my brother the day the Jensens moved two doors away from my house. He thought I was a boy, and when he realized I wasn't, he just kept on playing. He even bodychecked me, and told me I had good stick control. He sat with me on the bus to school, and never made a big deal about Tristan tagging along. Ever since then, it's been him and me. What kind of douche would I be to turn my back on him over some girl?

THREE

THE NEXT MORNING, I PAD THROUGH THE KITCHEN to stuff something in my mouth while I wait for Johnny to come up. He drives me to school on his way to work sometimes. Just me, because Johnny thinks Colby acts like an entitled jerk.

My mom's in there, dropping a tea bag into a blue mug. She

looks like a peasant lady from the islands about to go beat a rug with a stick out back, the way she's covered in some flowered summer dress with flip-flops on her feet. People usually assume she's my grandma, and sometimes that almost feels about right to me. It's like there's a hundred years between us.

"*Mãe bença*," I say, which is this respect thing younger people are supposed to do in my family, asking an older person for a blessing.

"*Deus te abençoe*," she says, which means God bless you. She turns to inspect me.

"Why you take you *irmão* clothes again? All the time, you take. It's not for you."

"This isn't Johnny's. It's mine," I say, except I totally stole the metal band T-shirt from him last week.

"You wear this and you *mãe* buy the beautiful clothes. It's no good."

I shrug. She shakes her head and moves closer to reach around me, grabbing the back of my school uniform pants by the belt and yanking them up.

"You wear clothes like you a *punk druggy*, Penelope. Why? Why you do this?"

"These aren't punk druggy clothes."

Switching to Portuguese so she can talk fast and easy, she goes into an explanation of what a *punk druggy* is, which basically translates to this: a punk druggy is a teenage douche who smokes cigarettes, does drugs, wears ripped-up pants too low, disrespects their parents, lies and steals, and—

"You not a boy."

Yeah, that. "I know. I didn't say I was."

She thinks that because I look like a guy, I must be trying to *not* be a girl. I don't speak enough Portuguese to be able to defend myself against that, so I shrug and sigh, and ignore what I can.

"You no wear that to the school."

"I'm taking it off when I get there. My uniform shirt's underneath."

She lifts a warning finger at me. "You watch out now." She always says that when she's warning me and Johnny not to do anything stupid.

Mom wanders into the hallway and starts yelling Johnny's name over and over. This is how she gets us to move fast, because it's the only way to make the yelling stop. I head for the front hall, taking a seat on the bottom stair to wait. Soon, I can hear the rumble of Johnny rushing up from the basement. He unties his bandanna, slicks back the brown hair that goes down to his shoulders, puts the bandanna on again, stretches his massive biceps, then triceps, shifts his muscle shirt, and finishes with a feel of his chin for its smoothness.

"João!" Mom says. That's his official name, the Portuguese equivalent of John, but he always hated how everyone mispronounces it *Jo-wow* when it should be more like *J'wah*, so he switched to Johnny a long time ago. I think he looks way more like a Johnny than a João.

"Relax, Ma. I'm right in front of you," he says, slipping his morning cigarette behind an ear. "I'm not deaf."

"Hey!" Dad says from over the upstairs banister. "*Respeito.*"

Johnny nods, but there's a sigh escaping his lips. Doesn't matter how old you are in my family, you always have to have respect for anyone older—especially your parents. Dad disappears back into the bedroom to finish getting ready for work. Mom fires a bunch of questions at Johnny. Stuff about how the patio stones are still leaning up against the house because he hasn't bothered to get started on the backyard work he said he'd have done by now.

"Whoa," Johnny says, lifting his arms like a shield. "I told you I'm busy at work right now. My business is the priority, man."

They dive right into an argument, mostly in Portuguese because Johnny's got a handle on the language. My parents' English is pretty rough, but they understand it well enough.

"I could do it," I say.

They both look over at the sound of my voice.

"Nah, man. I gotta level the ground," Johnny says.

"You could show me how to do it."

"No, no, no," Mom says. "You want job? I give you a job to clean with you *mãe*. This outside is you *irmão* job."

I'm not sure if by that she means that it's my brother's job since he does outdoor work for a living, or if it's his job because he can grow a beard.

"Ma, if Pen wants to help, what's the problem, huh? You think she's gonna hit her head with a shovel and cry or something?" Johnny says. She scowls, and he nods all exaggerated. "I'll get to it, all right?"

To me, she says, "You wanna learn the something? I teach you to do the stuff. I teach you to make the house nice. I teach

20

you to make *comida*. I teach you everything I know."

I don't say anything.

"You wanna learn? I teach you."

"I don't . . . uh," I say, but finding the least wrong-sounding way to say what I want to say isn't easy. She won't get it, regardless. "I want to learn to do different things."

"Ya, ya. You talk and talk just for the . . ." She starts over in Portuguese, saying I only want to do things that I know she won't be into, that she doesn't know anything about, and I do it all on purpose. When I try to respond, she waves me off and huffs and puffs her way back to the living room.

"Does she try to teach *you* how to do laundry and make food?" I ask Johnny.

He sighs like, *You know what she's like.* "Let's get outta here, little sister. I got a full day. I'm gonna pick you up at three fifteen later, so be ready out front."

Sometimes I wish I could ditch school and go work with Johnny, instead of having to wait all day to go help him after school. I'm pretty sure I learn a whole lot more being around him, anyway.

DURING FOURTH PERIOD, I put Mr. Middleton and his Shakespeare on hold to go take a leak. The hallway still smells like all the deep-fried stuff from the cafeteria lunch. When I walk into the bathroom, Blake is there, dropping a wad of paper towels into the garbage.

"Hey, Pen," she says.

She knows my name. Of course she knows my name.

21

There aren't that many people who go here, and I'm pretty sure there's only one of me at this school. I feel like walking right back out for a second. Guys don't have to deal with this kind of bathroom awkwardness. What if she thinks I'm here to take a dump?

"Hi."

"What class do you have right now?" she asks.

"English. You?"

"Math."

"Ew."

"Yeah. I'm not in a hurry to get back, but I've already been here picking at my face for seven minutes." She points to this red thing on her cheek that looks angry. I wonder if the mirror shows her how pretty she is. I really have to pee, but it's not going to happen when she's within earshot.

"We're doing Shakespeare so I pretty much want to poke my eyes out with my pen. That dude makes me hate reading."

She laughs, and it's a raspy sound that makes my lower back tingle. "Well, guess I better get back to class. See you later, Pen."

My name between her lips is the best thing ever.

"Yeah. See ya."

When I talk to her next, it'll probably be so I can hook her in for Colby.

WHEN THE LAST BELL rings, I take my time at my locker. Johnny won't be here for another twenty minutes. Outside, I wait a while, watching the city bus make its stop across the

22

street. Soon Olivia comes rushing out of the entrance doors behind me.

"I missed it, didn't I," she says.

"The bus? Yeah, it went by a minute ago."

Olivia drops her bag and then lets herself fall on the pavement, coming to a cross-legged position. I look around to see if there's anyone else here, but all the people are off by the side lot. She looks like someone whose house just went up in flames.

I edge closer to her. "What's going on between you two?"

"I can't talk to you."

"All right, well—fine."

"You seemed nice but I'm not stupid," she says. When I screw up my eyebrows, she goes, "You're Colby's *buddy*."

"So?"

"So . . ." She widens her eyes like I should know what she's talking about. Like I'm being dumb. "I knew what was going on. You asked me to hang out, and you knew what was going to happen. You know what he's like."

My mouth is all hanging open. "Uh . . . are you blaming me for—for whatever drama you've got going on?"

She shakes her head, tucks her black hair behind her ears, and drops her head into her hands. I take a deep breath, except all that does is make some of the anger from my gut rise up. "It's not like I'm responsible for what he does. You didn't have to follow me that day."

"Maybe you could've warned me," she says.

"You think it's my job to get in my best friend's way and mess up his game?"

23

"Maybe," she says, all weak. Then louder: "Yes, I do."

"Why—because I'm a girl, too?" I scoff, because she wouldn't be saying this stuff to me if I was a guy. She wouldn't expect me to owe her anything. "I have my own stuff to worry about. And you just admitted you knew better, but you still went for it." I'm looking at the top of her head. "I don't even know you. I was just trying to be nice."

Her head whips up. "Nice? That was you being nice?"

"It was supposed to be."

No sign of Johnny yet. I sit cross-legged next to Olivia.

"Fine. Here's some advice," I start. "Stay away from him."

"Yes, well," she says, while rising and dusting off her butt, "it's a little late for that. I already learned that lesson." She stares at the street and her face goes sad. "I have to call a taxi."

"Where are you going?"

"I'll figure it out."

Johnny's truck rumbles as it pulls into the lot. I watch it for a second, then go back to watching Olivia dragging her feet, her shoulders hanging low. The truck stops by me and I hop in. Johnny stares at Olivia as we drive by her, then he goes, "Who's that?"

"Just some girl."

"Nice."

"It's not like that. She's one of Colby's."

"Well, if you play your cards right," he says with a wink, "maybe she can be one of yours."

"Yeah, right."

I pull my phone out and text Colby: don't think u'll have 2 worry about Olivia anymore—took care of it

FOUR

LATER ON THAT WEEK, ON SATURDAY NIGHT, I slide the basement door open and step into Colby's room. I can tell something's off. For one, he's smoking weed right in his house, and the door's only slid open by a crack. There's music blaring, and there's a mess of papers and clothes all over the floor like he got into some kind of fight with random stuff. Although it's not like he has a pissy mom nagging him to clean his room all the time. His mom doesn't even come down here, so what does it matter that his big basement room's a mess.

He spots me finally, rolls off his bed and goes for the stereo, turning down the volume.

"Your parents are out?" I ask.

"Yeah. They had some concert in Toronto tonight, so they got a hotel room downtown," he says. "Tristan's on his way. Let's go sit outside."

"Are you all right, dude?"

"Yeah."

"You seem pissed or something."

"I'm fine. Just drop it, Pen."

He sweeps by me and goes out the way I came. I take another glance at his messy room, just in case I'll find some clue for why he's on edge, but there's nothing. So I head out, too.

If my parents had a balcony off the kitchen and they were standing on it, they could probably just see my head from Colby's backyard. But we don't have a balcony, and my parents are both asleep. My mom thinks I'm crashing downstairs with Johnny but I don't even think he's home yet. I haven't heard his truck. He's not answering my texts, so he must be with Jenna, this girl he's sort of dating when they're both in the mood.

Tristan shows up with his bag clanging like there's a Portuguese wedding reception dinner going on in there. He sets it down on the patio table where Colby and I are seated.

"What'd you bring?" Colby asks.

"Check it out." Tristan wags his eyebrows, digs into his backpack, and yells, "Whiskey!"

"Nice."

Tristan pulls out another skinnier bottle. It's got some stuff that looks pink.

Colby plucks the bottle from his hand. "What is that?"

"My mom likes it. It's some fruity wine." Colby shoots Tristan a look. "What? Alcohol is alcohol. Pen can drink it."

"Why me?"

"Because it's pink," Tristan says.

"Yeah, good one," I say. Since Garrett started hanging out with us, it's like Tristan doesn't think twice about throwing me under the bus.

"If anyone's gonna drink that stuff, it's you." Colby opens

the bottle, takes a whiff, then places it on the table in front of Tristan. "Go. Drink."

"I don't like wine."

"Drink."

"Why?"

"Because Pen is a loyal friend," Colby says, and I figure he must be talking about Olivia. "And you—well you got us a D on our science paper."

"I messed up the experiment. It's a legit mistake. It's not like you helped," Tristan says. He reaches for the whiskey bottle, but Colby gets to it first.

"Nope. The fruity stuff is yours." Colby laughs and puts the whiskey bottle between us. Tristan gets this pathetic look on his face. Colby waits and lights another smoke. I pick up the whiskey, watching the dark brown liquid sloshing against the glass.

"Seriously, take a chug," Colby tells Tristan.

It gets silent. Tristan puts his hand around the bottle and reads the label. I don't get why he doesn't just take a drink so we can move on to something else. He always makes it worse for himself.

"Okay, fine." Colby puts a finger on the spot where the top of the label starts. "Drink down to here. That's all you gotta do."

Tristan looks over at me, but I pretend I don't notice. I'm glad it's not me who has to drink the pink booze. It reminds me of when we were young, how whenever people did stuff to Tristan, he'd go all stiff and pretend none of it was happening. And the whole time, I was sort of glad he was the one getting picked on, because then it wasn't me getting asked why I was a boy with braided hair.

"Pass it over," I tell Tristan. "I'll drink the pink stuff."

"No," Colby says. "I told *him* to drink it."

"So? I said I'll drink it."

The bottle's on the table between the three of us. I go to reach for it, while Tristan stares all wide-eyed and quiet. Then Colby sticks his big hand out. "I said no!" He goes to grab the bottle before I do and ends up knocking it over. It shatters on the tiled ground between us, glass and fizzy liquid spraying our legs.

"Oops," Colby says with a grin. "You got lucky, Tristan."

Colby puts the wrong end of a new cigarette in his mouth and plunges its filter into the flame of his lighter. He inhales and makes a face. "These cigarettes taste like ass." He reaches for the whiskey and hands it to Tristan.

IT'S LATE AS HELL after Tristan takes off, and I figure I'll crash on Colby's couch and sneak home in the morning, before my parents wake up.

"Dude, it's so hot in here," I say. "Can we open the door and the windows all the way?"

He goes for the game controllers. "Yeah, do what you want."

So I walk around the room, opening what I can. It's mid-September, but the weather's all over the place these days.

"I've had it with girls, Pen. I'm done."

"What's going on?" I ask, pretty sure I know this is about one girl in particular.

No answer. He collapses on the couch and turns on the

TV. I sit on the other end. There's no talking while we pick our *Street Fighter* characters, and he decides which stage we'll fight in. I don't know why he picked that game, because I'll just end up kicking his ass and he'll get even more annoyed.

The fight starts and I knock his health bar down by half.

"Smoke," he says, handing me the joint he just lit. "You have an unfair advantage. I'm stoned *and* drunk right now."

I take a few tokes, and it's so harsh it makes me cough. I don't like the feeling of being stoned. It makes me all paranoid, feeling like my mom's about to sneak up on me, ready to drag me away by the ear.

I still manage to knock him out three times. He jams the buttons like that'll somehow give him skills.

"Of course a girl kicks my ass at *Street Fighter*," he mutters, and I get the urge to smack his arm for sounding like Garrett. "Because today wasn't bad enough already."

"What happened?"

"Girls can suck it," he says, chucking the controller aside. It hits me in the thigh. I take it and turn the game into a fight between me and an AI opponent instead. "I'm telling you right now, Pen, I'm not letting any girl mess with me from now on. I've had it. Getting in their pants isn't worth it."

Colby's words come out pretty clear, considering what he drank earlier and what he's smoking now.

"Are you talking about Olivia right now?" I ask.

"No one is talking to Olivia from now on," he says. When I don't reply, he goes, "You got it? She doesn't exist anymore."

I nod. Olivia should've listened to me when I told her to

29

stay away. She must not have, and obviously it just made things worse, but that's her problem.

Another joint sparks, and there's smoke everywhere. Even if I wasn't having the occasional toke, I'd still be buzzed off the fumes. It's so hot in here, and there's sweat collecting on my neck, under my hair. I pull off my hoodie, and now I'm a sweaty bastard in a muscle top. When I go to tighten my ponytail, the rubber band snaps, and the pieces get stuck in my hair.

"Can I borrow a shirt?" I ask.

"Yeah, whatever." He sighs before resuming his rant. "I just wanna have fun and get laid. That's all anyone should be into, right?"

"Well, that's cool, I guess. As long as you don't make the girl think you'd be into doing the boyfriend-girlfriend thing. You gotta find a girl who's into what you're into, I guess. A girl who won't get clingy, and just wants to mess around."

He nods like I spoke the truest truth, but then his face drops. "Wait—you think I led her on?"

"Olivia?"

"Any of them."

"I'm not there when you guys are alone, dude. I don't know."

"They lead *themselves* on, then they think they can trap me," he says. He reaches over the side of the couch and comes back with a bag of chips, handing it to me. "You think one might be different, then it's like, nope, same old. I swear, Pen, there are times I'd punch a girl if I was allowed."

"Uh . . ."

"Not, like, really hit a girl, or whatever. I wouldn't do that.

30

But sometimes it's like, if that girl was a guy right now, we'd settle this a different way, you know?" he says, waiting for me to nod along. "It's a good thing you're not like that, Pen, because then we definitely wouldn't be buddies."

"Yeah, true."

He nudges me with his elbow. "You sure you're ready for that crap? Girls are evil, dude. They try to change you, turn you into a pussy."

I shrug, tossing Cheetos into my mouth. I'm so ready for that crap, although it's not like finding a girl is as easy for me as it is for him. Finding a girl to take on a real date, to kiss, to talk with—that just sounds impossible sometimes. Colby's always known I was into girls, I never had to tell him, but he really doesn't get what it's like for me. Girls—no, not just girls— *people* don't even know how to talk to me, how to be around me.

Colby's looking at me funny through the smoke coming from the joint in his mouth. "What?"

"Dude, you look like such a girl under your hoodie," he says.

"I told you I need a shirt. Shut up."

I head for the dresser, picking through until I find a T-shirt that might work. At one point, Colby and I were almost the same size. But a couple years ago, he got more muscle and I got a layer of pudge and a chest. I throw on a black shirt, pulling my hair out from my neck.

Colby hitches his chin at the TV and says, "*Slashko*, co-op."

He swaps out the disks, then we sit on the couch and set up our offline campaign. I hate gaming online because of all the bull these dudes throw at me—like saying nasty sex stuff

31

over headsets, or talking crap about my gameplay, or just booting me out when they find out I'm a girl. I stick to gaming by myself, or with people I know, which is better anyway.

Colby gets us killed three times during a covert mission. We're supposed to infiltrate this alien camp in the sewers, then pick off the enemies without getting caught, but his aim is all over the place, so the alarms go off every time he shoots.

"Man, screw this game!" he says, flinging the controller.

"Chill. Just let me do it. I'll even get you the achievement. Don't shoot your damn gun until I tell you to."

One guy left to take out, and he's standing next to the alarm switch, surrounded by five German shepherds. I could use the plasma cannon, but for the achievement, it's pistol only. If I don't get him right between the eyes and quickly throw a bomb to take care of the dogs, he'll hit the switch, and the dogs will charge at me. It kind of bugs me that I have to blow up dogs— even if they're fake game dogs—but they're trying to eat me, so whatever.

I take out my pistol with silencer.

My gun's aimed.

The guy finishes talking on his walkie-talkie.

I take a breath. Time to pull the trigger—

But instead, Colby's touching me—raking his fingers through my hair, where it hits my back.

I miss the shot, and the dogs are on me.

What?

I'm not even sure it's happening at first, but then he does it again. I get goose bumps and jerk away. Because the only time

32

Colby ever touches me is to smack my shoulder or punch my upper arm. What the hell is going on?

"Why are you looking at me like that?" I ask. "You're creeping me out."

"It's like you're a girl, but you're not."

"So?"

"So . . . it might be kind of perfect, right?"

I feel funny. Guys don't look at me like this, just like guys don't look at each other like that, unless they're gay. Is this gay? I don't even know what to think because my brain's fried. There must be something else laced in that weed.

Colby's handing me the joint, so I take it.

All of a sudden, he's in front of me. His face is right there.

"Dude," I say. It's all that will come out.

"I'm just trying something," he says, too close to my face. "Just messing around."

And then a dude is kissing me. I'm kissing Colby.

FIVE

IT JUST FIGURES THAT THINGS WOULD GET ALL messed up and blurry. This is my life, confusing people, and I'm sick of it. Every time I think things are regular, something happens to remind me that no, things are not regular. *I'm* not regular. I'm some kind of glitch.

Johnny's basement sliding door has a lock and I have a key, so I can let myself in whenever I want without having to walk in through the front door upstairs. It's almost four in the morning. I head for the little bathroom, ripping off Colby's shirt and throwing it in the trash can by the sink.

In the mirror right now, it's my hair I'm staring at, pissed off because it's just hanging there over my shoulders when it's supposed to be tied back, out of sight. My thick, wavy black hair that goes all the way past the middle of my back—the one thing I've been too much of a pussy to do anything about. I hate it. At Christmas, I have to leave it loose or my mom gets mad. When family comes over, I can't wear a hat because it'll offend the guests if I look like a punk druggy.

Sometimes, something really messed up has to happen to make you realize you need to man up.

I go for the cupboard under the sink, pulling out Johnny's kit. Johnny has an undercut, and he gels or ties back the long upper half under his bandanna. Once a month, he takes out the clippers and cleans up the bottom half. Now that I'm standing here with the clippers in my hand, I have no idea where to start. There's just so much hair.

I make a ponytail with one hand, then grab the shears from the kit, and I cut. The longer it takes, the more I force the blades closed around the thick rope of hair, and the metal of the shears digs into my skin, strangling my fingers almost. It takes, like, twenty snips to make it through, and by the end I'm just pulling the last strands away from my head—I don't even feel it. It's in my hand now, all that stupid hair.

The thing looks like it came off the back of a horse, it's so long. I drop it into the trash can, on top of Colby's shirt.

I grab the shears again, and I start snipping, letting it all fall to the floor.

MY MOM'S ALL OVER me with the dirty looks on Monday morning, circling me with her hands wrapped around her belly. She's probably extra suspicious because I stayed in my room all of yesterday. I pad through the kitchen, my feet stepping on the hem of my school uniform pants. My head is safe under my hoodie. My mom's long graying braid is coiled and pinned to the back of her head, and the sight of it makes me feel guilty about what I've done, so I don't look directly at her.

"You know the wedding gonna happen," Mom says. "*Tia* Joana call me."

There's been rumors about my cousin Constance and her boyfriend getting married soon because she's gotten a little fat. Most of my family lives in Ottawa, but my mom's always in the loop because the aunts call the house every week and they gossip with my mom about everything.

"That's nice. Good for her," I say, because Constance is a little older than Johnny so it's not like it's a big surprise she'd be getting married. Everyone in my family gets married and has babies. Except for me and Johnny, I guess.

"You like the dress for the wedding? You like white dress?"

35

"Huh?"

"You like? The dress. It's nice. Like a *princesa*."

I bend into the fridge so I won't have to deal with this. My mom's always saying weird things like this, starting weird conversations I don't really want to be involved in.

"You know I make you dress when you old. I make nice white dress for you. I teach you, too."

"Okay, Ma."

"*Princesa* have the dress. They don't have the punk druggy clothes."

I put an apple between my teeth and hurry my butt out of the kitchen. "I'm not a princess," I say when she's behind me.

And then something happens. My hood. It's gone.

She yanked it off my head.

Right off my damn head!

Mom's hand is hanging in the air behind me when I turn, like it froze there from the shock of what it revealed. Her whole face scrunches up under the weight of her eyebrows and I know that if I don't move right now, I'll be getting a swat on the back of the head. So I back up until I'm against the wall.

She shakes her head and her lips go all tight. She puts a hand against her heart and for a second, I wish I hadn't done it.

"What you do? What you do, stupid girl?" she says. "Why you do that? You no like me. You no like you *mãe*. You break my heart. So many times, you break heart. No *respeito*."

I don't like when my mom cries. I like it even less when it's me who made it happen.

She shuffles toward the living room, her face in her hands,

36

rambling on about me.

She expects me to go after her, to tell her I'm sorry and maybe let her complain some more, but I escape to the front hall. My cell vibrates against my butt, and I already know who it is. I delete Colby's text without reading it. When he calls five minutes later, I press Ignore. Then I kill ten minutes eating my apple in the garage until I'm sure I missed our usual bus.

AT MY LOCKER, I have no choice but to pull down my hood because we get written up by teachers for not following uniform rules. I think about my mom's reaction earlier, but then I see myself in the mirror hanging inside my locker, and I smile because it's my real face in there. It's pretty sweet to see what I'm supposed to look like. Even if it's the ugliest haircut I've ever seen, it makes my face seem more legit somehow. It's a butt-load better now than it was Saturday. Saturday can go to hell.

The hallway empties fast now that the first bell's gone off. Colby and Tristan head over, because they don't give much of a crap about being late for class either. They're in my peripheral vision. I keep them there until I'm sure they've both seen the change, and I don't have to see any weird looks they might've had at first glance.

"I legit thought you were a guy just now, Pen," Tristan says. "What the shizz happened?"

"I got gum stuck in my hair, like way at the back against my scalp, so, you know . . . I dealt with it."

I picture this big wad of purple gum melted into my hair, gluing my head to the pillow. The more I see it, the more real it becomes in my mind until yeah, this could so be why I had to cut all my hair.

I look at Colby. He'd have to be a pretty big idiot to not know what the deal is. I'd thank him for it, if I didn't feel like punching him in the chin. "Gum, huh?" he asks.

"Yeah, gum."

Garrett and a couple of other guys move past us. They don't stop, but Garrett's big dumb face breaks into a smile and he points at me over the rush of people between us. "Penelope got a makeover! I'm gonna call you . . . Steve from now on."

"He's the biggest donkey-crotch ever," Tristan says to me before wandering off when Trent—this tall kid with huge curly brown hair and fifties-style glasses—waves him over.

Colby and I exchange this look and maybe it takes all I have to not look down. When he raises his eyebrow, I keep my face blank.

"All right then, gum. Let's go with that," he says. "Whatever."

I nod, then we break eye contact.

I figure from this point on, we've got an understanding: Saturday night never happened. Gum is the reason I finally cut my hair.

I'M THE TYPE TO get stared at. Always have been. So today wasn't as bad as I thought it would be. Most of these people have seen me every day for the past two years and it's not like I ever looked girly enough to *not* cause people to wonder about me. There might be a bit of shock at first, but then it's gone and

38

heads turn back to the front.

Home is worse. It starts at dinner. My dad won't let his eyes land on me for more than a second, like I'm some big dent in his car he can't afford to get fixed. My mom's in a mood, sighing and slamming cupboard doors. It's like—I don't know—almost like the meaning of this haircut is heavier than my long ponytail used to be.

"Can I eat downstairs?" I ask.

"No. You sit here," my mom says, then she curls her lip up in disgust while her eyes drift over my forehead.

I hear gunfire coming from Johnny's TV. He's probably eating fried chicken and playing *War Zone 3* at the same time. I should be there, but I wasn't allowed to go downstairs today.

"People gonna laugh," Mom tells me, pointing her fork at my head. "You want people laugh at me and you *pai*?"

"They'd be laughing at me, not you."

She starts grumbling about how her children do everything they can to break her heart and make life hard. Dad shakes his head, but I'm not sure how much of it is because he agrees with Mom, or if he's just pissed off because she's upset. When my mom's upset, everyone suffers.

"What everybody gonna say? What Constance say?" Mom says.

"What does my hair have to do with that? They all live, like, four hours away from here. They don't have to see it," I say.

"What you say, huh?" Mom turns to Dad and goes off on him about how everyone's going to say my parents have no control over their kids, that they're not strict enough. She says there's no way my hair will grow back in time for when everyone comes down for a visit on my dad's birthday.

"Ana, we eat now." Dad tells her I'm doing okay at school, that I do what I'm told at home, and even if my hair looks stupid, it's not the worst thing in the world. "We eat now."

"How you know?" Mom says to Dad. "You work work work, after you sit and watch the *televisão*. You don't know nothing, Duarte. I know. I see and I know." She turns to me. "I know what you do, Penelope. I see you."

She doesn't see me.

Right now, we're right above Johnny's head. With my heel, I smack down on the linoleum three times.

"Hey," my dad says. "Stop. You eat."

But it's too late, because the TV's quiet now, and soon, Johnny's stomping up the stairs.

"What's up?" he says when he appears in the kitchen, looking over at me. He gives me a hitch of the chin, and then his eyes go wide when he realizes. He stares at me like my head is some weird painting you have to stare at for a while to truly appreciate. I curl my shoulders over my plate, looking down.

"Why you here?" Dad asks.

"You do this, João?" Mom asks Johnny. "You do this stupid cut the hair?"

Dad tells Johnny to answer.

"He didn't even know I did it," I say.

"What's the problem? So she cut her hair—what's the big deal?" he says. "Are you the one wearing it? No."

"João, *respeito*," Dad warns in between forkfuls of chicken.

"You go away. No food for you today." Mom says she's getting tired of him stepping everywhere with his big feet when he's not welcome. To me, she says, "You stop be like you brother. He no good."

"What? I'm no good?" Johnny says.

For a second, Mom looks sorry, like maybe she screwed up her English, but then she just goes with it. She directs her rant at Dad now, going off about how Johnny's been setting a bad example for his little sister and that now I'm trying to copy him because I don't know any better. Dad agrees to that because as much as my mom has it out for me, Dad has it out for Johnny.

"All right, man," Johnny says to me, pointing to the hallway. "Let's go for pizza."

"Hey! What I say?" Dad says. He tells Johnny he better watch himself, or he could find himself on the street. "You wanna get outta here, João?"

This isn't the first time they've threatened to kick my brother out—it's, like, the fifth time just this year—but every time they do it, there's a sinking feeling in my gut. I know for a fact they could follow through on their threat at any given time—they've done it before.

Mom looks at me and says, "You see? You brother he no good. He no smart."

Doesn't matter what Johnny does, he'll always be the punk druggy who dropped out of high school to hang out with his buddies and smoke weed. Our parents don't care about his business because to them, it's not a real job—it's not a safe job at Dad's packaging company with benefits and paid vacation and all that crap.

"This has nothing to do with Johnny, Ma. He didn't do it," I say. "It's just hair."

"You cut you hair to be the boy. It's no good. I tell you now, I want no more." She says she can't take much more and things are going to have to change. Then she asks Dad what he thinks, and he does this big shrug that doesn't really mean one thing or the other.

It's not that things are going to have to change—they're changing already.

I bring my half-eaten dinner to the sink, then I go past Johnny and head to my room. I shouldn't have called him because he always ends up getting blamed for everything. I should've known that. Why can't I just take care of myself? I'm such a pussy.

Upstairs, I check my phone. There's a text from Colby: Y u gotta b such a girl about this? It's done. Just move on.

Me: not being weird—i moved on

Him: Don't buy it. Gum in yr hair my ass.

Everyone wants something different from me. It's like one second, I should be a better dude. I should stop being such a girly douche, and I should just man up. Then, it's the opposite: I'm too much of a guy, and it's not right. I should be a girl, because that's what I'm supposed to be.

The thing is, I'm not a boy, but I don't want to be *that* girl either. I just want everyone to screw off and let me do my own thing for once.

SIX

THE NEXT DAY, AFTER SCHOOL, TRISTAN AND I meet up online to play a couple co-op missions. After that I spend twenty minutes looking over my weekend English homework and decide to pack it back into my schoolbag without doing any of it. At least I tried.

A text comes in. From Colby: Mall after dinner? As soon as I finish reading it, another text comes through, this one from Tristan: Colby says mall l8r. Can u pick me up maybe?

I reply to Tristan first: i'll let u know in a bit

I text Colby next: i'll meet u there

Meanwhile, I head down to the basement. The bottom of the stairs is where the kitchen starts. Past that is the living room, and then Johnny's bedroom. On one side of the bedroom is the entrance from the backyard and on the other is the bathroom. The only real light that could come in here is through the patio doors, except there's an ugly, old quilt tacked up to cover them. The rest of the tiny windows are lined in black garbage bags, and the floor is all concrete with patches of area rugs. My parents act like Johnny's lucky to have his own apartment, like it's some amazing little home they gave him for free, but it's just the place where all our old crap ends up. Still, I wish I lived down here. If my parents ever decided to kick me out, I'd just pack my stuff and head down.

Johnny's lifting weights with the music blaring. He spots me and nods.

"Can you drive me and Tristan to the mall in a bit?"

"Not like that. You gotta let me deal with that thing on your head first, man," he says.

"You can fix it?"

"Can't get any worse," he says, grinning when he puts the forty-pound weight down next to the couch. He points to the bathroom. "Go."

I plant myself in front of the mirror and let the ceiling light shine on what's left of my hair. The clipper goes on, and Johnny makes a psycho-killer face through the mirror, holding the clipper to my head like it's a chainsaw. I grin, and then more hair starts falling off my head.

AT THE MALL, TRISTAN, Colby, and I head for the Gamer Depot. I'm pretty sure none of us have any money to buy anything, but Colby goes in. Blake is behind the counter. I probably would've known this if I shopped here for my gaming stuff. But I don't because everything in my house comes from Walmart. But there she is, shooting price tags at a stack of Xbox games with this sticker gun thing. She doesn't see me. I flip my hood up and hustle after Colby and Tristan.

Colby hitches his chin toward the front of the store. "Go work your magic."

"Right now?"

"Uh, yeah?"

"But . . ." Not Blake. "What do I ask?"

"Since when do you need help with that? Just get her to come over."

"What about . . ." Bringing up Olivia would be dumb. "How come you're all of a sudden into Blake?"

"Because she's hot? And I heard she's not with that guy anymore."

"What guy?"

"Some guy who would pick her up after school. I don't know. Just some guy."

"Oh."

"All right, what's up?" Colby says. "Because it kind of seems like you're trying to mess up my game."

Tristan's in front of the Nintendo console, playing through the demo game. Colby's glare bores into me. What would happen if I told him I like her? If I said, Can you just back off this one, because I'm sort of into her, how would he respond?

Really? You? Ha!

So? I already told you she's mine.

Come on, Pen. That would be a waste of a hot girl. It's not like she'll ever be into you.

You're into her? Then maybe I'll let you have a turn after I'm done.

I sigh and head off toward the front counter.

"Excuse me?"

Blake looks up. "Oh, hey, you."

The way she says that, like I'm somebody . . . "Hi."

She smiles and reaches for a pack of licorice, shoving a red stick into her mouth and biting off the end. I throw a glance back at Colby, and in my head the words get all jumbled up.

"Can I help you?" she asks after a couple seconds of weird silence.

"Uh . . . do you know if *Rusted* is out on PlayStation yet?"

"It's an Xbox exclusive, and the release date is October twentieth. You can preorder it, though."

"Oh, right." Obviously I already knew all that. I'm just nervous as hell, and now there's nothing left to do but follow the plan. "So, my friend Colby, he's looking for a new first-person shooter to try out."

She doesn't glance around to see if he's near. She's looking right at me. What if I say something dumb? She's so pretty. She's even prettier now that she's talking to me.

"Well, you've got your classics—*War Zone 3*, *Target*, *Slashko 2* and *3*, but stay away from the first one, because there were some pretty severe game-design flaws with the controls, and the glitches were insane."

All of that was so hot, I just want it to keep going. But then I realize it's my turn to talk, so I stop nodding and say, "*Slashko 3* is awesome. I have it on Xbox."

"I'm an Xbox girl, too, for first-person shooters especially. Although Nintendo wins everything."

"Colby figures Nintendo is for little kids."

"He must be quite the idiot then," she says, and it makes me grin. "No one messes with Nintendo. I'm into retro gaming,

46

too. It's made me appreciate solid gameplay over sharper graphics."

I nod. "Like eight-bit side-scrollers for the NES, right? I'm into that, too."

A massive smile spreads on her lips. I watch her hands while she goes through the stack of games in front of her, and I look at her mouth, where the piece of licorice dangles from the corner of it.

"Okay, so here's the deal. Colby thinks you're hot and he wants me to talk you into coming over there." I pause, looking for a reaction. She takes a bite of her licorice. "I don't think you should do it, though."

"Huh," she says. "Why not?"

"Because he's kind of an ass and you can so do better."

Her eyebrow goes up. "How come you're telling me this?"

"You just don't seem like you'd be the type to, uh . . ."

"The type to what?"

"To waste your time with idiots."

She nods. Her eyes are shiny with something that looks like a smile but doesn't show on her lips. She goes, "Want a price sticker?"

I have no idea what she means, until she picks up the price gun and aims it at me. I extend my hand, palm out. She grins and flips my hand over. She shoots and swipes the gun against the back of my hand. I go tingly where she touched me.

"Twenty-nine ninety-nine," she says.

"Cool."

"Want a sale sticker?"

"Sure."

She peels a red circle off a roll and hands it to me. "Ten percent off."

"What if I decided to stick them on a full-price game?"

"You don't seem the type to pull off such an idiot move."

Her eyes do the twinkle thing again and it's like my stomach falls into my shoes, in a good way. I press the sticker against my shirt, as if it's a name tag.

The store phone rings. Blake puts her gun down and runs a hand through her hair. It's like a curtain of messy waves around her face. I watch her mouth move as she talks. The call ends and Blake says, "Tell him to get *Slashko 3*, and then tell him you tried but I have a boyfriend."

"Okay," I say, thinking about that guy. Some guy. Of course she must have a guy. But still, I have to ask: "So, um, *do* you . . . have a boyfriend?"

"No. Do you?"

"Do I have a boyfriend?"

"Well, girlfriend or boyfriend."

"No to both. But that's not really—I mean, I'm not looking for a boyfriend."

"Neither am I." Blake nods with a grin. "Righteous hair, by the way. That style wins everything on you."

"Uh . . . thanks." I'm lucky Johnny's got skills with the clippers. "So hey, do you game online? We could exchange gamertags or something."

"Yeah. Do I have you on Facebook?"

"I'm not sure." Of course we're not Facebook friends. If we were, I'd be able to do more than stare at the thumbnail of her profile pic. I could creep all her pictures and just . . . think about stuff.

"Add me," she says with this little smile I'll be thinking about for the rest of the night.

She does a two-finger wave before going back to her stickering job.

I walk back, pulling Tristan by the sleeve on the way.

"What the shizz?"

"Abort," I tell him.

"Why? What happened?"

"The mission failed. Gotta regroup."

Back in the PlayStation section, Colby hitches his chin up at me and goes, "So? Is she coming?"

"She can't leave the front. She says to try *Slashko 3*."

"*Slashko* rocks," Tristan says.

"I don't give a crap about *Slashko*," Colby tells Tristan. To me, he says, "I think you're just losing your touch."

"How?"

"Look at you," Colby says, pointing to my head. "They used to think you were one of them. Now, they think you're trying to be one of us."

"I am . . . one of us."

"You know what I mean. Anyway, whatever. Blake isn't really worth my time. Garrett told me she had crabs," Colby says. "That's why she got dumped by her boyfriend."

"I bet Garrett's the one with crabs. He's always scratching his balls."

Colby cracks a grin, then shrugs. "Better be safe than sorry. Besides, she's not really that fit."

My eyes narrow, but I keep all the words inside my mouth. If he wants to act like Blake is suddenly not thin enough for him—which is total bull because he knows exactly how hot Blake is even if she's not skinny like most of the girls he's usually into—then good. At least it'll keep him away from her.

"You should've let me give you a decent haircut," he says. "Fauxhawks are so five years ago, dude."

My hand goes up to feel the back of my head, where it's buzzed super short. Fauxhawks could be thirty years ago and I wouldn't give a crap, because I think it looks pretty good.

The three of us make our way through the store, passing right in front of the counter. I sneak a glance at Blake, and she's looking, too. I pull out my wallet so she can see, and I peel the stickers off my shirt and hand so I can put them in my wallet. Her eyes—everything shows up in her eyes. I'm so glad I have enough balls to look into them.

SEVEN

ON SATURDAY MORNING, JOHNNY WAKES ME UP
with a tap on the head. I'm sprawled on his couch with my face
stuck to one of the cushions. "Wake up. We got work to do." It's
as early as a school morning. We grab leftover fried chicken
from the fridge and head out to the garage to lug bags of gravel
down the slope to the backyard.

We're both in black T-shirts with our sleeves rolled up over
our shoulders. I have a sweat mustache, and Johnny's got a cigarette hanging from his lips.

"You think if I keep doing this, I'll get pipes?" I ask Johnny,
feeling my squishy upper arms.

"You'd have to do it every day."

We each have a shovel and we stab them into the grass,
pulling up chunks of it. There are worms and snails under
there and I kind of feel like crap for destroying their home and
murdering them. I wonder about picking them out and bringing them to the other side of the yard, but then I think about
how only a pussy would be sitting here thinking about picking
bugs out of the ground to save them.

"You had pipes in grade ten."

"That's because I've always lifted weights," he says. "Plus,

I've always been a Portuguese stallion, you know?"

"Yeah. And I'm more like a chubby pony."

"Nah. You're a . . . I don't know, man. I don't really know anything about horses."

We dig some more. It looks like we scalped the part of the yard against the right side of the house.

"I'm getting tired of the NES emulator. I've been thinking about collecting retro gaming stuff," I say. "Think we're going to get paid for this?"

"Ha!" he says. "That's funny."

"Yeah. You're right. Forget it."

A text from Colby comes in: Xbox @ my place later

Me: can't—working outside w/ my bro

Him: Whatever.

My fingers are already typing something that starts and ends with the *F* word. But I delete it because now there's a Facebook IM alert. Blake must've accepted my friend request, and now she's messaging me. She's right there, under my fingers.

Her: Know that coffee shop across from St. Peter's?

Me: yeah

Her: I'm meeting Robyn later, but I was thinking of checking it out before that.

Me: that sounds like fun

Her: Maybe I'll run into you there sometime?

Me: maybe—like after dinner?

Her: Like at 7. ;-)

"You gonna stand there and text, or are you gonna help me?" Johnny says.

I reread the conversation one more time before shoving my phone into my pocket.

"Hold this," Johnny says, and he hands me his half-smoked cigarette. My face is going to split open with the grin Blake caused. Johnny walks to the middle of the dirt patch and crouches to stab stakes into the ground, while I think about later.

Mom comes shambling down the slope of the side of the house, carrying a basket with what look like sheets and bed-spreads.

"Ma, man—you're gonna fall." Johnny rushes over and takes the basket from her hands.

"Ya, ya, I fall and you no do stairs on the side and you say 'I do it, *Mãe*. I do it!'" Mom says, talking about another project Johnny was supposed to do last year. He keeps his mouth shut and takes the basket to the clothesline. She waddles over to it and digs into the pile of sheets. "You come help. I teach you."

"But I'm full of dirt," I say.

She points to the hose, and waits until I've rinsed my hands.

I know it's only hanging stuff on the clothesline, but still, I'd rather be digging and working on my biceps, or checking my phone again—just to make sure that conversation with Blake actually happened.

We spread sheets and pin them up. I'm quiet, stealing glances at Johnny while he pours sand over the dug-out rect-angle. When the basket is empty, I head back over to Johnny. Mom watches us a while, then she announces that she and Dad are going to the *churrasqueria* tonight.

"You come?" she asks us.

We haven't gone out to the restaurant in over a year, mostly because it's boring as hell to sit there for two hours while my parents catch up with all the Portuguese people who are in and out of there, either dining in or picking up takeout. And there's also the fact that I'd get nagged about looking like a punk druggy.

"I bring you *comida*," she says before Johnny or I have to shake our heads. This must be her thank-you to us for the work we did.

"Potatoes, rice, lots of hot sauce," I say.

"Chicken," Johnny says. "A lot of chicken."

"Ya, ya," Mom says.

My parents are probably going to be out most of the evening now. That means I can meet Blake at the coffee shop without having to make up some lie about hanging out with the guys.

I need a massive shower, though, because I'm pretty sure there's dirt in my ears.

USUALLY, I DON'T CHECK myself out in the mirror. Mostly because without clothes on, I weird myself out. Maybe everyone thinks they look funny naked. My body is fine, I guess, but I wouldn't want anyone to see it. Especially not Blake. Not, like, with the lights on at least. And it doesn't have anything to do with the fact that I'm sort of pudgy. When I have my clothes on, I feel normal. When my clothes aren't on, it's like I lose something important about myself. When I think about someone else seeing me like this, it feels like they'd actually be seeing some other person. Like it wouldn't be me they'd be looking at.

It's not like I want to be looking at a boy's body in the mirror. It's just that a girl's body is so . . . girl.

When I get back to my room, I find fifty bucks in an envelope on my bed with a fake independent contractor invoice from *J. Oliveira Indoor & Outdoor Handyman*.

THE COFFEE SHOP IS pretty dead for a Saturday night. I should take a leak before Blake gets here, so there won't be a chance of us needing to go to the can at the same time. I hang around the bathroom door, making sure the coast is clear. It would be great if I was better at holding my pee. Maybe it's like other muscles, and the more you work it, the stronger it'll become.

"Um, that's the ladies' room," someone says from behind me.

The door falls against my shoulder. When I turn, there's a lady standing there, looking like she wants to get by me. She makes an awkward face, lifting her shoulders. "Oh, I'm sorry . . ."

She sweeps past me, and I move over. I should've pissed before I left the house.

There's stuff online about trans people and bathrooms. That's what would come up when I'd search about people who avoid public bathrooms. A couple years ago, I used to be like,

But I'm not trans, so why are people still jerks when I try to go take a piss? Then I realized I don't have to be trans to still confuse people with the way I look. I had my hair then. Now, there's nothing left that makes me a girl, except for the fact that I am one. But I guess that's not enough.

BLAKE AND I ARE sitting on the curb out behind the coffee shop. There are two feet between us. I mostly look at her legs because it's the only thing I can stare at without seeming obvious about it. Besides us, there are two Dumpsters and three recycle bins out here.

"So, how'd you get into gaming?" I ask.

"My dad. He has a few retro gaming consoles."

"Which ones?"

"A ColecoVision, and a Commodore 64," she says. "And an NES. That goes without saying."

"Your dad sounds awesome."

"He doesn't game much anymore because he's always working. But I inherited all his stuff. Robyn keeps saying I could get so much money on eBay for it all, but I'm keeping it."

"That's smart," I say. "It's what I would do. Plus, you'd probably end up selling to resellers. I hate resellers." I watch enough gaming YouTubers to sort of know what I'm talking about. "They jack up prices for everybody."

"That's true. You know, we get so many people asking if we sell retro stuff at the Depot. I keep telling my boss we should do that," she says. "So what are you playing right now?"

"I'm replaying the anniversary edition of *War Zone* with my brother. I'm playing *Crypts* with Tristan. And I'm doing a second play-through of *Slashko 3* with Colby."

"Do you play by yourself ever?"

"Sometimes. Not often, I guess," I say, wondering if that means anything. "You?"

"I mostly play alone. I don't like playing online."

"Same."

"Guys are disgusting on there," she says.

"I know, right? There was this nine-year-old kid from Colorado I used to play *Crypts: The Beginning* with a couple years ago. His dad would come on headset to talk to me and make sure I wasn't a jerk messing with his son. He was a pretty cool kid, decent gamer."

"That's adorable." The smile Blake gives me makes me feel a little gooey inside.

"Yeah, well, you know . . ." I shrug.

Her boots look like they lace up all the way to her knees. The silver rings on her hands, the black nail polish, the one freckle near her left wrist—those are Blake details. I wish I could look at her face that closely, so that I could see what Blake details are going on there.

"So *Slashko 3*—where are you at?" she asks.

"Just took down the guy in the sewers."

"That's a tough mission."

"Not really. Well, unless you want the achievement."

"That's what I'm talking about."

"So you got it? On the highest difficulty?"

"You think I'd take the easy way and get him with the

57

plasma cannon?" she says. "Pistol, with a bullet right between the eyes. Grenade for the dogs. Got it on my first try."

"That's just so . . ." So hot, is what it is. "Wow."

She does this little shrug like, *No sweat*, but with that grin on her lips, she doesn't look cocky at all. Just badass. She runs her fingers through her hair to mess it up like she just got caught in a gust of wind, and it makes my own fingers tingle with the urge to touch it.

"How come we've never hung out?" she asks.

"I don't know. We've never been in the same classes?"

"I was in your biology class last year. And your media class."

"Oh." I wasn't sure she realized. "Um . . . well, maybe it's because I always sit at the back of the class."

"Maybe."

I put a hand down on the concrete between us and her hand is so close that I can almost feel the heat coming off of it. We talk about music. She likes metal bands with girl singers. "Not the kind with demonic screaming, though," she says. I tell her about being stuck between metalcore and the old-school rock stuff Johnny's always forcing on me. "So one second I'm blasting Asking Alexandria and All That Remains, then I'm nodding my head to Def Leppard and Skid Row."

I even tell her about my parents' obsession with this Portuguese singer who's released, like, thirty albums so far with the weirdest song lyrics ever.

"Like what?" she asks.

"Like, *The little boy who lives in my belly, he wants fish, fish, fish.*"

She laughs. "And I thought I was bad."

"At lyrics?"

"Yeah," she says. "I sing."

"For real? Like, in the shower?"

Now, in my mind, she's in the shower and she's naked and there are soapsuds everywhere. It's awesome.

"Like, in a band."

"Yeah? Do you guys play shows?"

"Not yet, but there's a Battle of the Bands on New Year's Eve. It's at the community center. Five bands total."

"You guys are playing? That's amazing."

She shrugs and her cheeks go red.

"What?" I say.

"I can sort of only sing if no one's looking at me."

That's the cutest thing I've ever heard, and I hate using the word "cute," even in my own head. I want to tell her that she shouldn't be scared because even if all she did was stand there, mute in front of a microphone, it would probably be epic. "Maybe you just need to practice in front of an audience a couple times. Even a small one."

It's really hard to keep acting cool when I'm turning into a puddle inside.

"What time is it? I'm meeting Robyn at nine," she says, and right away I know it's time to go.

EIGHT

AFTER SCHOOL ON MONDAY, IT'S JUST COLBY AND me at the mall food court. In front of Colby are two deluxe bacon combos with extra fries and cheese sauce. I have a regular bacon combo with eight packets of ketchup.

I wonder if Blake told Robyn about me. If there was anything to tell.

"What?" Colby says, nudging me with his elbow.

"Nothing, why?"

"Because you're acting like Tristan," he says, "all fidgety and annoying."

I shrug. I must be doing something to make it obvious there's a tiny Blake tickling my brain.

"Did you watch 8Bit Destruction's new video yet?" I ask Colby.

"Damn," he says, hitching his chin to the left, totally ignoring what I asked. "Check out that girl. I'd ask you to go work your magic, but . . . well, you know. You're kind of useless now." The word replays in my head, *useless*. Just because Blake won't fall for his crap suddenly makes me useless? Not that it happens often, but the girl doesn't always take the bait, and I've never been considered useless for it.

Colby dips a wad of fries in cheese sauce and he says, "You should come over Saturday. We can smoke. Garrett's hooking us up."

"I'll see what my mom says. She's been extra bitchy lately."

"I already told him to lay off you and Tristan," he says, "so don't get your panties in a bunch."

"Man, why are you saying stuff like that to me? Seriously, dude."

"I'm just messing with you because *you've* been extra bitchy lately, Pen," he says, and then he laughs.

"If anyone's been . . . anything lately, it's you."

"What? What have I been like?" The way he's looking at me—it makes me regret bringing this up because—what if he thinks I'm talking about that night? I do not want to talk about that.

"You've been weird about this Olivia stuff," I say, not that I meant to come out with that either, but it's a butt-load better than the alternative. "Like one second nothing's going on, and the next you're ready to lose it on her." He stares ahead, his brow heavy. I should probably drop it, but—"I thought . . . I mean, you guys hooked up for what—a week?"

"So?"

"So . . ." I hate the nervousness that's sparking in my gut right now. It feels like I should've never brought anything up. Questioning Colby is always a stupid move. "Well . . . you knew it was her mom's car that day."

"And?"

"And maybe it wasn't just a week of hooking up?" I say.

His jaw clenches, and he finally turns to look at me. It makes me back up just a little. "You're talking to her."

"I'm not!"

"You're listening to her shit then. Same thing."

"She hasn't said anything to me, but I'm not stupid. Something's up, and you're keeping it a secret."

"Keeping secrets? Seriously, dude? Spare me the girl talk," he says, which makes me crush the fry between my fingers. "Besides, what I do is my business anyway. Unless I ask you for something, you don't need to try to worm your way into my shit, got it?"

I sigh and watch the mangled fry between my fingers until the hanging part breaks off. This Blake stuff felt like keeping secrets, something he'd be pissed about. But maybe that can just be my business. Maybe he can just leave it all alone unless I ask him for something. I wish that's how it worked.

"Whatever that girl says about me, it's bull. And if she keeps on trying to mess with me," he says, and I stare back at him with his weirded-out expression, waiting for him to finish, "well . . . anyway. She is no longer my problem. I already told you she doesn't exist anymore, so drop it. I'm serious, Pen."

It looks like he's about to say something else, but then his face changes. He pulls his shoulders up and ditches his second burger. "Guess I don't need you anyway. Here she comes."

"Good thing. Since I'm useless and all."

"Suck it, Pen," he says quickly, because there's a girl in front of us now. A girl with wavy brown hair, shiny powder on her eyelids, and big hoop earrings. Her face is okay, I guess, but everything about it says snob. She pulls up the sleeves of her striped sweater.

"Are you Chris?" she asks Colby.

"Maybe. What's your name?"

"Avery. My friends think you're this Chris guy from Castlehill Alternative."

"Nope. My name's Colby."

She shifts her weight to the other foot, like she's deciding whether to stay or go. "Cool."

My burger and I make ourselves as small as we can.

"So, you go to Castlehill Alternative?" Colby asks, palming his chin. She shakes her head, so that means she goes to the public high school.

Castlehill Alternative is where the messed-up kids go. The ones who can't handle regular school. I could've ended up at Castlehill Alternative if things hadn't worked out when I met Colby years ago. Elementary school wasn't always that great for me and Tristan. I'd take off randomly from school a lot. The principal would call my parents, but it was always Johnny who found me. He'd take his beat-up white car—that's what he drove before he made enough money to get the truck—and drive around the neighborhood until he'd spot me on the sidewalk. I wasn't really going anywhere specific. Maybe I just figured Johnny would end up coming to get me.

It backfired big-time when Johnny got kicked out for almost a year. I should've known better and just taken whatever came at me.

Colby and this Avery girl exchange words over my head,

and I'm mostly listening to the sounds of my own chewing.

Colby says, "You smoke?"

She shakes her head.

"You wanna start?" He flashes her one of his grins and she smiles for the first time.

Man, why can't I be that smooth talking to a girl?

"Is your, um, friend coming?" the girl asks, right when I'm catching a piece of onion before it falls out of my mouth.

"Yeah," Colby asks. "Pen's got nowhere else to go."

I could just go home, but instead I'm doing what I usually do, and I follow.

COLBY'S THE ONLY ONE smoking. We stand against the concrete wall, next to one of those cigarette-butt ashtrays that look like mailboxes. I sip the rest of my Coke, chewing on the end of the straw. That Avery girl left her friends behind; I'm third wheel now, which isn't unusual for me, except today it sucks. I kick an empty can of Sprite around until Colby flashes me a look that says he'll shove the can up my butt soon.

"You guys go to St. Peter's?" Avery asks, like she's only now realizing we both have gray uniform pants on.

"Yeah." First word I've spoken since she appeared.

Colby checks his cell phone. I pull mine out, then Avery does the same—it's like a yawn.

"So, what kind of stuff do you guys do?" she asks.

I think of Blake and wonder about all the cool stuff girls could be into that they're not obvious about. "Gaming. Do you game?"

64

She shakes her head and shrugs. "My little brother does, I guess."

"We're not losers about it," Colby says, nudging me with his elbow. "Pen is, but I'm not."

Yeah, that's why he goes nuts when I kick his butt at *Street Fighter* and tries to explain why it wasn't fair that I won, while he pops old-school *Double Dragon* in and challenges me to rematches until none of it is fun anymore.

"So you're, like, a girl?" Avery asks. "Like a gay girl?"

"Uh . . . ," I say, staring back at her, pulling the straw in and out of my cup, making it squeak against the plastic lid. Colby takes a drag, and exhales the smoke in swirls.

"I just didn't want to assume," Avery says, frowning.

"Assume I'm a girl? I am, so that's cool," I say.

"Do your parents know?"

"That I'm a girl?"

Colby snorts a laugh.

"That you're gay," Avery says.

"I don't really know. I guess it's obvious," I say, but I don't think of myself as being gay, because that word sounds like it belongs to some guy. *Lesbian* makes me think of some forty-year-old woman. And *queer* feels like it can mean anything, but like—am I queer because I like girls, or because I look the way I do? Maybe I don't know enough words.

"You never told them?"

"No."

"It's not really a big deal," Colby says. "Kind of boring, actually."

That's why I've had respect for Colby, because he's always acted like the way I look and who I'm into is just as interesting as it would be when it comes to anybody else—so basically not interesting at all.

She says, "Isn't it hard to be religious? Do you go to church?"

"Religious?" What does that even mean? She's making me picture people holding their hands up and praising the lord. My parents go to church on Sunday mornings, and there are rosaries draped over the Virgin Mary statue in the living room and the framed pictures of my dead grandparents—does that make *me* religious? I don't believe we came from Adam and Eve, and I don't believe in doing things just because an old book says so. "Nah, I'm not religious."

"So how come you're at a Catholic school then? Don't they say anything about it?" she asks, like this is some kind of interview.

"I guess if I went around doing queer things in the hall, they probably would," I say.

"For Pen to be able to do queer things in the hall, she'd first have to have some game," Colby says, winking at me like it's a joke. My eyes get all narrow and I clench my teeth. This is what I get for bringing up Olivia earlier. He pats my shoulder. "Better watch out for Mrs. McCallion, though. Our principal is a Jesus-loving psycho."

"So you're not like that guy on TV. The one who used to be a girl?" Avery asks.

Colby laughs. He's always more of a jerk when he's trying to

66

impress a girl, and I usually cut him some slack. Usually it's in one ear, out the other. Usually.

"I just wanted to know if you're a transgender guy. I was going to say that I'm cool with that," she says.

Colby laughs some more. Avery's eyes dart between Colby and me.

"Relax, man," he says to me. "I mean, you can't blame people for thinking you might be one of those. You've looked in the mirror, right?"

"Why do *people* care so much?" I ask. "Should I put a bow in my hair, you know, to clear things up?"

"I'm just saying, people are gonna ask questions. You can't blame people for wondering what the deal is."

"I'm . . . going to go," Avery says. "My friends—"

"No, wait," Colby says.

"I have to go find my friends," she says, pointing to the doors. Then she drifts away, fingers typing on her phone.

Colby shakes his head while he lights a new cigarette, then he turns to stare me down. "Dude, you better stop getting in my way. All of a sudden you're really screwing up my game."

"I didn't do anything. I was just here—because you told me to come."

"Yeah, that's my point. It used to be good when you were around, but now . . ." He shakes his head with this condescending fake look of disappointment. "First you mess things up with Blake. Now you tell this one that we're douches who play video games all the time, and it becomes all about your identity crisis. And Olivia—well, let's not even go there."

67

I have nothing to say back to him. It's not the way he makes it sound, but it's not wrong either.

"Now I'm gonna go find that girl," he says. "So I'll catch up with you later."

"Yeah," I say. "Later."

"We good?"

"Yeah," I say, my back to him, "we're good."

When I'm on the bus, he texts me: Old school Street Fighter on Thur?

I stare at the screen, then shrug.

Me: ok

Him: U b Ken. I'll b Ryu. I'll still kick yr ass.

Me: yeah right—i'd kick yr butt even with Chun-Li

Him: I'll take that bet. Winner buys pizza.

Me: gonna snap yr head with Chun-Li's mega legs

Him: Hey would u do Chun-Li?

Me: if she wasn't a bitch

Him: She would be. She thinks she's so big & bad cuz she does 8000 leg-presses a day.

Me: how many can u do?

Him: Like . . . 4, easy. :P

That makes me laugh out loud.

NINE

sitting on his couch watching a bad remake of some horror movie that was already shitty to begin with. Colby hasn't texted me about later, which is good because I don't feel like going anywhere today.

Johnny stirs next to me. He stares at the credits on the screen and wipes his face. After thirty seconds of being motionless, he jerks up and stretches. With a bandanna, I wonder if I'd look like a mini-Johnny.

"Can I ask you something?"

Johnny turns off the Xbox and Netflix disappears. "Sure. What's up?"

"Well, um . . . it'll sound weird."

"Okay," he says.

"Um . . . nah. Forget it."

"All right, then."

He wanders into the bathroom, just off the living room so I can see him standing in front of the mirror, checking his face out before putting on some deodorant. I stare for a while, feeling like an idiot.

"Okay, fine. So, do you, um, think that I'm trying to be a

69

guy?" I look up and meet his gaze.

"Are you *trying* to be a guy? Are you telling me you're my little brother now?" he asks.

"No."

"Is Ma saying stuff to you?"

"No."

"Is anything weird going on at school or something?" He says it all innocent, but he's watching my reaction.

"No. Nothing I can't handle."

"Good. Because you know you just have to say the word and—"

"I know," I say. "It's nothing like that. I just have a question."

"Shoot."

"Well, like—why do you think people think that? That I'm trying to be a dude."

He looks totally annoyed. "People are always thinking stuff about other people. Let 'em do their thing, and—you know—in one ear, out the other. If it gets to be more than you can ignore, then you tell me and we deal with it."

"I don't get why it's such a big deal to people, the way I am. I know it's confusing or whatever, but—"

"You're just gonna act the way that comes natural, little sister. How many times do I gotta tell you to toughen up and stop listening to everybody else—especially Ma and all the people like her."

I nod. When people keep acting like I'm the one who's wrong, it starts to feel like they're going to be right no matter how unfair it is.

"And I mean, you in a dress? That's what's scary." He laughs. "Listen, man, have you seen me in a suit? Or those damn shiny shoes *Tio* Adão wears? Can you see me working at the factory with *Pai*? Marrying some lady so I can make babies? Come on. I let nobody else decide what kind of dude I am. You shouldn't either."

"Yeah, but . . ."

"But what?"

"The difference is that no one would look at you weird if you decided to do that stuff. Because you're allowed. You're supposed to."

"My buddies would look at me weird. *I'd* feel like a douche, and that matters more, right?" He waits and I think. It's like it all knocks on the door of my mind but it doesn't actually go inside. "Look, just because people look at you funny, doesn't mean you have to change anything. Screw 'em. Even if it's your own mom giving you hell for it. You don't have to change. Unless you want to. You wanna wear a dress?"

"Hell no."

"You want your ponytail back?"

"No."

"You wanna give me my shirt back?"

I look down at the gray skater tee I'm wearing. "No way."

"There you go. Leave it alone. Worry about you. Everyone else can worry about themselves," he says. "But for real, man, you gotta stop stealing my stuff."

"Can I borrow it?"

"I got a reputation. I can't be wearing the same stuff as my sister, man. I just can't be doing that."

"Because I'm a girl?"

"Because you're twelve."

"I get it." I roll off the couch and jog over to the stairs. "I guess I'll just keep the shirt then. Thanks!"

AFTER DINNER, STILL NO text from Colby. I send him one as I leave the kitchen, then my phone crashes to the floor and the battery pops out of it.

"Shi—shoot . . . uh, balls!"

"What? Why you crazy?" my dad asks, coming up behind me, probably on his way to the living room recliner. "Balls, balls. You no say balls."

"I'm not."

He tells me to go be crazy up in my room, then he screws up his eyebrows. "You hair look stupid."

"Thanks."

"You wanna be a tall girl with this?" he says, running his hand over the top of the fauxhawk; then he flattens the whole thing down against my head. "You wanna be tall, you get big shoes."

"I don't wanna be tall. I want cool hair."

"Cool hair, cool hair," he says with a smirk. "It's dirty hair."

"That's gel."

"Gel. You wash it. It's dirty."

I pretend to fuss after it, fixing the spikes so they all point in the same direction—straight up. My dad rolls his eyes and wanders into the living room. That's when I notice my mom watching from the kitchen.

"You come here," she says.

"Why?"

"I make *massa*. I show you how." All of a sudden, it's super important for me to learn how to bake sweet bread all by myself.

"But I'm going to Colby's soon."

She tells me to do what I want before turning away.

UPSTAIRS, I SHAKE THE crap out of my mouse to wake my computer up so I can get on my NES emulator. There's a Facebook message from Blake, just sitting there all fresh from four minutes ago.

Her message: Hey Pen. :-)

Me: hi, hey—i'm here—r u there?—sorry i missed yr message—hello?

And then I erase it all and start over, without the creeper factor: hey—what's up?

One entire minute later, her: What r u up to?

Me: not much—u?

Her: Same, actually.

Me: cool

And then there's silence, and it's my fault because I answered with one word.

Her: So . . . what if we were to hang out again?

I throw a fist pump in the air, then type: well then i think fun would be had

Her: i think so too

Me: so . . . was that a hypothetical type of scenario?

I don't even know how I'm coming up with this stuff. I sound so much more chill than I feel right now.

Her: I'm thinking it could be a real scenario.

Me: real is good—so um . . . maybe i should run into u @ the Gamer Depot sometime?

Her: I'm thinking we actually leave our houses & purposely meet somewhere to do the hanging out.

Me: that sounds like an awesome plan—when

Her: Tonight?

Me: good idea—where

I have no idea where she lives. We figure out that we live on opposite sides of Castlehill and neither of us can walk an hour in the cold to meet halfway. The buses go every half hour, but we'd have to transfer at the Castlehill Transit Station. That'll take an hour and it's already seven. On a school night, too.

Her: It's not looking good . . .

This is not going to go down this way. I can figure this out.

Me: i have a brother—he drives

Her: Feel like coming over then?

I close my eyes because I can't believe my amazing luck tonight. I'm going to Blake's. I'm going to her house, even if lightning strikes me or a bird craps on me. She invited me over.

I dial Johnny from my cell.

"What?" he says.

"I need a ride. I need a ride so bad. Please, please, please."

He sighs into the phone. It shouldn't be too much of a hassle

74

because he does the outside work at the McKinley buildings, which is right by Blake's house; he knows exactly where to go. I rush around my room, swapping jeans, spraying cologne on both sides of my collar.

"I'll pay you!"

"You mean, I'll pay myself," he says.

"Yeah."

"Fine. You got five minutes."

"Three, man! That's all I need."

I end my Facebook conversation with Blake, then sprint to the bathroom to put on a fresh layer of deodorant and brush the crap out of my teeth and my tongue. You never know. My hair's not too bad. I gel the stray pieces into place, then spray the whole thing so it won't ever move again.

I'm going to Blake's. I made it happen.

TEN

HALFWAY UP THE DRIVEWAY, I STALL. THE DOOR opens wide and Blake's there. I'm like a dirty raccoon caught in the garbage bins. I need to man up.

Blake's hair is in two loose, messy braids behind her ears. *That's* how you do braids.

"Come in!" she says.

Inside, there are dark hardwood floors, a carpeted spiral staircase, and art on the walls. It's not, like, rich-people fancy, but it's a butt-load fancier than linoleum, Portuguese roosters, and thick lacy curtains covering every window so that you can't actually see outside.

"Want me to hang up your coat?"

When the zip-up hoodie comes off, I feel kind of weird about the striped button-down shirt I slipped over my tee. It makes me feel too dressed up. I watch my hoodie draped over Blake's arm, wondering if it'll smell like her later.

"Want something to drink?"

I nod, and follow her to the kitchen.

"Pepsi? Water? Orange juice? Uh . . ." She bends into the stainless steel fridge, but it's not like I can see her from where I'm standing. Still, I think about her shirt riding up and her jeans getting tight around her—"Or milk? That's all I got."

"Pepsi."

She hands me a can with her left hand and I reach with my right. My fingers are over hers, not for long but still. My phone launches into the *Ninja Turtles* theme. Blake grins while I fight with my pocket to dig inside it. It's a call from Colby. I press Ignore, put my phone on Vibrate, and shove the thing back in my pocket. "Sorry."

"Follow me." She heads back the way we came, pulling open a door. We take the stairs down to the basement. There's a family room with a massive sectional couch, a TV, and a fake fireplace. I'd so live down here if this was my house. Blake puts her can of Pepsi and her cell phone on the coffee table, then moves to the TV unit to open its doors. There are shelves of video game consoles and rows of games in boxes or just loose cartridges.

"Oh, man," I say. "Wow. Can I look?"

"Of course."

"I've been thinking about starting my own retro collection."

"You should do it," she says. "Although you won't find much decently priced. All the thrift stores have caught on and they're overpricing everything."

"Do you watch YouTube a lot?" I ask. She nods. "Me too. I watch that more than I watch actual TV."

I point to systems and ask questions, and she's got all the answers. She shows me the three Nintendo handhelds— the majorly old-school Game Boy that doesn't have any color besides the greenish-yellow background and the gray graphics, the Game Boy Advance that has color, and the newest DS, which I've been dying to try.

"Wow. You're really into *The Legend of Zelda*, huh?" I say, pointing to the sword-wielding main character, Link. "I played him in Smash Bros. at Tristan's house. I don't have any new Nintendo consoles, though. I just never thought the *Zelda* games would be that good."

"Are you crazy? If Nintendo puts out new *Zelda* games almost as much as they put out *Mario* games, isn't that a pretty good indicator of how righteous these games are?"

I smile and maybe my cheeks get hot because I'm getting schooled about gaming stuff by a girl. A girl like her. "Okay, fine. Yeah, I'm an idiot."

"Smash Bros., huh? So you're definitely a beat-'em-up type of gamer, then."

I nod. "And hack-and-slash games. First-person shooters, too, obviously."

"The *Zelda* games are adventure, puzzle games—no, don't make that face. They're absolutely amazing."

I reach for one of the smaller boxes, a more recent *Zelda* game for the handheld system I really want to try.

"Good choice." She passes me the handheld console and the game, then we go back to the couch to start this thing and drink some Pepsi. The cut scenes are long as hell, but the story sounds kind of cool. It becomes obvious pretty quick how much I suck at this game because I get annoyed at not knowing where to go.

"See, this is why I like playing with other people," I say.

"I like relying on myself, on my own skills. Besides, the whole point is to explore everything, meet different characters, and try things out because then you end up finding what you need," she says.

"I just kind of charge in there and mash buttons."

"What do you do when you get your ass kicked?"

"This is why I like playing co-op. I charge in there, and if I get in trouble, they have my back. And vice versa."

"That's not really brave, you know? In these games, you have to learn and make sure you gained all you can before you go up against evil. You have to grow into your powers and truly know you're the hero. That's how you make sure you kick some serious ass. All by yourself. Like I do."

My mouth opens, but there's nothing in there except for a smile. She laughs the sound I've been playing in my head for days when I hand her the console to take over. She's so pretty, and now I get to steal glances at her while she's busy with the game.

"Okay, fine, this is pretty cool," I say, watching her go. "I guess I don't have enough patience. Which is probably why I get so pissed off playing my NES emulator."

"I get pissed off, too, don't worry."

A little while later, I point to a closed door with a poster of a rock band I like on it. "What's in there?"

"That would be the band room."

"Band room? You practice here?"

She pauses the game. "Yeah."

"Can I see?"

She nods and gets up. Her shirt is loose and cut so that it's longer at the back. Around her neck are three or four silver chains and the bracelet on her wrist looks like barbed wire. She is so badass, I can't even handle it.

My phone vibrates six times in a row, which means it's a phone call. I check it in case it's Johnny, but it's Colby again. Ignore. I never told him I was definitely coming over tonight, and he didn't bother getting back to me until now. Besides, it's not like he hasn't bailed on me a thousand times before.

A white furry thing darts out of the band room when Blake goes to turn on the light.

"That's Dove. She's my cat, except we're not friends. She doesn't like me."

The cat glares at us from the stairs and hisses before disappearing.

"Damn, she really doesn't," I say.

"I don't know why, either. She only likes my mom. Whenever she's not home, Dove hides."

Blake turns on the light and we step into the band room. It's about the size of my parents' bedroom. At the far end is a set of drums. Then there are a couple big amps laid out against the left wall. There's a mic set up on a stand with its thick wire leading to another amp at the right of the room. The walls are covered in music posters, and some of the bands in them are ones I like. Beside me is a big sofa that faces where the band would stand.

"Wow. This is pretty sweet. How often do you guys practice?"

"A couple times a week usually."

I take a seat on the couch. "So, how'd you get into singing?"

"It all started with choir," she says, diving into a story about the elementary school she went to, back when she lived in Ottawa. "And then last year, Charlie and Billy put an ad online looking for a girl singer and a bass player. At first, we used to practice in Billy's garage, but it was cramped in there so my parents said it was okay that we move everything in here."

"So, those are some guy's drums?"

She nods. "Charlie's. The drums are a pain to move, so it would've been nice to have practice at his place, but he lives in an apartment building. It's not far from here, so he can come and check on them and practice if he wants—as long as I let him, of course."

"He lives in the McKinley buildings then?" I say, and she nods. "My brother does work there."

"Oh yeah? So, how old's your brother?"

"Twenty-six." I talk about him for a bit.

"Sounds like he wins everything."

"He's pretty cool."

"I don't have any siblings. Charlie and his brother are constantly fighting—like until something breaks or bleeds. Two weeks ago, they got a noise complaint over one of their fights. The cops and the super showed up at their door. Charlie was texting me through the whole thing. I think they're crazy."

"Me and my brother aren't like that. Johnny's always been cool. Once, when I was little, we built a fort and I thought we were gonna move in there, it was so sweet."

Blake smiles and curls a leg under her. We just keep talking, about anything, and all of it is interesting to me. And when I tell her stuff about me, it seems she's into it.

"You're really pretty," I say without meaning to. The shock makes me choke on my spit. Blake's smiling like she's not embarrassed at all by what I just said. That makes me even more nervous. "Uh, so are you just friends with a bunch of guys then?"

"No. Robyn's my best friend and she's a girl," she says. "And I've been hanging out with this new girl since we teamed up for the photo diary project."

I'm pretty sure there's only one new girl in grade eleven this year. "Olivia?"

"Yeah. You know her?"

"Sort of," I say, and Blake looks like she's waiting for more but I don't want to talk about Colby right now. "She . . . uh. She hung out with people I know. So, is Charlie your boyfriend?"

"No. Not anymore."

That goes right for my chest and takes all the words out of my head. This Charlie guy she keeps talking about was her boyfriend. His drums are in her house.

"Oh. Well, that makes sense," I say. He's the Some Guy Colby was talking about.

"It does?"

"I just mean—well, he seems like the kind of dude someone like you would be into."

I pull out my phone and pretend to stare at it. Colby keeps texting suck it over and over. When I look up, Blake's making a face, like I'm something impossible to figure out. Or maybe from where she's standing, I just look like a friend. I always look like just a friend. Just some girl.

WHEN BLAKE GOES TO grab her drink from the other room, I send Johnny a text. My mom probably thinks I'm at Colby's, but she still expects me home by now.

Johnny replies with: Gonna swing by in 20 min. Be out front.

Blake reappears. Looking at her makes my back go tingly, and the tingles turn into chills. She takes a seat but instead of being completely at the end of the couch, half of her is on the middle cushion. There's less than a foot between my knee and her left thigh. That's what I focus on while she checks her phone.

"Feel like playing *Mario Kart* or something?" she says when she's done.

"Yeah, but my brother's picking me up in about fifteen minutes."

"Already? But you just got here."

"Yeah. I figured your parents would probably be home soon and think it's weird that I'm here," I say. "And it's a school night and all."

"Why would they think it's weird you're here?"

"Just because they don't know me, I guess."

"My parents are nice to strangers."

When she walks out, I leave a few feet between us. It seems like the more I want to be near her, the farther away I stand. She probably smells the massive crush evaporating off my skin.

We head to the staircase, me hanging behind. I swear, she keeps slowing down so I'll gain on her. Or maybe I can't keep track of my legs right now. She flips the basement light off, and the glow from the top of the stairs is all there is. My arms are all tingles, like they're trying to tell me something, so I shove my hands in my pockets.

At the bottom of the stairs, Blake stops.

"You're not going to try anything, are you," she says, her back to me.

I can't tell if it's a question or a statement. But it gives me goose bumps. Why can't I just go for it?

She pauses, takes a step back so that her back is almost against me. Her hair is right there, and I want to touch it. "Can you put your arms around me?"

83

"Yeah."

My hands go up to her waist, palms and fingers flattening the material of her shirt against her sides then her stomach. Then her back is against my chest. My face is in her hair. It smells pretty, like berries. When she moves her head to the right, mine goes to the left. A little more and my chin would be on her shoulder. She rests her arms on top of mine.

Time passes and we stay like that.

She moves in my arms and I feel like she might get away. So I kiss her ear. It's kind of awesome to feel a shiver move through someone and know I'm the one who caused it. I just can't believe this is happening because not five minutes ago, I was pretty sure she'd never think of me that way.

I think maybe she could be my girlfriend. I don't want to be *her* girlfriend, though. But there's this part of me that totally knows I could be her boyfriend. I don't want her to think of me as a boy, or a boy substitute, though. I want to be a boyfriend who is a girl. I have no idea how to explain that stuff to anyone, let alone a girl I like. I just wish it was already all understood.

She pulls away and whispers, "Let's go."

She grabs my hand. We're holding hands now.

The whole way up the stairs, I think about how I might be asleep right now. How can this be real? It's so intense, my heart is beating too fast. Maybe it's Blake. Maybe she's the reason this is so nuts.

Or maybe this is just me being a total girl about it.

ELEVEN

WHEN I WAKE UP IN THE MORNING, I WONDER IF I
made last night up. But then I see my clothes draped over my
chair. On my cellphone, Blake's text from last night is waiting
to be read over and over again. She texted: *I so wish you could've
stayed longer, Pen.* I'd texted her back: *Me too.* What would've
happened if I'd stayed?

I stare at my hands. They touched her. My skin remem-
bers. My lips were on her ear. I think that might've been a
dumb move. I never pictured myself as the type to kiss a girl's
ear, but it was right there and—yeah, it was dumb. No one's
first kiss with a girl is between their lips and her ear.

On the bus, Colby tells me to suck it for wasting his time
last night. I tell him I fell asleep on Johnny's couch. He doesn't
buy it. Whatever.

At school, I don't talk to Blake. I don't even look at her.
Things are different the morning after. Sometimes they're
better, but other times they feel wrong. Sometimes you regret
doing something so much because it made you realize things
about yourself—like that you never wanted to do that thing in
the first place.

So I give her space. And I hope to hell she doesn't actually want it.

After the lunch bell, I'm at my locker putting my books away when she heads over. I make myself look at her. There's a smile on her face. And she tucks her hair behind her ear— *the* ear.

"I sort of have something to ask you," she says.

"Okay, shoot," I say.

"I just wanted to know if you're free to hang out in two weeks, on Saturday, October first, around four to be exact."

"In two weeks? That's in forever. But yeah, I'm totally down for that."

"Really?" She gives me this wide grin. "Robyn can't come, but I invited Olivia, too."

My face wants to bend into some expression that would make it clear how weirded out I am. I give her thumbs-up with both hands, hoping it'll make up for my face. "So what is this October first thing, anyway?"

"I have band practice that day. It's sort of a big deal because we're rehearsing at the community center. Charlie thought it would help to have a practice in the hall where the Battle of the Bands is going to be on New Year's, so we're inviting a few people to sit in."

"So you want me to come stare at you while you sing?"

"You are *not* allowed to stare at me!" She twists the end of a chunk of her hair. "I also have a favor to ask: Will you tell me if I suck? Robyn always lies to me and says I'm great."

"Robyn's smart." I grin, making myself hold eye contact

with her. It's kind of awesome that she cares what I think. "I'm pretty sure you'll rock no matter what."

She's the one who looks down now and her cheeks go pink. It makes me feel badass. I wish some part of me was touching her. Whenever she's near, my fingers tingle. Facing her again. I grin like a moron. She grins back. Last night flashes in my mind.

I follow Blake to her locker. For just a second, it's almost like I'm walking my girlfriend to her locker. I'd carry her books if she let me. I wonder what she sees when she looks at me. Outside of school—outside of her basement, surrounded by regular people, by her friends, by tall dudes with beards— she'll realize I'm not a guy. She'll also realize I'm not exactly a girl either.

AFTER BLAKE GOES TO find her lunch table, I wander away from the cafeteria, avoiding my usual table. Colby and Garrett are sitting with Tim and Ray, these two guys in grade twelve. Tristan's sitting at a table near the microwaves with Trent and Kyle, so that probably means Garrett and the others were being jerks. I watch Olivia finish up in line, carrying a little container of fries. She walks along the tables, not looking at anybody. Blake and Robyn wave and call her name. Olivia's head pops up and she smiles and waves back, but she keeps walking.

When she gets close enough to the hallway, I call her name. She looks weirded out by the fact that I'm here. "Can I talk to you?"

She stands there, holding the cardboard container with both hands. "What is it?"

"Not here," I say. "Follow me."

In the west hallway, there's a chapel that never gets used for chapel-y stuff. Inside, there's a small supply closet, a tiny room with a lightbulb that swings from the ceiling. It's always locked, except it doesn't latch, so most of us know to wiggle the knob and push to get it to open. There's a big painting of the Virgin Mary on the back wall, a couple fold-out chairs, an altar, crates of candles, and a bunch of other boxed stuff used for mass.

We stand inside, and Olivia closes the door behind her.

"You ever wonder why this chapel is even here?" I say, and Olivia's eyebrows go up. "I mean, it's not like we have a priest here, and mass happens in the auditorium. Like, what did they think when they built the school? That a bunch of us would want to come pray between classes?"

"Praying doesn't work," she says.

"Praying definitely doesn't work."

I'm thinking about my mom and her Mary statue, thinking about all the prayers she must've had about me. I wonder what Olivia's thinking about.

"Okay, so Blake invited me to her thing next week," I say. "I think I want to go."

She might be a little relieved. "Oh. Well, I can tell her something came up."

"Why?" I say. "Blake said you'd feel weird going alone."

"I think I'd feel weirder going with you."

That's kind of harsh. "Why? Because people will think you're weird for showing up with a girl who looks like a boy?"

She seems panicked, like she wasn't thinking that at all. "No! That has nothing to do with it."

"Well . . . what then?"

She holds her hands out like, *Are you serious right now?* "You really think I want Colby to hate me more than he already does?"

"He's not coming. He doesn't even know I talk to Blake."

"Yes," she says, "he does."

My eyebrows go screwy, and now I'm the one giving her my own are-you-serious-right-now gesture. "How do you know?"

"Because he told me."

"How? When?"

"Sometimes he calls me."

He calls her? He wants me to threaten her to stay away from him and he *calls* her? What the hell. "Okay—what is the deal between you and him? Because obviously you didn't listen to the advice I gave you."

"It's not that easy," she says.

"How is it not easy to stop hanging around someone who makes you feel like crap?" I ask. "You said you learned your lesson."

"He's different when it's just us. And I know that sounds stupid, but things were complicated, okay?" she says. "You have no idea."

"What was complicated?"

She rubs her eyebrows obsessively, like she's trying to

smooth them into place even though they're super thin and clean to begin with. "What's going on? Did he put you up to this?"

Paranoid—both of them. She rests her things on the edge of the altar and looks down, putting her hands on her hips, and it just doesn't look good. She tries to act all tough, but under the surface, she always seems ready to lose it and bawl.

"It's bad," I say. "Isn't it."

"It's fine."

It's not fine. Her face says so.

"Olivia?" I ask, and it's like time stops. Because I'm not an idiot. This whole mess—it has to be bad enough to account for everything that's been going on, for the way they've been acting. What if it's big—really big?

"It's fine," she says to the ground.

"Olivia," I say again. "Are you—are you pregnant?"

"What? No!" she says, all exaggerated. I felt like crap for even asking, until her gut reaction crumbles, and fear makes her features freeze.

"Because you were sick," I start, watching her eyes dart between the floor and the walls at her side. My heart starts pounding. "And Colby's worried you're going to talk shit about him, and you guys have obviously had some secret thing going on this whole time." She says nothing. "And . . . he told me."

"He told you." It's not a question. She closes her eyes.

"No," I say. "But I think you just did."

Is this really what's been going on this whole time? This is bigger than big. It's massive.

90

"I'm not pregnant, okay? I'm not," she says, and it sounds like she's about to cry. "I thought I was, but I'm not."

"Why did you think you were?"

"Because we didn't use anything, and I was so worried. He just said it wasn't his problem, that I should stop freaking out." Her words are coming out fast, like she's afraid I might start yelling at her. "But then I was late, and I took tests. I guess I panicked too soon. But he got really mad at me for it, and now it's all a mess. He's different. But I won't say anything about him. Believe me, Pen, okay? I want this all to be over."

I could say I believe her, or tell her I'm sorry, but right now, I'm just stuck thinking about that night, and about how their mess spread over to me. Olivia wasn't there that night, but it was about her. She has no idea what her panicking too soon about being knocked up caused. And I don't know who, out of the three of us, I'm more pissed off at right now.

"Are you sure it's over now?" I say.

She frowns, probably because my tone changed. She nods and says, "I'm sorry."

She whips the door open, and it slams into a box of candles. She's gone before I can tell her I'm sorry, too.

TWELVE

THE NEXT DAY, THE NOISE DOWNSTAIRS STARTS
right around lunchtime, when the first carful of family pulls
up to my house. Soon the smells of all kinds of different foods
start making their way up to my room. Today is my dad's
birthday—he's fifty-five—and the family's over from Ottawa.
Worst timing ever. My head is full of Olivia and Colby.

My mom comes up to my room, which she doesn't do often.

"You wear hat," she says. "I want no one see the hair."

"Okay."

"You watch out now, okay?" she says. "I want you no make
hard for me *e* for *Pai*. I want you to be good girl. This no joke,
Penelope. *Respeito.*"

"I'm not making things hard," I say, but she closes her eyes
and holds her hands up like she won't argue.

"You stop," she says. She tells me she needs a break from
me. "Not today, okay? Not today."

I turn my collar up and reach for the black baseball cap
hanging on the inner doorknob to put it on, flattening my
freshly styled hair. The smile on my lips says, *Are you happy
now?* She whirls around and I close the door behind her, maybe
a little too harshly.

BY DINNERTIME, THE WHOLE clan is here and I can't get away with staying up in my room anymore. Johnny's old bedroom is full of suitcases and the blow-up mattress is set up next to his old bed. There are, like, fifteen people here, and most of them take an hour asking me how school is and if I'm being a good girl and helping my parents around the house. Anyone walking into this house without knowing us might think we're all angry at each other. We talk with our hands, slap our knees, and act like every piece of news we share is unbelievable.

"Get outta here, Duarte!" my uncle Adão says to Dad, switching to Portuguese to talk about overtime laws in Canada. "You crazy!"

The women are in and out of the kitchen, bringing things to the table, and then serving their husbands like the men won't eat unless food is brought to them. My aunt Joana is the worst, not even sitting down to eat until she's sure my uncle Adão has everything he needs. I don't really know if this is a bad thing or not, because I don't know who's making who do what. Maybe my aunt likes it, being a servant.

When my mom tells me to set up the kids' table, it makes me pissy, knowing she's going to make me sit with the little ones. The kids' table is made up of two fold-out tables set up side by side in the hallway outside the dining room, and the other five kids who end up around it are all way younger than me. Marc's on his phone. Sara, Katie, and Amelia are talking about whether or not my mom has colored thread so they can make friendship bracelets they saw on Pinterest. Madison, who's too young to care about that, lines up these tiny dog and cat figurines in front of her plate and then changes her mind and puts them back in this pink purse hanging over her shoulder. Madison's baby brother, Emanuel, gets to sit at the big-people table in his high chair.

I spend an hour staring at my phone, flipping between Facebook and texting Colby. I picture telling him I know about Olivia, just to see what he'd say. Marc tells me he's texting his girlfriend. When I ask what they're texting about, he says, "It's private. Okay, don't tell my mom and dad, but it's dirty—good dirty. Hey—your bathroom upstairs has a lock, right?"

"Aw, come on! That's disgusting. Keep it in your pants. You're twelve," I say.

"Almost fourteen," he says, then he's not listening anymore. That kid thinks he's the next Cristiano Ronaldo—without the soccer skills.

"Penny, I want ketchup!" Madison says.

She's, like, six years old, but still. "Dude, don't call me that."

"Pen, I want ketchup," she says.

"Fine," I say, kind of glad for the excuse to get away. I head for the kitchen, where my cousin Constance is grabbing a plate and scoping out the casseroles on the stove.

"Your brother's a horndog," I tell her.

"My mom says he's dating an older woman."

"What? How old?"

She grins. "Fourteen."

"The boy must have game," I say.

We grin at each other, then she digs into the potato

94

casserole. "Look at your hair—it's so short! How's school?"

My hand goes to my head while I look around to see if Mom is within earshot. "You can tell it's cut?"

"Of course!"

"Well, can you, uh, not tell anybody?"

"It's a secret?"

"Not really. But my mom hates it, so . . . you know."

"Gotcha," Constance says with a wink. "Oh, I sent you guys an invitation to the wedding in the mail. You should get it soon."

"Oh. Yeah. Congratulations."

She squeezes my arm, while her other hand holds a plate overflowing with wedges of potatoes sprinkled with *pimentas*. "You bring Colby along if you want. He's such a little hottie. You're old enough to bring a date."

"Oh. Um . . . okay."

My dad's parked in his recliner with the remote in hand, which means the cousins can't watch TV so they keep bugging me to let them play with my iPod or my phone. The baby never cries because he's always in someone's arms, usually my mom's. She makes baby noises at him and he smiles. I really hope if he decides he likes dolls, my aunt Manuela won't turn out to be like my mom. The four aunts and my mom gather around the baby while they talk about their kids. I already know my mom won't be sharing any stories about hers.

JOHNNY COMES UP AFTER dinner's over and we're all eating cake. He comes to sit beside me on the couch, a heaping plate of food in his hands. When my aunts and uncles ask about his job, he lays it on thick about all the extra work he's gotten through his new Facebook page. Dad watches him with narrowed eyes, while Mom disappears to the kitchen to make coffee for everybody.

Johnny nods to Dad's unwrapped present sitting in its box next to the recliner. Everyone chipped in for a brand-new TV. I'm pretty sure we're both thinking gaming on that thing would be awesome—not that Dad would ever give up his spot in front of it.

"I wasn't sure you were gonna show," I say.

"I get my balls busted if I come, and I get 'em busted if I don't. At least this way I get food, you know?"

"Yeah."

My uncle Adão goes, "Hey, João. You no work at factory yet? Money money with the overtime, huh?"

Johnny gives me a look like, *Here we go.* "Nah, I'd rather work for myself. Grow my business."

"Oh, you big business man!" *Tio* Adão says, downing his fifth beer. "Big Shot Oliveira! Why you not give you *pai* a job, huh? Big big shot."

"Ya, ya." Dad laughs, then says Johnny's a big shot living in his parents' basement.

It goes quiet and Johnny gives a twisted chuckle while he finishes his mouthful. So I say, "Johnny does the mayor's property, and he has the contract for all the apartment buildings in Castlehill. Plus, he gets recommended by real estate agents all the time. He's the best in this town. And in Crestonvale, too."

"Forget about it," Johnny says to me. He points to his ear.

"In one ear, out the other—remember?"

"No good," Dad says, then he goes off about how the mayor is a crook who drives around in a Mercedes he pays for with the taxes he gets from my dad. Dad says if Johnny was smart, he'd take the job at the factory with the benefits and retirement package. "And you go buy a house."

"I'd buy a new truck before I'd buy a house," Johnny says to no one in particular. He dips corn bread into the runny stuff at the bottom of his plate.

"No smart," Dad says, and my uncle nods while taking a swig of beer.

"Okay, okay," my mom says, which is her version of "enough."

"You got a girlfriend, Johnny?" my aunt Jacinta says. Johnny shrugs as a response, which is smart because Jenna isn't the type of girlfriend you'd want to answer questions about.

"A good-looking man like you—I'm sure you've got someone special," *Tia* Valerie says. She's my uncle Francisco's wife, and he's got his hand on her thigh. Sara and Amelia scroll through an iPad at their feet, not paying attention to their parents at all. "You must be getting close to moving out and starting a life."

"Oh yeah," Johnny says. He leans over to me and whispers, "You know, because what I got right now isn't a life, huh?"

Tio Adão says, "You gotta get good job to pay for the babies. Cut grass no give the money for the baby."

I don't know why they always go off like they think all Johnny does is mow lawns as if he's some kid my age trying to earn a couple extra bucks in the summer. What he did with the mayor's property ended up being photographed for the paper. Plus, he does all the repairs and painting of the vacant apartments waiting to be rented at the McKinley buildings.

"What about you, Penelope?" *Tia* Jacinta says.

"Penelope—what you doing? You got the boy*friend*?" *Tio* Adão asks.

Now all the adults are looking at me. Except for my parents.

"No," I say.

"You no get a boy*friend* when you look like João, huh? Small One Johnny!" he says with another drunk chuckle. "Snip snip you hair. Scary tough girl!"

Mom gives me a sideways glare like, *Happy now?* Constance looks like she feels bad for me, wincing while she leans into her fiancé.

"I got gum stuck in it."

"You little tough girl, Penelope! Small One Johnny!"

"Not really."

"Yeah, you tough girl." My uncle lifts his beer like he's toasting the fact that I'm a tough girl and he drains the rest of it.

"Hey," Johnny says, meeting my uncle's drunken gaze. "Lay off her, okay? *Pare, agora.*"

"What you say?" Dad's eyes go right for Johnny, like how dare he talk to his uncle like that.

My uncle laughs and says, "You tough big brother, huh? Big man."

Johnny puts his plate on the coffee table, then he leans back and stares at Dad. The vibe changes. People are getting up and moving around, the girls rushing toward the dining room, my aunt Manuela bouncing the baby up and down, the other aunts clearing off the last of the dishes. Constance and her fiancé escape to the kitchen.

I send Colby a 911 text.

There's always some kind of argument when we all get together. My mom's going to lose it on me for being the cause of it this time.

"What?" Dad says to Johnny. "You wanna say something? Say."

It sounds like a dare.

"I said nothing. You guys are the ones talking," Johnny says.

"Big tough man," *Tio* Adão says, except he's not as drunk–happy as he was a second ago. "I tell you, Duarte, my kids no tough like this. My kids . . . they got the *respeito*."

"Let's just go," I tell Johnny. "There's cake."

"What?" Dad says. "What you say?"

"We're gonna go get cake," I say.

"You house is you house, Duarte." *Tio* Adão's shaking his head like he's disappointed in his little brother. "In my house, *I* say. I say this, I say that. No one say nothing in my house. Nobody tough in my house but me. I pay the money, I say."

"You want another beer, *Tio*?" Johnny says. "You wanna drink some more? *Outra cerveja, Tio?*"

My uncle's laughing, but his eyes shift over to my dad, like he's waiting to see how his little brother's going to handle this.

"Hey, *esse é o seu tio. Respeito!*" Dad says, pushing to his feet.

It's like the whole house goes quiet, even though mostly everyone isn't even in this room. My dad rarely raises his voice.

"Yeah, yeah. Respect," Johnny says, standing up. "You know, for a word to mean something, you gotta do stuff to back it up."

"João Oliveira! You come in my house, no say hi to nobody, eat my *comida*, now you tell me what to do?"

Johnny's face hardens. His eyes close, and his jaw tightens. I want to say something, but all I can do is bounce my foot like crazy. Finally, he gets up and gives this fake smile. *"Desculpe. Pai bença. Tio bença. Obrigado por comida."*

Dad and *Tio* Adão don't give him a response because it's pretty obvious Johnny wasn't really sorry, that he was just saying words.

The doorbell rings, and Johnny takes off.

THIRTEEN

THERE ARE ALL KINDS OF EXCITED GIRLY NOISES coming from the front hall now. Colby appears in the living room doorway, hitching his chin up at me. I knew he'd get his butt here right away when he saw the 911.

"What's up, Portuguese people?" he says to no one in particular. "I'm starving."

"Hey hey, Koo*bee*!" my uncle says, raising his beer. "What you do, huh?"

"I smelled the fish from my house so I came over," he says, which makes everyone smile with pride, because *bacalhau* is our thing—especially the way my mom makes it.

Everyone starts trickling back into the living room. My aunt Joana comes with a fresh beer for *Tio* Adão. My family's always liked Colby. He nods and laughs at the right times even if there's only Portuguese flying around the room, and at the table, he always takes seconds of everything. The aunts think he's such a nice boy, but I think they're basing that on the fact that he's got a nice-looking face and he smiles a lot.

"You like tough girl, Koo*bee*?" my uncle says.

"Uh . . . sure," Colby says.

"You like the tough girl. This cut hair no good. Penelope

look like a boy. You tell Penelope she be pretty girl like her *mãe*. You nice boy, you tell her," *Tio* Adão says.

I pull my baseball cap low to cover my eyes. "Oh man. This is messed up," I whisper, knowing Colby can hear me.

"Yeah, okay. I'll tell her," Colby says.

My uncle raises his beer and laughs. "I like you, Koo*bee*."

"Thanks," Colby says with a wide grin.

"You want some food?" I ask him.

He nods, and we head to the kitchen. My mom's Saran-wrapping food but she figures out what we're here for, so she starts loading fish on a plate for Colby.

"You *mãe* no make this for you, huh," my mom says.

"Not like this," he says. "This fish is awesome. It's that *pimenta* stuff."

"*Pimenta moida*. I make. It's good, huh?" Mom's scowly face turns into a smile and she piles more fish. It's the perfect moment for me to say, "Can I go to Colby's?"

"It's black outside," she says.

"Just for a bit," I say.

"Just to eat some fish and watch a movie," Colby explains. "Can I have bread, too? Did you buy it from that place again? Man, corn bread rocks. Can I take some fish for my dad? He loves it, too."

She slices a big wedge of the bread and wraps it in a clean dish towel. Then she adds more fish to a different plate she gives to me, and shoos us away, saying, "You watch out now, Penelope."

Colby winks at me as we escape the kitchen.

"Drunk uncle?" he says as we slip into our shoes.

"Yeah. And brother-dad drama," I say. "Thanks. You know . . ."

"No problem, dude," he says. "Got your back."

WHEN WE GET TO Colby's, we go through the front so we can give his dad some food. Mr. Jensen is this super tall dude who looks like an older version of Colby, but with a bald head. He rubs his hands together when I hand him a plate with fish and says, "Good job, son. Don't tell your mom. She doesn't want me eating fried stuff." He turns to me and says, "Give my compliments to the chef. Is your brother home? I wanted to check with him about next week's work."

"He just went out," I say.

Mrs. Jensen comes in and narrows her eyes at Colby's dad with a piece of fish halfway into his mouth. "I'd like to thank you for feeding your father more crap and making him fat. Thank you."

"You're welcome, Mom."

Mr. Jensen finishes chewing fast. "Honey, I was just having a little—"

"I don't care. I don't want to hear it, Tom." Mrs. Jensen walks out the front door, letting it slam behind her.

Colby waves me over and we take the stairs down to his room. I sit on the couch, holding a plate of smelly fish. Colby pulls the patio door open halfway and stands there going through his pockets.

"That fish is gonna be awesome later, when I get the

munchies," he says, pulling out a joint. He sparks it and sucks on it for a while. We're not worried about getting caught because his mom's out, and Mr. Jensen secretly smokes weed, too. Colby found his stash last year.

"So what was going on at your house?" he asks.

"Same old crap. My dad taking hits at Johnny, and my uncle egging my dad on."

"Your brother should move the hell out."

"Yeah, but rent's really expensive. And my parents would always be calling him back over here to do all this work."

"Then maybe he should just stop answering his phone for a while," Colby says. "Your cousin was checking me out again."

"Constance?" I roll my eyes. "Yeah, whatever. She's, like, twelve years older than us."

"So? Every time I'm over there, she's all over me."

"You wish."

He laughs. "Anyway. Thought you'd want to know that even though you almost screwed things up for me, I still managed to score with that girl from the mall."

"I wasn't the one saying all kinds of dumb stuff to scare her away."

He glares at me from where he stands with one foot out the door so he can blow smoke outside.

I take a breath, thinking about Olivia, about how I could just tell him I know. But my mouth stays shut.

"You've kind of been a pain in my ass the last couple of weeks, Pen," he says.

"What if *you're* the one who's been extra pissy lately?"

"What are you talking about? I'm no different." He stares me down from behind a curtain of weed smoke that's trapped inside. "It's you that's got something up your butt. And I think I know what it is. It's a girl."

"Huh?"

"I saw you yesterday with Blake. Not that I hadn't already figured. You really gotta be less of a douche about this, Pen." He knows. "I can't blame you. You don't have any game yet. I haven't taught you how to be cool."

"Nothing's happening. We were just talking."

"Yeah, sure," he says, offering me the joint, but I shake my head. "It's not your fault. Everyone acts like an idiot when they first start getting some. But listen, when you get a girl, you can't go all pathetic and ditch your buddies. Only jerkoffs do that. It's a question of loyalty and respect."

Respeito. I know all about that. "I wouldn't ditch my friends."

He chuckles, finishing with the roach. He slips it into his pack of cigarettes as he lets himself collapse on the opposite end of the couch. "You say that now, but just wait till a girl goes all whiny, guilt-tripping you into going to her place all the time to, like, watch her paint her nails. Trust me, I know what I'm talking about. I've never let a girl get in the way of my loyalty, right?"

"Yeah." This Olivia stuff was happening behind my back almost the whole time. Maybe he thinks that means she hasn't been getting in the way, because he never ditched Tristan and me, never disappeared. But that would be complete bull because he did let it get in the way—he let it screw everything up between me and him.

"You just gotta be ready. Girls try everything to get in there and stir up some shit. If I didn't put my foot down, these girls would've messed with my life so many times. I tell 'em to suck it. You gotta be tough. Even if you're not a guy, it'll probably work the same way. Guaranteed Blake looks at you and sees a dude—why else is she only giving you the time of day now that you look like that?" He pauses to shoot me a look like, *Am I right?* "So she'll just be acting like a regular girl about it. This is why you gotta remember where your loyalty lies."

"So—okay, wait, let's say I did have a girlfriend, then what?"

"Well, first," he says, "you don't bring her to hang out with us. That's just sad. No one wants to watch two people rocking their nastiness together. Plus, girls are annoying as hell when they're near the dude they're messing around with. Trust me, it could get ugly."

"You bring girls around all the time."

"They're not my girlfriends—that's the difference. They're just girls I'm working on hooking up with, so they're totally different. Once a girl's got you, she turns into something else. Trust me. You remember Leslie? Bailey? Alisha? Remember what they were like before I told them to take a hike?" Colby doesn't mention Olivia.

"Yeah."

He lights up a cigarette and hands that to me. "Blake already thinks she's hot and badass, so she'll be way worse than the average hot girl. And because you're technically a girl, well—just be ready for whatever bull goes with that."

"Like what?"

"This is Castlehill, dude. In real life, hot girls want guys. That's just how it is. I mean, maybe that girl Gina in grade ten could go either way, because she's super fit, but she's got half her head shaved and she wears those ugly boots. Otherwise, think of the decent girls at St. Peter's—they're all into guys. There are a few who pretend they're into girls, but only when they're trying to be all feminist about it, you know, like 'I don't need penis,' when really they think we're gonna feel all threatened and start doing everything they ask just to get some." He gives me that *Am I right?* look again. "The ones who are for-real into girls are the fat ones, the ones who look guyish, and the angry girls, but even then, it's usually because they're pissed off that they're not hot enough to get one of us to look at them. So, like, who the hell knows what Blake's deal is." He points a finger at me. "I'm not saying you should stay away from her, but just know it could turn around real quick. So, rock that while you can, *if* you can."

I can't help it, I give him a full on crooked-eyebrow, you're-full-of-it glare. But it's not like I can say he's wrong, because he knows way more than I do about this stuff. It all just sounds really messed up. Maybe I just don't want him to be right.

"Remember Jess Gallagher?" he says, then flashes me a look of challenge. "Right? How long was she a dyke for?"

"You don't even know her. She's two years older than us, and she's gone to college. How do you know what she's doing now?"

"Answer the question, dude."

"Maybe she's bi."

107

"Temporarily dykey, attention-seeking, confused straight girl. She's with Ike's brother now, going on a year."

My answer is a roll of the eyes, then I shove the fried fish under his nose, and he digs in.

"Are we playing something or what?" he asks.

"Yeah. Let's play."

He heads for the stack of games. His phone beeps with a text. It's lying on the couch next to me. Olivia's name appears on the display, along with a couple words of the text: *I swear. It's fine now—*

I probably shouldn't, but I take a chance. "Dude, why is Olivia texting you?"

He shrugs, still busying himself with setting up the game. His back is to me. "Because she's crazy. I'm about to change my number, I swear."

"Well, what's going on? Why is she crazy?"

He hands me the controller, picks up his phone, and flings it onto the bed behind us, then sits on the opposite end of the couch. "I told you. She's, like, in love with me. This is why I'm telling you to watch yourself with Blake. You never know what kind of crap these girls can pull just to keep you hooked in."

"You think Olivia was going to make stuff up, just to hook you in?" I ask.

"Uh, yeah," he says, like I'm naïve. "You know how easy it is for girls to run their mouths and have the guy look like an ass? Nobody questions when girls say things, even if it's total bull."

I wonder if Olivia's texting because she feels bad that she jumped the gun with her late period, or because she feels bad for lying about all of it thinking it would keep him around.

"Well, do you need me to talk to Olivia again? Do you want me to tell her to back off?"

"Nah," he says. "It's fine now."

FOURTEEN

JOHNNY'S BACK BY SUNDAY EVENING TO SEE THE family off, and there's no more talk about what happened to make him storm out in the first place. We go through our good-byes, cheek kisses for everyone. Monday morning, Johnny drives me to school.

"It kind of sucks when everyone visits," I say.

"Tell me about it."

There's no music on, and it's raining. Johnny's heavy on the gas, and everyone around us is driving slow.

"You think Constance will move out, now that she's engaged?" I ask.

"Maybe. Who knows."

"You'd think she'd want out of there, with *Tio* Adão for a father. I don't even get how she's been able to stay there this long."

Johnny pulls into the coffee shop for his morning caffeine, and the truck bounces over the curb. "You want something?"

"No, thanks."

I don't like when he's quiet like this, because it's impossible to know what he's thinking about.

AT LUNCH, TRISTAN AND I head for the computer labs to print out our English assignments. He tells me about this idea he has for a video game.

"So then basically, these dudes would be hopping through time and doing all this shizz they shouldn't be allowed to do," he says.

"Like what?"

"Like changing things, important events that happened in history."

We sit side by side and push our USB sticks into the computer. A couple people come into the lab, but they go sit way at the back.

"That sounds pretty sweet," I say. "But how would that be a video game? What would you do?"

"What do you mean? It would be so legit, to, like, be able to go stop Martin Luther King Jr. from getting shot, and to warn all these people about the tsunami before it hits."

"Yeah, for sure. But I still don't get how that would be a video game."

The printer at the end of our row starts spitting out pages. I head over to get them, handing Tristan his copy.

"It would be a story-based game, I guess," Tristan says.

"Or it could be a kickass book," I say. "You could write it."

"I don't know how to write."

110

"You could learn."

"Yeah . . . maybe," he says. "But I don't really like English class."

"Yeah, I think English class is the reason I don't like reading." I sign out of my computer account. "Are we done?"

"I gotta fix Colby's before I print it. He messed up almost every question."

"I'm surprised he actually did any of it."

"Listen to this: *'Come, you spirits that tend on mortal thoughts, unsex me here / And fill me from the crown to the toe top-full / Of direst cruelty!* What is Lady Macbeth saying here? Explain.' Colby wrote, *'She's saying she's pissed off because she's sexually frustrated. She wants a man to fill her.'* He can't be serious."

"I didn't really know what to answer for that either. I looked online, though, and found something about Lady Macbeth not wanting to be weak anymore," I say. "In that book of yours, you should make it so the character goes back in time and takes Shakespeare's feathered pen away. Then we could read something else. In actual English."

"Sometimes he says some pretty legit stuff, though. What Lady Macbeth is saying is that she wants to be tough and ready to fight, and to be able to do that, she thinks she needs her girliness to be stripped away by some magical force."

"Really?"

"Yeah."

"Oh. Well, I still don't get it." But maybe I kind of do.

"Uh . . . ," Tristan says, rolling his chair next to mine.

"Why is that Olivia girl hanging out by the door? Does she think Colby's with us? He says she's a creepy stalker."

I turn to see Olivia peeking into the lab, looking right at me.

"No idea," I say, turning away from her. "Are we going? I'm starving."

"I gotta finish this."

"Just leave them. They're *his* dumbass answers."

He gives me this look like, *Yeah, right.*

"I'm leaving," I say. "Come find me when you're done."

I slip my binder under my arm and head for the door. Olivia waits against the wall, and I sweep right past her.

"Pen?"

I stop, letting the breath I'd been holding deflate. "He's not with us. He's already in the caf with Garrett."

"It's you I want to talk to," she says.

"Why?"

Her gaze darts all over the place, like she thinks she's about to get caught doing something bad during school hours.

"I can come meet you in the supply closet after I grab my lunch," I say.

She nods, then gives me a smile, but it fades when I don't return it. I'm not trying to be a jerk, but all these secrets and lies between her and Colby—it's like I'm caught in this thing I know nothing about, and I'll end up paying for it.

TWO CHEESE SANDWICHES IS what I got for lunch today, because my mom's still mad about the weekend. I'm so hungry that the sight of them makes my mouth water. Half a sandwich is stuffed in my mouth when I get to the supply closet. Olivia sits on an overturned crate.

"What's up?" I ask.

She keeps watching me eat, and soon it creeps me out. She seems to notice and snaps out of it, looking at the carpeted floor instead.

"You want half or something?" I say. "It's just cheese and butter. Not that exciting."

"It doesn't look like a regular cheese sandwich."

"Oh, that's because it's St. Jorge cheese on a bun," I say. "It's Portuguese cheese. It kind of tastes like feet."

"It looks good."

I uncover the second sandwich and wave half of it at her. "Just take it! For real."

She does, and she looks even more pumped about it than I felt a few minutes ago. She eats it by picking little chunks away with her fingers.

"So what do you want—besides the sandwich?"

"Would you . . . ," she says, hesitating. "Do you like photography?"

"Photography?"

"Yes. Taking photos."

"I don't know—I've only ever taken them with my phone. Why?"

"I wondered if you'd want to take my place for the photo diary project—you know, the one for the school anniversary party in November," she says. "I don't want to leave Blake hanging."

"Oh. Would she be okay with that?"

"You like Blake," she says, totally ignoring what I asked. My blank face probably makes me look guilty as hell. "Do you like her enough to be her partner for a project?"

"Probably." Then I snort like, *Who am I kidding?* "Totally."

Olivia's hands are clutched together as if she would have been ready to beg me if needed, and right in front of that painting of the Virgin Mary, it looks creepy and appropriate. "Thank you! Thank you so much."

She looks kind of sweet and easy to be mean to. What was Colby doing with a girl like her?

"Why are you bailing from the project all of a sudden?" I ask.

"I've got too much on my plate right now," she says. "Blake talked me into it, but I should've never signed up."

"I was there on Saturday night, when you texted Colby," I say.

Her face drops, and so do her hands. "I just—I don't want him to be so mad at me anymore. I want to make it right. I wish I'd never said anything to him, but he won't let me take it back."

"It just makes him madder, you know, the more you try to make it better," I say. "It's already all screwed up, and it probably can't be fixed."

She wraps her hands around her waist, rocking back and forth. Her face changes, crumples. I think she's going to cry for a second, but the way she swallows, the look of panic in her eyes, the way her mouth is open—oh, man.

She pukes between her feet.

I watch the puddle, listen to her gasp for breath.

"You're sick," I say.

"It's fine!"

"It's not fine," I say. "You lied."

"No! I'm fine. I'm just intolerant to . . ." She gags into her hands, and more chunks come out.

"You really *are* pregnant."

FIFTEEN

THERE ARE TEARS IN HER EYES, BUT I DON'T know if they're real tears, or if they're just from the puking. She wipes her mouth and I look away because it's barf and it smells like feet.

Colby knocked up a girl.

"You're pregnant," I say again.

We joked about this happening. It happens on TV, or to girls who go to other schools.

"You can't tell him, Pen," she says. "Please."

"So it's for sure?" I flatten my hand against the back of my head obsessively, like I'm trying to smooth the hair that's too short to actually need to be styled. "Are you sure that it's for sure?"

"I've been taking tests since my period was due to come back. They were negative. Three of them were. But then," she says, and her bottom lip sticks out like a little kid who wants to cry, "the one I took on Friday wasn't negative. The doctor at the clinic said it's not a mistake, that it takes a little while for it to show up. She said there's some kind of hormone or protein and if there's a positive, then it's positive." She presses her palms against her eyes and sniffles. "It's positive. I shouldn't be telling you this because—well, because now you have to keep the secret, too."

This supply closet is getting smaller all of a sudden. She looks up at me, and some of her hair is stuck to her cheek.

"Olivia—you're pregnant. You can't hide something like that," I say. "And secrets always find a way of coming out."

"I just need time to think."

"Do your parents know?"

"Of course not. My dad and his new wife are gone for a year to set up his company's UK office, and my mom didn't want me to go. And my mom . . ." The way she says it makes it clear I don't have to ask for more information. "I just need time."

"Time for what? What are you going to do?"

"I'm going to fix this," she says.

"How?"

"You have to promise not to tell him," she says, ignoring my question. "Please, Pen."

I reach for a box of pillar candles and I place it between Olivia's legs, right on top of the puke to cover it. She looks shocked. "We can't leave it like this!"

"Why not?"

"It's a mess. It's contaminated. And in here? It's a disgrace."

I shrug. "It could be worse."

She lifts the box and makes a face, then puts the box back. I want to pull the door open because it feels like I'm inhaling puke even if it doesn't smell much anymore, but if I do that, someone could see. Olivia reaches into her purse and comes out with her vibrating phone. She holds the screen out so I can see Colby's name and number flashing across it. "You didn't tell him you were coming to talk to me, did you?"

"No way. All he knows is that I talked to you that one time out front, and only to tell you to back off and leave him alone."

She looks hurt, and it makes me feel like crap. "Something is wrong with Colby."

"You mean besides the fact that he's a douche?"

"If he's such a douche then why are you friends with him?"

"He's like that to girls. Not his buddies."

"You're a girl," she says, then looks confused. "Aren't you?"

"Yeah, but it's not the same. Obviously."

She nods, even though it looks like she doesn't understand. "You'll keep the secret, won't you?"

"I'm supposed to pretend I don't know this is happening?" I say, and she nods.

She stands and dusts her gray uniform pants off, as if she'd been sitting on a dirty curb outside. My eyes keep wanting to drift low, to her stomach, as if I'll be able to see some kind of proof. She's thin, and there's nothing really there.

"What'll happen when you start looking . . . you know?

He'll know you lied when you said you panicked too soon."

"I'm going to fix things before it gets to that, okay?" she says.

"Fix." I try to catch her gaze, but she won't let it happen. "You're going to get an abor—"

"It's fine, Pen. It's my problem."

Colby told her that—that it's her problem. "You're going to fix it all by yourself?"

She doesn't answer.

I stare at the ground, at the dark blue carpet, and in my head, I try to picture what would happen if I told Colby any of this. He'd be pissed. He'd be worse. Who would it help? It wouldn't help Olivia. It sure as hell wouldn't help me. Sometimes with Colby, all he leaves room for is lying. Or maybe not saying anything isn't actually lying.

"What happens now?" I say.

She tries for a friendly grin. "I'm going to talk to Blake about the photo project."

"Okay."

She glances one last time at the box of candles, then she turns to me. "You'll keep the secret?"

"Yeah. I will."

MR. MIDDLETON SURPRISES EVERYONE during English class by deciding to forget about teaching and going with a movie instead. A really, really old *Macbeth* movie.

"There's a newer version, sir," Tristan says.

"I know that, but why would I sacrifice the pleasure of

seeing your faces take in the beauty of a seventies film?" Mr. Middleton says.

Throughout the entire movie, I steal glances at Colby. I think about stuff. About whether or not I can pretend this never happened. About whether or not I can pretend I don't know. That I don't know more than he does. But then I remember if there's anyone who can pretend stuff didn't happen, it's me. Stuff that makes me feel like crap gets pushed to the back of my mind until it's not part of my life anymore. Pretty soon, that messed-up night with Colby will have faded, and this Olivia stuff will, too.

The bell rings before the movie is over, and Tristan actually looks bummed. We rush out of class. Colby and Tristan break away from me when we reach their lockers. After that, I'm dodging bodies and pushing through them. My elbow knocks Blake in the boob.

"Oh man, sorry," I say, coming to a stop. "Oh, wow. I can't believe—sorry."

"You're in a rush."

"Nah. I just really like when school's done."

She smiles, and then it doesn't matter that we're stopped in the middle of a hallway filled with chaos. People just move around us, and it's a blur. Her hair is all swept to one side, and her eyelids are smudged in so much black, it makes the blue of her eyes so . . . there. She's saying something and I'm staring.

"Sorry, what?" I say.

"I said Olivia told me about the project. Her mother sounds

119

like pure diarrhea," she says, and laughter busts out of me. She grins.

"Sorry. It's not funny. It's just . . . pure diarrhea," I say.

"It's so much more righteous than calling someone a bitch, because, well . . . what's worse than pure diarrhea?"

"Really contaminated, infected diarrhea," I say. It echoes in my head, then I get visuals. "Oh, man. I can't believe I said that. I don't even . . . uh . . . yeah. I'm just gonna go away now."

"No!" She puts her hand on my arm for a moment. It's not skin on skin because of my sleeve, but it might as well be. "I was slightly pissed when she told me she was bailing, but then she told me you were going to be my new partner. I think that wins everything."

"Oh . . . yeah?" I say, and she nods. "Well, me too."

"It means we're going to have to hang out, I guess."

"Yeah. We're gonna have to."

"Maybe Saturday? After my rehearsal?" she asks.

I open my mouth to let the "yeah" spill out of me when I feel a smack on my back, below my neck.

"Are you done yet?" Colby asks, his hand dropping from my back. "We're gonna miss the bus, and we don't wanna be late."

"Oh, uh, yeah," I say, wondering what this thing about us being late is about. "I just need a minute. I'll be there."

"We don't have a minute. Remember Avery's bringing Sienna. They're meeting us at the mall at four."

Blake's just standing there while Colby talks at me, and I have no idea what he's going on about because we're not going to the mall. I don't know anyone named Sienna. Blake's watching Colby with this look on her face like whatever he's saying is stupid to her. When her attention is back on me, it's like she's waiting for me to say something.

"Yeah, um." That can't be all I have to say. "I guess I'll talk to you . . . soon?"

"Maybe," she says, and there's an edge to her tone. "Bye."

"Yeah, later," Colby says to her, then to me, "Dude, let's go."

The back of her head gets smaller and smaller.

"What'd you do that for? Who's Sienna?" I ask Colby while I head for my locker.

"I don't know," he says, waiting while I get my bag ready. "Made her up."

"Why?"

"Because you don't wanna keep looking like a desperate idiot. She has to feel like you have plenty of other choices. Like you can do better."

"Why?"

He shakes his head like I'm clueless. "Because she has to want you more than you want her. You want her to end up calling the shots?"

"I just wanted to talk to her."

"So then talk."

"I was." My locker slams louder than I meant it to. "And then you came and messed it up. Now she's pissed at me."

"You'll thank me later," he says, following me. "I know what I'm talking about."

"You don't know as much as you think you do," I tell him. "That's the problem."

He stops. "What did you say?"

"Nothing." I keep walking.

Up ahead, Tristan's almost at the exit. I shout his name before he goes through the door. While I head over to him, I pull out my phone to send Blake a text: sry—colby's a prick as usual—i hope u still wanna hang next weekend.

"Wow, dude. You need to relax," Colby says, catching up to me. "If this is how you're gonna act after one two-second conversation with some girl, then we are going to have a problem."

I ignore him all the way to the bus, where I sit next to Tristan. The whole way, Colby bumps the back of my seat. Blake still hasn't replied by the time I get home.

SIXTEEN

FRIDAY NIGHT, JOHNNY AND I HEAD TO THE PIZZA place for the special on the garlic pizza. On the way, we stop at Walmart to get more Halloween stuff for when we decorate the front of the house. October doesn't even start until tomorrow but we have to take control of the decorating before Mom tries to beat us to it with her pumpkin cutouts and fake spider webs for the porch railing.

At the store, we pick up a couple severed hands and a foot,

six foam tombstones for the lawn, and a cheap Michael Myers costume. We're going to stuff the costume with blankets and make a dummy to sit on the porch, with the bowl of candy in his lap.

When we get to the truck, I stuff the plastic bags on the bunk behind my seat.

Johnny keeps burping at the wheel, which is stinking up the truck, and we haven't even gotten to the pizza place yet.

"That smells like it came out of your butt." I roll down the window.

"What—sorry, man. It's that damn fish."

Johnny hits the brakes when a couple of kids start shuffling across the street randomly, like they're taunting the cars to come close. "Man, what is it with these kids? That's just what I need, to run over a couple of dumb idiots and have to deal with their crying mothers. You better not jaywalk, Pen."

"I don't." Not in front of cars, at least. "Hey, so do your friends ever get pissed off at you for having a girlfriend?"

"Not unless I start acting like a douche bag." Johnny glances my way.

"How do you know you're acting like one?"

"You don't know at first, but your friends do. It's like you change."

"Change how?"

"I don't know," he says, with a sigh like thinking of an answer is too much work. "Like . . . ditching your buddies. Letting the girl run your life. Getting all moody. Spending all your money on dumb stuff. Letting all kinds of drama follow you everywhere. That kind of thing. But that usually comes with dating a girl who's a douche bag."

"But what if you change for the better?"

"If you have douche bag friends, that won't matter," he says. "You just gotta be cool and ask yourself if what's going down feels all right, or if it makes you feel worse. Then you do what you gotta do."

We pull into the pizza place, and Johnny squeezes his big truck into the only free spot left.

"Think you could drive me to this thing tomorrow?" I ask, before we open our doors to get out.

"What kind of thing?"

"Blake invited me to this rehearsal thing for a gig her band has."

"Whoa, she's in a band? That's pretty hot. Does she have an older sister?" He wags his eyebrows. "What does she play? Is it an all-girl band?"

"She sings. And no, it's just her and a bunch of dudes. Tall dudes with beards."

"They all got beards? Like long, metal beards? Not those dumb hipster beards, please."

I shrug, because I don't feel like explaining what I meant.

"I'm gonna have to get a taxi license soon. You put too much mileage on my truck." He asks me what time it's at and then says he can drive me there on his way to meet the guys but that I'll have to figure out how to get home. "Maybe one of the beards can drop you off."

INSIDE, WE ORDER A large. It comes with too much cheese all bubbly on top of lots of layers of meat smothered in garlic sauce—totally perfect. I get garlic dip, because I won't be kissing anyone tonight, and Johnny gets barbecue sauce.

It takes a while before I clue in to the laughing going on next to me. It's not regular laughter, just these clipped little chuckles of dudes egging each other on. I sneak a glance to my right. There's a table of guys and most of them are looking right at me. Great.

"I'm getting a grille for the front of my truck," Johnny says.

He gets all into it, and I'm almost listening, going "Oh yeah?" here and there, to keep his attention on the conversation, and not on the idiots next to us. They probably thought I was a dude, and now they realize I'm not. It would be nice if there were a few other girls in this damn town who looked more like me.

". . . working for this contractor. Who doesn't wanna make more money, right?"

"Oh yeah?"

Johnny gives me a funny look. "What's your problem?"

"Nothing. I'm kind of full. Can we go?"

"I'm gonna hit the can first." He snorts at the look I give him. "I gotta take a leak."

While Johnny's gone, I pack up the rest of the pizza. No one but those guys seems to be staring at me; they're all busy enjoying their pizza night. My ears get so sharp when stuff like this goes down; I can tell when those guys are saying stuff about me. I think one of them might be one of the jerks from the movie theater Colby and Garrett took on last spring.

A bunch of *F* words, including the word "fag," drift over to my ears.

I get up.

"That's nasty, bro. Isn't she a girl?"

"No idea. They'd still be fags, though."

"No, wait. That's a girl. Remember?"

Johnny's not back from the bathroom. What if he heard that stuff? When I'm by myself, I can take that crap because soon, it fades away and it's like it never happened. But when there are people with me—well, that's when it goes from being annoying to being embarrassing. It goes from me rolling my eyes to me wishing I'd never stepped out of my house at all.

Screw those guys.

"He's my brother, idiots," I say, before turning. I throw over my shoulder, "Don't ever talk shit about my brother."

They laugh louder.

"Are you packing?" one of the guys asks. Haven't heard that one in a while. At least one of them is definitely from the movie theater last spring.

I walk away, meeting Johnny as he comes out of the bathroom. He reminds me of Dad, the way he rubs his chest to soothe the indigestion.

"Are you packing?" those guys keep calling out.

"Let's go," I tell Johnny.

"What's going on?" he says.

"Nothing. I'm going to the car."

Johnny stays put. The door is just to the right, and I have my fingers on the handle. Johnny's spotted the guys. He looks back at me.

"Just forget it," I say. "Let's leave."

"What is that, packing? Packing heat? They think you're carrying a gun?"

I shrug. No way am I going to be the one to tell him it can also mean a girl who goes out wearing a strap-on rubber thing just for the hell of it. When those guys said that to me last spring, I went home and Googled it like crazy until I found what they were talking about. It's not like I have any interest in putting anything in my pants that wasn't already there to begin with, but I guess girls who look like guys are also supposed to want the proper equipment.

Johnny storms out ahead of me, and I let out a giant sigh, following after him.

But then he slams the truck door and meets me on his way back over. He throws me the keys. "Go to the truck."

"Don't go back in there," I say, but he's already flying inside the pizza place.

He heads for the douche table. Back in the truck, I can see everything unfold through the window. I'm full of dread and guilt. Johnny should know better by now. But mostly, I'm the one who should know better than getting him stuck in situations like this.

Johnny pounds over to the guys with his shoulders straight out. It's his badass walk. He stops at the table and then his mouth moves. The guys are just sitting there with dumbass smiles on their faces, but they fade when Johnny leans over and pulls open his jacket a bit. Then it's all over. The guys don't look over my way, even as Johnny walks out.

I breathe a sigh of relief as he hops into the driver seat and fires up the engine.

"What'd you tell them?" I ask.

"I told 'em I was packing." He pulls his jacket open, and in the inner pocket sticks out the handle and part of the blade of a massive butcher knife. The big plastic knife with fake blood we just bought for Michael Myers. Johnny revs the truck and peels the tires out of there.

"Maybe you shouldn't do stuff like that," I say when we're cruising down Wilson Avenue past all the department stores.

"Stuff like what?"

"You know—stepping in to defend me or whatever."

"I'm the older brother," he says, looking over at me while we wait at a red light. "It's my job."

"Yeah, but I'm not a kid anymore." I don't look at him. "I can take care of myself."

My eyes are on the road flying by through the passenger window, and Johnny says nothing more.

SEVENTEEN

LATER FRIDAY NIGHT, I HEAD TO COLBY'S. I PUSH
the gate to the backyard to find Garrett there, too. I suck it up
and head over to join them, sitting in the empty chair between
the two. Colby gives Garrett his joint, then he pulls out a cigarette.

"What's up, Penelope?" Garrett asks. "Oh, my mistake. I
mean Steve."

"Ha ha," I say, rolling my eyes.

"Garrett was just going on about this chick he banged yesterday," Colby says. "I don't believe any of it. Who'd wanna get
with that face?"

"You talk all you want, Colby. I've got quite the skills."
Garrett wags his eyebrows and does some nasty thing with
his tongue. "So we went back to her place but her parents were
home, so we hid inside her parents' trailer. This big thing
parked on the driveway. It was like our own hotel room. Anyway, we had some drinks," Garrett says. "So, we're in the tiny
bed, and I'm right about to score and she gets all freaked out."

"Figures," Colby says.

"Why'd she get freaked? Were you being your usual self?"
I say.

Garrett flashes me a dopey grin and continues, "I sorta forgot to bring a condom. So, I was right about to . . . you know, and she goes 'Stop!' and gets all worried about getting pregnant. I told her I'd pull out before, but she was paranoid, saying it doesn't work."

Colby's eyes are on me, and mine are on him. It can't last long because I feel the truth starting to change my face.

"It doesn't," I say to Garrett. "It doesn't work."

He shrugs and brings the joint up to his lips. "It's worked for me enough times."

"Well, you've probably just been lucky. Luck runs out," I say.

"So, then what'd you do?" Colby asks.

Garrett says, "I put my jeans on and ran to the corner store. Got a box of rubbers and ran back. A man's gotta do what he's gotta do—am I right?"

Colby smacks Garrett's hand, then takes another toke before passing it to me.

"You like that, Steve? You like living vicariously through our guy stories?" Garrett asks. I'm pretty sure I like Penelope better than Steve.

"I don't need to live vicariously through your made-up stories," I say. "I got my own stories."

"Oh, yeah?" Garrett leans forward. "What are you waiting for? Spill it! This is the whole point of being friends with a dyke."

Colby tokes and watches me through the smoke.

"As if I'd tell you," I say.

130

Garrett laughs this lazy, stoned sound. "You save it all for your diary? *Dear Diary, today I touched a boob. It made me feel gooey inside. Love, Steve.* Ha! I think you're full of it. You've got nothing to tell, do you, Steve?"

"I've got nothing to tell *you*," I say. "Think what you want."

A couple tokes and my mind goes a little hazy. Garrett takes a few more shots at me, calling me Steve, and then Colby starts a story about the girl Avery from the mall. I lean back in the chair and let my head fall to stare at the sky.

AN HOUR LATER, SO much weed has gone around that I wonder how the cops weren't called here by smoke signal. I haven't smoked any more but I still feel weird. It must be getting to me by secondhand.

"Ike and them are meeting up soon," Garrett says. "We going?"

Colby shrugs. "Maybe later."

Garrett sighs and pretends to be super bored. I check my phone a couple times. Nothing. Not that I'm expecting anything.

"Hey, hey, Pen, I got an idea," Garrett says. "Show us your boobs."

"Oh, give me a break."

"If I had some, I'd show you."

"You *do* have some," Colby says.

Garrett pulls his shirt up to show his slightly flabby man-boobs. "These aren't real. It's just from all the McDonald's I've been eating. Come on, Steve. You're not even using them."

"The Steve thing is getting old," Colby says.

"It's genius," Garrett says.

"Right. I look like a guy so you call me a guy's name. That's so genius," I say.

"You're a guy with real girly boobs," Garrett says. "Come on. Let me see."

"Just because she cuts her hair doesn't make her any less of a girl," Colby says. I look over at him, not sure if what he said is a compliment or an insult. Maybe it's nothing at all.

"I just wanna see some boobs!" Garrett says.

"Dude, screw off. Why don't you show us your junk, huh?" I say.

He looks interested. "What, you wanna see it? I'll show you mine if you show me yours."

"You're nasty. What's wrong with you?" I sit up straight, ready to take off. "Your mom definitely dropped you on your head when you were a baby."

"That's why his face is like that," Colby says.

"Hey!" Garrett crosses his arms. "You guys are so mean! My feelings are hurt. I think the only way I'll cheer up is if I see some boobs."

Colby gets a text, so the conversation stops. Garrett pulls out his Baggie of weed and starts squeezing tobacco from a couple of cigarettes and pulls off the filters, probably because he ran out of papers. He mixes a couple flakes of weed with tobacco and stuffs some back into one of the cigarettes, twisting it into a tight joint.

"You're being pretty damn stingy with those," I say.

"They're for that little creep in grade nine. He can't tell the

132

difference," Garrett says. "My brother used to do that to me all the time, sell me fake stuff. We all have to learn those harsh lessons, am I right?"

He does the same to the second cigarette and then puts them back into his pack. He hands me a regular cigarette. I take it.

"That was a peace offering," Garrett says.

"Yeah, whatever."

Colby puts his phone down and reaches for the cigarette between my fingers. He lights it, takes a couple drags, then places it back between my fingers.

"All right, guys. Are we meeting up with Ike, or what?" Garrett says.

Colby and I ignore him. Colby's definitely distracted, and he keeps shooting me weird looks.

"This is boring. How can we make this interesting . . . ? Oh—I know! With one very important question," Garrett says. "This is serious business. I'm doing research."

"What?" Colby asks.

"Okay, so would it be gay if Pen screwed a guy? Think about it for a minute. *Would* it be gay? It's confusing, am I right?" Garrett says.

All I know how to do is sit here and clench my teeth. But I'm not going to run away. I say, "I don't know how it works either."

"Garrett, man, you're so pathetic," Colby says.

"This is legit," Garrett says. "It's research!"

"Research for who?" I say.

"For me. It's a personal project."

"Why don't you go meet up with Ike and them?" Colby says.

He gets up from the table and points to the side gate. "I'll text you later and let you know if I'm coming."

"Finally! I'm out of here!" Garrett says. To me, he says, "For real, though. Would it be gay? I think it would be. Especially if the guy were to call you Steve while it was going down."

Garrett sticks his tongue out at me and wiggles it between his index and middle finger. I give him the finger and head for Colby's room.

I SIT ON THE couch at the foot of Colby's bed, staring at the TV even though it's not on. Colby throws his cigarettes on the bed, then peels his jacket off before taking a seat next to me.

"I love this movie," he says, then laughs. When I don't respond, he rolls off the couch to go flip on the stereo. Rap music starts playing low. He stands there for a minute before saying, "Damn, I'm baked. Wanna play *Street Fighter*?"

"Okay."

"Why don't you stay over tonight?"

"I can't."

Colby turns and slides his hands into his jeans pockets. His eyes are on mine like he knows it'll mess me up. Being stared at always messes me up. I don't like the feeling spreading through me. It's nasty.

"Stay," he says. "Come on. I kicked Garrett out. It's just us."

Oh, man. Not again.

"I was thinking of trying something," he says. "Maybe mess around."

This is that night happening all over.

EIGHTEEN

HE RAN HIS FINGERS THROUGH THE WAVES against my back that night, like he was trying to give me chills. I've seen him do that kind of thing to girls before. And it worked, because I got goose-bumpy. I wasn't really sure I *wasn't* into it. It's hard to remember what I was thinking that night, but it all just didn't seem like such a big deal.

It was a huge deal. Because I felt like a homo. For the first time ever, I felt really queer. In a bad way. His hands were on me, and the feeling got worse. The feeling I get when I see myself naked in the mirror—that feeling, times a hundred. He touched me, and I turned into the kind of girl I'm not.

Now, while he stands there, staring at me, waiting to see if I'll be into doing a repeat of that night, I think about that feeling. About losing who I am and turning into someone else.

"We don't have to kiss if you don't feel like it. I'm cool with that," he says. "Kissing just gets in the way."

He presses his hand against the front of his jeans, the way I see all the guys around me do when they're adjusting their junk. It's never something to pay attention to. Tonight, though, I'm the reason for it, and it's nasty.

That other night, Colby grabbed my hand and flattened it

against his crotch, and at the same time he shoved his hand down my pants. I was thinking, *How the hell did he do that so fast?*

This is gross and it needs to stop.

I pulled away and told him we were done. I said, "Yeah, no. This is weird. Sorry." He laughed and called me a prude. Or maybe he called me a dude? I can't remember. Then it was over, and I said I had to go.

We were both going to pretend the messed-up stuff never happened. And now he wants to go there again. What the hell is wrong with him?

Who the hell is the queer one right now?

I STARE AT THE carpet and shake my head. Hell no. My fists ball, nails digging into the skin of my palms. I hate feeling like a homo.

"What?" he asks. Then he sits next to me. "You didn't tell anybody, did you?"

"Are you kidding?"

"Okay, good," he says, moving to his bed. "Look, I think we should do it. Last time was kind of weird, but listen, I know what I'm doing, and obviously, you need to get laid. Doesn't matter how guyish you are, you're still a girl."

I can't even believe what I just heard. "Huh? I mean—what the hell are you talking about? This is the most messed-up thing ever."

"What—because of what Garrett said? He was just messing around. He doesn't know anything."

Colby hops over the foot of the bed, landing on his usual corner of the couch, arms folded against his chest, eyes on me. "Here's the thing: girls make things complicated. I learned my lesson, believe me. I'm done with drama. This is why you're so perfect. A dude, but a girl, right?" He wags his eyebrows, and I inch myself back a little. "Come on, man. People get horny. That's all this is. Why don't you just let me rock your world? It's not like you're getting any otherwise. You're sexually frustrated. Even if you're into girls, doesn't mean you can't get some on the side. It's just messing around. It's just fun. I won't tell anyone."

My face feels like it's stuck in the expression I make when I don't like something I'm eating. "Yeah, if that was true, then you'd also be seeing if Tristan wants to mess around on the side. Or Garrett."

Now he's doing the same face. "You're a girl, and I'm a guy." I stare back at him like, *For real?* He nods like he figured it all out. "Oh, okay. Are you afraid you're gonna find out you're bi or something?"

"Uh, no. I know what I'm into."

"Yeah? So . . . are you into sucking me off or what?" He laughs.

"Oh man, Colby. You're disgusting." I stand up and rub my face.

"I'm just kidding. Relax," he says. "Look, I'm not gonna laugh at you, if that's what you're worried about. I'm not gonna tell any—"

"No! Stop talking. Stop trying to flip this into something

I'll suddenly be into. I'm not." There's no expression on his face, like none of it made it through to him. "I think Garrett's right—this whole thing is gay. Like homo gay. I like girls. Girly girls. I don't like guys, and I didn't think you did either."

I don't know why I said that. I must be an idiot.

Colby puts his hands on his knees and his features drop. "Don't try to act like I'm a fag. You're a girl. You've *always* been a girl. You kiss like a girl, and when my hand was down your pants, I felt—"

"Shut up!"

"You think you're so tough, huh?" He snorts a laugh, but it feels like the whole room gets dark. Colby's pressing a fist into an open palm, grinding it. "Get over yourself, Pen. You don't get to be a guy now, just because you look like that. You better watch yourself. For real. You don't wanna be on my bad side. You don't want me to really start treating you like a guy. Trust me."

"I can't believe you're saying that stuff to me. To *me*."

"You're asking for it."

"You've been full of it this entire time," I say, turning to go. "I'm out of here."

"This better stay dead, Pen. Stay out of my way with your identity crisis stuff and go back to normal. You're not gonna get another chance."

By the TV stand is a tall stack of games, and when I walk by it, I whip the thing over with a smack, sending game cases flying against the wall. After that, I'm out of there, thinking it wasn't his face, but at least I got to hit something.

NINETEEN

WHEN MY PHONE RINGS AT NINE ON SATURDAY morning, I wake up remembering last night. It's an unknown number. But I pick up anyway.

"You sound like you just woke up. This is too early, isn't it?" Olivia says.

"How'd you get my number?"

"Sorry. Blake gave it to me."

"Oh." I sit up in bed and wipe the crusts out of my eyes. "What do you want?"

It sounds meaner than I wanted it to.

"Oh. I just wanted to check in about this afternoon," she says, her voice coming out small. "I'm sorry. I shouldn't have called."

"I—I can't talk to you right now."

She hangs up before I can even wish I'd said something different.

FOR AN HOUR NOW, I've thought about everything. It's like my head is too stuck in last night to be able to also be in today.

I have to ditch Blake's show. That's all I know.

I make it halfway down the stairs before I hear angry

139

voices. The basement door is half-open. I push it some more, glancing around in case someone's there. My mom can't be far away, if she's not down there already. I hear my dad's voice. He almost never goes down to Johnny's place. It's mostly Portuguese coming from down there, something about pulling a knife on some kids at the pizza place. Oh, man.

This is it—it's happening again. Going out for pizza wasn't worth this.

"It was a goddamn joke!" Johnny yells.

"*Não* funny, *é louco*. You crazy man," Dad says.

Johnny says that it actually wasn't a joke, and that the jerks deserved it. "I'm the only one who pays attention. That hasn't changed, huh? You guys don't see. You don't even try to look. *O pai e a mãe não vê. Não vê* nothing."

I want to rush in there and tell my parents to back off, to punish me instead. It's not Johnny's fault that he gets in trouble defending me. But I'm too much of a pussy to move from this spot.

"*Estúpido*." Dad says that Johnny's a psycho for pulling a weapon out on children. He says he had to find out about Johnny's dumb stunt from one of the delivery guys at the factory. "You want the police here again?"

It fills me up with anger, thinking about everything. Why didn't we just order the pizza and hang out downstairs? I should've used my damn head and realized this kind of crap was going to get worse the moment I cut my hair.

"Come on, *Pai*. You care more about this guy than you do about what his kid did to yours?" Johnny says, then he repeats

140

that the guys from the pizza place deserved it. "You let it all happen, then you blame her."

"I tired, João. Okay? *Cansado*. No more." My dad says he's sick of Johnny making him look bad, and trying to act like he's the man of the house. He says, "You wanna act crazy? What I tell you before, huh? I say you get outta here."

My fingernails are digging into my palms. This is bull.

"*O pai sempre diz a mesma coisa!* Always the same thing. You know what would happen if I left," Johnny says. "*O pai sabe o que vai acontecer.* It's not gonna go down like it did last time. You know what would happen this time. *O pai sabe.*"

What would happen this time? What would be different this time? Part of me wonders if he'd take me with him.

"I know? Nothing happen. This my house. I say in my house!" Dad's voice gets out of control. I jump. "This son—my son—got no *respeito*! No more. I can't no more. *Saia da minha casa*, João. I tired of everything."

Saia da minha casa—that means . . . get out of my house.

"Fine," Johnny says. "I'm out."

My mouth hangs open, and I stare at the purple half-moons dug into my palms. What's different about this time is that he's not putting up much of a fight. He's just taking off.

MY MOM PUTS A hand around my wrist, pulling my arm up to look at my hand. She tips her head toward the kitchen.

"No. Not you bus*iness*, Penelope," she says. "Come."

She drags me to the kitchen. I'm so mad my eyes sting. We sit at the table, listening to the shouting going on below us.

"You let you *pai* talk to João," Mom says.

"Whatever."

"João got big big mouth, big head. He gotta shut up his mouth. He gotta stop being crazy. Stop being *estúpido.*"

I stare back at her. "Whatever, Ma."

Her face goes all mean. *"Tu não quer saber o que tu faz para trazer problemas para o seu irmão?"*

"I already know what I did. I already know it's my fault—trust me. You don't have to yell at me about it."

"I no yell. Listen. You cut you hair, you get people laugh," she says. "You go outside like this, what you think gonna happen? I tell you. I tell you this all the time." She asks how I can expect people to understand something that doesn't make sense. "João no need *problemas de sua irmã.* You *irmão* he need to grow up, be a man. You grow up and be a woman."

Things get quieter downstairs, and I picture Johnny throwing his stuff into garbage bags, getting ready to finally be done with the crap this house is full of. Maybe I should go help him.

"I tell you when you no try to be good girl, the other people they gonna have to . . ." She gets tongue-tied here, so she starts over in Portuguese, telling me when I insist on not being a good girl, I'm making things harder not only for myself, but harder for everyone around me. She says I should be bending for other people instead of expecting everyone else to bend for me.

"I already know all this, okay?" I say, my voice harsher than I meant it to be. "You can stop explaining it to me. I'm not stupid. I already know."

There's pounding up the stairs now. Shouting. Johnny's the first one up. I leave the kitchen before my mom can try to pin me to the table. Dad makes it up the stairs, winded.

"João!" he yells.

Johnny stomps around the front hall. "It's done. This shit's been going on too long."

"I tell you get outta here long time ago," Dad says; then he says Johnny should've never been allowed to come back.

"Believe me, I didn't wanna come back," Johnny says.

"Well, then why did you?" I ask. "Huh? Why the hell did you bother coming back?"

He goes quiet. Dad's finger is still up in the air like some kind of warning. All this yelling, and when I ask a question, everyone goes mute.

"Leave. For good this time," I say. Johnny's looking back at me like I'm not speaking clearly. "Just go."

They're all staring at me.

"Come outside a sec, okay? I gotta tell you some stuff," Johnny finally says.

Dad looks ready to say something but I beat him to it.

"I don't need stuff explained to me like I'm stupid. I get it, okay?" My voice is louder. "You're old enough. You have a job. And you hate it here. Why would you stay? There's no reason. There's no reason at all for you to stay here."

Johnny's looking around like he's trying to find a reason, but he's coming up empty. I can't stop clenching my teeth and staring at that statue of Mary, picturing myself dropping it on the floor and watching it shatter into pieces.

"You need to cool off," Johnny says, tapping my shoulder. I whip his hand off. "Don't touch me."

"Pen, man," he says. *Calma.*

"I don't need to calm down," I say. "I'm done calming down, okay? Get outta here." He holds his hands up like I usually do when he's losing it in front of me. "Get out! Don't be a pussy. Leave."

Johnny gets in front of our parents, but he turns to look at me. His biceps are huge, ready to bust. "Don't be a stupid little hothead, Pen. This family's all about talking shit about everyone else and then going off about *respeito*. Bunch of hypocrites."

"You're one to talk," I say.

"Que desgraça," Mom says. *"Nosso filho é uma desgraça."*

At being called a disgrace, Johnny pretends to wipe his hands and shake the filth off them before whirling around.

Then the door slams. He's gone.

TWENTY

NO ONE COMES UPSTAIRS. NO ONE TRIES TO TALK to me. Not even with a text. There's nothing to do, and I'm so damn ready to blow. So I take a shower, and I throw on some clothes. There's a basket of folded laundry on my bed. I knock it over. Just because.

My phone starts playing the *Ninja Turtles* theme, but it's not Johnny. Good—last person I want to talk to is him.

"Hey, you," Blake says. Those two words and the breath rushes out of me. "I was doing some vocal exercises, but I keep thinking I feel a little tickle at the back of my throat. So, I decided to relax and play some *Zelda*, which made me think of you. You're coming later, right?"

"Um . . . I'm not sure yet," I say.

"What do you mean?"

"Sometimes my mom says yes to stuff, then she changes her mind."

There's silence for a moment, then a sigh. "Well, that's sort of not cool. You live like that? With someone saying you can do something then turning around and taking it away?" she asks, and her voice takes on this edge.

"I can't really control what my parents do," I say.

"Well, do you tell them they're not being fair?" she says.

That makes me laugh. "Yeah, you don't really know my parents. You don't *tell* them anything. They decide. It's their house. Respect and all that."

"That sounds like some crazy stuff right out of the fifties or something."

I snort. "It's not crazy. It's how a lot of parents are. Especially in European families."

There's more silence, and it feels weird. I don't want to be annoyed with her, because it's Blake. But I sort of wish I hadn't answered the call.

"Well," she starts, letting another sigh go, "I get it if you can't show up. Just make sure you warn Olivia."

Olivia—crap.

"I'm going to try to make it, Blake," I say.

This awkwardness is the worst.

"Just in case, I'm going to assume you're not coming, so that way I won't look for you."

"But I want you to look for me."

There's just the sound of her breath on the other end, and it makes me wish I'd just said I was coming. Because I think seeing her would make things better.

"I should go," she says.

"Oh."

This isn't better at all.

OLIVIA LOOKS NICE, I guess, but a little too nice for this kind of thing. She's got this shiny purple top on and her hair's pulled back in a loose bun. We stand side by side at the terminal, waiting for the bus that'll take us to the community center. I've got my white Portugal soccer sweat jacket over a white tee, jeans, and white sneakers. I was pretty sure I looked all right when I left home, but now that I see myself reflected in the terminal windows, I don't know. I think I might be trying too hard to channel Cristiano Ronaldo or something.

"This is a little weird," Olivia says.

I don't even know why she still wanted to come to this.

"Yeah. I guess it is," I say. My texts probably weren't enough to make things better. "Look, I'm sorry I was a jerk. I was in the middle of family drama." So maybe the family drama hadn't happened yet, but I'm not going to tell her I was having Colby drama.

"What kind of family drama? Is everything okay?"

"Someone's gone. It's all right."

She touches my arm. "Oh my god, Pen. Like . . . passed away?"

"He's not dead," I say. "He just took off. It needed to happen."

"Your dad?"

"I wish." He could take my mom with him, too.

Olivia makes a face like she's tired of not understanding when I talk.

"It's just my brother. He's old enough to get a life, so it's not a big deal."

There are other kids our age and younger walking in front of the terminal where Olivia and I are standing. Some of them—maybe most of them—probably think we're on a date or something. Any girl who stands near me has to deal with that. I take a couple steps away, leaning my butt against the frame of a bike rack.

"Plus, Blake's pissed at me," I say. "I probably shouldn't even go to this, but I didn't want to bail on you."

"Why is she mad?"

"She doesn't want me wasting her time."

Olivia's head tips to the side. "She said that?"

So I give her a two-line summary of that phone call. "I don't know why she even invited me to this thing."

"She's disappointed that you might not have shown up," Olivia says, her eyebrows up like she's waiting for me to clue in. "She probably had butterflies thinking about seeing you today, and then you said you might not even be coming."

"Butterflies?" I say, and Olivia nods.

After that, I scroll through my phone for a while, wishing Blake would text, but feeling like too much of an idiot to text her.

"So, is Blake's band good?" Olivia asks.

"I don't really know, actually."

"What's the band called?"

"Uh . . . I have no idea."

Olivia lets out a little laugh and zips up her jacket. I stare ahead, at the random Saturday Castlehill people waiting around for the same bus we are. The sky's kind of gray, like the sun's not even going to try to pretend to stay up until dinnertime.

"I'm actually looking forward to this. I've never seen a real band play," Olivia says.

"You've never been to a concert?"

She shakes her head. "You?"

"Yeah. I've seen a few." I stop myself from naming the ones Johnny took me to because I don't want to think about him.

"Should I take notes? I brought a notepad in case."

That makes me laugh. "I think just listening and then telling them if it rocked or not will be enough."

On the bus, we sit together on one of the back benches. A few people our age get on, three guys and two girls. They're loud and that makes me shrink down toward the window. As they head to the back, they notice me right away.

They fall onto a couple benches, and keep throwing glances my way. Their grins are definitely not the friendly kind. I pull out my phone to scroll.

"When people can see you're doing something wrong, they're really mean," Olivia says.

"Huh?"

"If they knew my secret—if they could see it—they'd be awful to me. Right now they can't tell, so I'm safe," she says, shifting in her seat a little to look over at me. She said the word "if." But she's talking again before I can ask her about it. "You're not safe ever, are you? People can always tell with you."

Up ahead, those guys are making jokes and the girls laugh. I can't tell if they're about me, but they probably are. "Yeah."

"Did you look like a boy when you were little?" she asks.

"Pretty much."

"You're not a boy, though, right?"

It's now that I can kind of see why Colby might've called her to talk. There's something about her really soft voice, and her tone, like she just wants to tell the truth and isn't going to judge anything. Like she's not even able to be mean if she tries.

"Nope," I say. "Sometimes I think things would probably be easier if I was."

"How do you know you're not a boy?" she asks, and when I make a face, she goes, "Because my friend Lily's cousin from Minnesota is transgender. He always knew he wasn't a girl, but he says he just never said anything about it and let everyone think he was."

It's hard to come up with an answer to her question. When

I think about that stuff in my own head, I don't usually end up anywhere because I don't ever think it through to the end. Everything's always made me wonder if I was supposed to be a boy. When I was really little, I even thought maybe I was born one and then some weird circumcision disaster happened and my parents decided to take home a little girl instead. But the older I got, the less that made sense to me. Because—

"I don't feel wrong inside myself. I don't feel like I'm someone I shouldn't be. Only other people make me feel like there's something wrong with me."

Her staring at me is making my face feel hot. "I don't really understand why you're friends with someone like Colby."

"Well, I don't really understand why you're . . . whatever you were with Colby. So I guess we're even," I say.

She nods like, *Fair enough*. Then she pulls out a little bag full of Halloween candy and chocolate.

"I like that you're such an honest person," she says.

I've never thought of myself as being honest. It feels like I'm full of it most of the time.

"Thanks," I say. "I like that about you, too."

She opens the little bag and holds it under my nose. I don't need to be asked twice to eat chocolate.

TWENTY-ONE

THE COMMUNITY CENTER HALL IS LIKE A DARK, dingy church basement. It's this building that's attached to the bigger rec center where the pool and skating rinks are. This is not the kind of place where people get married. It's more of a retirement or anniversary party kind of place. There are round tables sprinkled around the room, and the windows are covered by heavy drapes. At the far end of the room is a corner with sound equipment. It's not a stage exactly; I guess more of a platform. Blake's band is set up there. At the tables, there are some other people our age or a little older. I don't know most of the faces except these two other girls from our grade. There are a lot of guys who look like they're in grade twelve or maybe even in college.

We walk in together and pause to scan the room. What if Blake throws me a dirty look and won't talk to me? It helps to know that however messed up and nervous I feel, Olivia's got to be feeling way more out of place.

"Are you really up to being here?" I ask her. She looks confused, so I add, "You're not gonna puke or anything, are you?"

She pulls open her purse and there's another bag of

chocolate, plus lots of packages of soda crackers. "If I snack all the time, I don't feel as sick."

Should we even be talking about the secret? Should I be pretending it's not really happening? When I look at her, it just doesn't seem real that she could actually be pregnant.

"This place is a little," Olivia says, chewing on the inside of her mouth like she's looking for the right word, "run-down."

"Totally."

A couple people are looking over at us, but all I see is Blake up there. She looks hot in these black cargo pants that are all tight and bunched at the ankle, while her feet are in these black heels. She's setting up her mic, looking like she's trying to find the best spot for the cord not to trip her. The guy with the bass is a super tall black dude with thin dreads that fall into his eyes, and he's plucking a couple notes that don't go with the chords the guitar player's messing around with. The guitar player's a fat white guy with reddish hair; his face is all pierced and he's playing a riff that sounds pretty sweet. The last guy must be Charlie. He checks the amps, moves Blake's mic stand forward, and then motions for the guitar player to go more to the right. Then he grabs his drumsticks and settles behind the kit.

Why would I even step out of the shadows? There's no competition between me and him.

"Can we sit near the front, but to the side? I like being able to see well," Olivia says, and we go.

"Guys!" Charlie shouts. Instruments quiet. "It's four o'clock. I want to start. We only have two hours."

Olivia makes her way to the tables off to the right of the fake stage, and a few people notice us. Olivia and I take a seat.

Blake looks over and smiles.

"Hey!" Blake says, coming to sit with us. She leans into me and it's enough to make me almost fall over, but instead, I square my shoulders and decide not to pay attention to anyone else right now. Her words are in my ears. "I'm . . . sorry," she whispers. "I get cranky when I'm nervous."

"It's okay," I say, staring at my hand resting on the table.

"I really wanted you to come over tonight," she says to the side of my face, still so close to me.

"You did, huh?" I pull away to look at her. She nods. "That would be pretty awesome."

"Sorry, audience. Our singer's holding everything up," Charlie says, super loud, into his portable mic.

Blake gives him the finger by pretending to scratch her cheek with it.

"Good luck," I whisper in her ear. "You're gonna rock this."

For a second I think she's going to kiss me, the way she looks at my mouth. But she just grins and tiptoes up to take her spot with the band.

"Okay, guys, well, thanks for coming out. We are Drowning in Shadows," Charlie says from behind his drums, and we give a little clap. "Yeah, so, uh, just let us know how it sounds. Whatever."

"That's a very depressing band name," Olivia whispers in my ear. It makes me laugh.

Now Blake is standing in front of her mic. The spotlight

above shines on the four of them. She looks nervous, just standing there, tapping the fingers of her left hand against her thigh and staring at the ground. Charlie raises his sticks above his head and counts to three. Then the band starts and it sounds good—like real music. These guys are sort of awesome. I relax in my seat a little. Blake nods along with the beat and her eyes close. She looks so good, with this silver top, and her arms left bare.

"They're good, aren't they? They must practice a lot," Olivia says, leaning over. "I was so scared they were going to be awful and I'd have to lie."

"Same."

Blake sings now, and I can't move anymore. The rasp in her voice disappears when she's singing higher notes, unless she strains. Then, when she goes low, it's smooth. She's loud and totally hard about it.

Her eyes are closed most of the time, but that's okay because I'm staring at her mouth. By the time the song's over, I don't care about anything except kissing her.

THE BAND DOES SIX songs, and Blake sings all of them. When the show's over, people gather around to talk to the band. Even though I'm dying to talk to Blake, I stay put at the table with Olivia.

"I wish I could've been in a band," Olivia says.

"Why can't you?"

"I don't sing very well. And my fingers are too short. I'd need a child's guitar," she says, fanning her hands open to

154

show me her small fingers. "I think composing the score for films would be fun. Sometimes I watch these films and the music totally changes the tone. Do you know what I mean? Like, if they'd scored it differently, the movie would've been darker, or funny, or sad."

"I never thought about that. I wonder if it works the same for video games."

"Definitely. It's all about writing a piece of music that will add to the story. Create atmosphere," she says. "You and Colby are really into video games."

"Apparently he's not cool with girls knowing that about him. But yeah, we are."

"He thinks you're the best gamer he knows," she says. When I give her this look like, *Are you for real?* she nods a bunch of times, like a little kid who thinks the faster they nod, the more they'll be believed.

"Well, I am. But I'm surprised he said that," I say. "What else has he said about me?"

Now she's shaking her head. She pretends to zip her lips. "See that girl over there?" Olivia points to one of the girls from our school. I nod. "She wears her uniform skirt really short at school so everybody can see her underwear—have you noticed that?"

"Yeah, that's kind of Morgan's thing." The guys and I have all seen her underwear, on many occasions.

"Last Thursday, I could've sworn she was wearing the same polka-dotted ones she wore the day before."

"Ha!" I cover my mouth. "Maybe she has two of the same?"

155

"Maybe, but then she should space them out."

I'm laughing my butt off. "I think it's funny as hell that you look at her crotch every day."

"Accounting is just so boring," she says with a small shrug. "Blake looked really good up there, didn't she."

"Really, really good."

Soon Blake click-clacks her way over, thumbs hooked into her front pockets. She slips into the same spot she was in before going up, and our knees touch.

"Okay, lay it on me," she says.

I open my mouth but Olivia beats me to it. "I think your mic needs to be turned up a little. You shouldn't be afraid to get closer to it, even when you do your louder parts, because the instruments can drown you out. But overall, this was stellar. Do you guys have a CD yet? I would buy it. Your lyrics are pretty sophisticated. Who writes them?"

"Wow—thank you," Blake says, her face lighting up. "Charlie's the word guy."

"Really? I was hoping it was the bass player," Olivia says, looking down. "He just seems . . . I don't know."

"That would be Elliott. He's bass, but he actually composes most of the melodies," Blake says. "He plays guitar too, so he comes up with these chord progressions, and then Billy takes over to rip the hell out of them. Eventually we're hoping to add another member to play rhythm so Billy can really focus on lead."

Olivia gives a smile. "That's impressive."

"We're packing up. Can you guys stick around?" Blake says to me.

"We can help," Olivia says.

"Uh, I can help with the heavy stuff," I say, throwing Olivia a glance. Our eyes lock and the light in hers dims a little.

"I can sort out the cords and microphones or something?" Olivia says.

I think we both know people who are pregnant aren't supposed to lift heavy things.

AN HOUR LATER, EVERYTHING is taken apart and packed away in Elliott's dad's work van.

"When did you start writing music?" Olivia asks Elliott, while we're all standing around waiting for the community center guy to come get the key.

"I started taking guitar lessons when I was ten, and playing other people's songs was fun for a while, but I was always hearing my own tunes in my head, you know?" Elliott says.

"They're really great songs," she says, and he smiles.

"The lyrics are mine," Charlie says.

"Are you a poet?" she asks.

Charlie puffs up, palming his scruffy chin. "I just like to let the words flow."

"Liar!" Blake says, throwing a weak punch to his arm. "He drives himself crazy over each word and then changes his mind a hundred times. *I'm a wordsmith, babe. You can't rush me.*"

Babe. I know they used to date, but still, it doesn't feel good to hear that. I'd been wondering about calling her babe, and now it feels like the word is taken.

Next Olivia's asking Billy how long he's been playing guitar.

"Since I was three or four. My stepdad's in a band," Billy says, lighting up a cigarette.

"You're very good," Olivia says.

"Thanks," he says.

The *Ninja Turtles* theme breaks out from my pocket and for a moment, it makes me feel like the little kid in a group of cool kids. Elliott laughs and says, "I so approve of that ringtone."

I smile and nod knowingly, and then I'm backing away from the group and answering the call because it's my house.

"Where are you?" My mom sounds annoyed or suspicious about something, but that's the way she always sounds.

"I went out with my friends."

"You no tell me," she says.

"It's daytime and it's the weekend, Ma."

She tells me she thought I was hiding in my room this whole time, and she expected me home today, that my bathroom needs a good cleaning.

"I'll do it tomorrow." I can feel her rolling her eyes because when my mom's decided something needs doing, it has to get done right away. She tells me to be home for dinner. That's in less than an hour. "I'm grabbing pizza. We're going to the movies later."

"No, no," she says.

"Why?"

She tells me she doesn't have to explain herself to me.

"Ma, come on. It's Saturday," I say, looking over at everyone standing around. My eyes linger on Blake, watching her mouth move while she says something that makes Olivia crack up and Charlie shake his head and grin like she just took another shot at him. I'm not going home. "I'll be home tonight, okay?"

"Penelope Oliveira!"

"Am I in trouble?"

"In trouble," she mutters. She says it has nothing to do with being in trouble, that it has to do with kids doing as they're told.

Blake glances at me just then, head tilted and a side grin on her lips. I can't believe I'm standing here arguing with my mommy because she wants me to come home.

"Fine," I say.

When I get back to the group, Elliott's asking Olivia something and their conversation gets quieter. Olivia's doing this shy smile for him so I look away. Blake shivers next to me. Time's going by too fast. I wish I could put my arm around her. I wish I could at least open my mouth and ask a decent question or something.

"I'm glad you came," Blake says, when Billy and Charlie dive into some conversation about having a pickup installed into one of their acoustic guitars and how much that'll cost. "And I'm really glad you're coming over."

"Me too." With that, I reach into my pocket and turn my

phone right off. When I get in trouble for this later, it'll totally be worth it. "You kicked ass. You guys could totally record an album."

"Yeah?"

"For sure. Your voice is just . . . well, I don't really know how to explain it, but it's got a lot more going on than just being able to hold a note."

One of her fingers hooks around mine. Icy skin against icy skin, but it's the warmest thing I've ever felt.

Charlie looks over at us then. I wish I could know what he sees when he looks at me. Does he see a girl pretending to be something she's not? Because nothing I'm doing, nothing that I am is about pretending.

TWENTY-TWO

ELLIOTT TAKES OLIVIA IN HIS VAN BACK TO Blake's, while I hop in the back of Charlie's little car, Blake next to me. Billy rides up front with Charlie. At Blake's house, we unload all the equipment, making a hundred trips to and from the basement.

I wait for Olivia while she's in the bathroom—the fourth time she's gone today already. She comes out looking regular.

"You okay?" I ask.

She nods. "Elliott offered to drop me off on his way home. He's so nice."

"Yeah, he seems all right."

"I don't think I should talk to him," she says.

"Because of Colby or because of . . . the other thing?" I ask.

She makes a face like she's annoyed with herself. "Of course I can't talk to him. What's wrong with me?"

It makes me wonder if maybe for an hour, she forgot how seriously messed up her life is right now. I forget all the time. Nothing looks wrong right now, so it makes it seem like nothing actually *is* wrong.

"Olivia," I say, making sure to lower my voice. "Do you know what you're going to do?"

Her cheeks get flushed. "I won't talk to him. But a ride home would be nice."

"Uh . . . okay," I say. "But that's not really what I meant."

She doesn't acknowledge what I said, staring off at a framed photo on the wall of two people decked out in wedding gear, sporting old school–looking hairdos, and smiling at the camera.

"Well, obviously you don't want to be talking to me about this stuff—which I get—but maybe you should be talking to someone." When I realize that what I just said could be taken the wrong way, I add, "But not him. When he thinks someone's a threat—well, you already know what he's like." She won't look up at me now. "Say you wanted to decide stuff, I just don't think letting him in your head would help. Things would get all twisted and confused."

When she still won't look up, I say, "Trust me. I know what I'm talking about."

"I'm not confused." She takes a deep breath and shakes her hair out. "I know that much."

OLIVIA TAKES OFF WITH Elliott not long after Charlie and Billy leave, and now it's just Blake and me. She brings me upstairs, down the hall, and into her room. The walls are pink with big angry streaks of black spray paint. The curtains are black, and so is the bedding. There are photographs everywhere—some overlapping one another in collages, some framed, and some stuck in the edges of the big mirror next to her closet. There's a shelving unit filled with records—like old-school, massive records.

"I don't think I've ever really looked at one of these in real life," I say, heading over to pull one out—a soundtrack for a movie called *Saturday Night Fever*. "Where'd you get all these?"

"My uncle. People are always throwing stuff out like it's not worth anything anymore," she says, pulling off the big dangly earrings she had on. "So is it just me, or is Elliott into Olivia? I'm pretty sure she's into him, too."

"Yeah." I can't help it, I say it with the wrong tone. Blake looks over from the edge of her bed. Oh, man—does she think I'm jealous? "Just, uh, well, she's on the rebound, and I'm sort of looking out for her."

"Elliott's a really good guy."

"Yeah, he seems cool." I flip through the records, not really recognizing any of the band names. "You're allowed to be up here with someone, with the door closed?"

She laughs. "Yeah. Why, you're not?"

"My mom likes to spy."

"Come," she says, patting the spot next to her.

I sit on the edge of her bed and she gets up, only to return with a handheld game system. When the game starts up, she hands it to me. It's the same game I tried that time in her basement.

"You really want me to like this game, huh?" I say.

"*That*'s to swing the sword, and *that*'s the action button," she says, pointing them out for me. "This is one of my saved games. I'm about halfway through. This game wins everything. You won't be able not to love it."

So I steer this character around a field, hacking monsters and tufts of grass to find money and items. The whole time, Blake is next to me, against me. Her feet are bare since she ditched the heels downstairs, so every once in a while, I look at her sparkly blue-painted toes and think feet aren't supposed to be this interesting. I also think that if I were a guy, I probably would've made a move by now. The thing is, I have no idea if I should be making a move or not. It's not clear what's going on. The rules are clear when it's boy-girl. If I was a dude, I'd probably be saying something to make her smile and blush, like, *How am I supposed to kick ass at this game when you're all pressed up against me, smelling like that?* And then maybe I'd touch her on purpose, trying to get her to make eye contact with me so I could see what's reflected there, which is how I'd know she's into it. But this—the way things are because it's me—well, it's all blurry to me.

"You're pretty good," she says.

"I'm just riding around on a horse now," I say.

"Hand it over. I'll take you to where the action is."

She teleports the Link character to some dungeon, and hands the game back to me. "No, you do it," I say. "I want to watch you." She uses a bow and arrow to get rid of enemies and her aim is perfect. She's all squinty-eyed and nibbling her bottom lip, hardly taking any damage while she fights with her sword and all kinds of other weapons.

Somewhere along the way, I stop looking at the screen and I just look at her. I want to learn all the lines of her face. Maybe she'll let me. Maybe she'll want to look at me, too. I'm in a trance, staring at her lips now. My hands tingle and my eyes blur from the blink-less staring.

Her lips are really pretty. I might die if I don't touch them soon.

"You're staring at me," she says.

"Yeah—uh, no. What?"

She's still looking down at the game. "Do you want to kiss me?"

"Uh . . ." My heart goes nuts.

She presses Pause and puts the game down next to her, before shifting her weight toward me. Her cheeks are flushed now, and her breaths are deep. I don't want to crowd her, so I lean in a little, my eyes darting between her eyes and her lips. And then I'm kissing Blake. It's happening. It's close-mouthed and it's soft at first. I'm thinking too much, thinking it's going

164

to end here, but then it doesn't. It keeps going. I don't know who reaches for who first, but somehow, we're holding hands.

THIS—US KISSING—IS giving me mini heart attacks over and over. She makes little noises, which make me have to hold on to bigger noises that try to force their way out of my throat. I don't know how late it is, but it feels like time stopped and sped up at the same time. I just want to be next to her, to have her be super close to me all the time.

"Is this real?" I say.

She smiles all wide. "It better be real, or else we're having the same dream."

"Like in *Dream Warriors*."

"What?"

"The third Freddy movie, where Kristen can pull Nancy into her dreams so . . ." I roll my eyes at myself. "I'm just going to shut up now."

She laughs, and then she lies down on her side and pulls my hand so I'll go down with her. I can't believe I'm here, in Blake's room, kissing the crap out of her. We're getting better. I sort of know her rhythm and what she likes. And, well, what she likes is what I like.

"Blake!" It sounds like it's coming from right behind the bedroom door—a woman's voice. I hop off Blake, smooth my shirt, reach for my hair to fix it as though I still have my long ponytail to slick back. Then comes a knock. "Don't spend the evening in there. Your dad's expecting your help."

"Okay!" Blake says, and she's holding a finger up at me,

165

laughing without a sound. "Be right there!"

There's nothing more from the lady, who must be Blake's mom. I'm in the far corner of the room, hands in my pockets. Blake's laughing.

"Do your parents know you're up here—making out with a girl?"

"I really hope not." She comes to stand close to me. I try to move back, but there's nowhere to go.

"No—I mean, do they think we're just friends having some friend hangout to work on a project? They don't think there's something going on, do they?"

"I don't know what they think," she says. She touches my wrist. I flinch. "Pen, are you freaking out?"

"Kind of."

"Why?"

"Well, say your mom freaks out, and she comes at me with a broom."

Blake gives me this look that's barely holding back a laugh. "Aw, you're actually nervous. That's kind of adorable."

"No, no it's not." I feel dumb, but if my being a douche is going to cause her to look at me that way, with her sparkly eyes, then maybe that's okay. "I need to know how I'm supposed to act. Around your parents."

"Just act normal," she says.

"I don't want to embarrass you. I don't want to do something stupid, you know?"

She does this thing, balling her fist and putting it against her heart. My mom does that too, but only when she wants us to know we're breaking her heart. With Blake, it feels like something to smile about.

DOWNSTAIRS, BLAKE'S MOM WHIPS back and forth through the hallway, a phone cradled to her ear. She's a tall, skinny lady with blond hair to her shoulders, but other than the hair, I don't see much resemblance between her and Blake. The white cat darts down the stairs next to us, hissing. Blake's mom waves at me when we get to the main floor, and she winks in between saying "uh-huh" and "absolutely." Blake takes my hand and leads me to the kitchen. I let go when her dad comes into view. He slices an onion while something sizzles in a skillet on the stove behind him.

"This must be Pen," he says. "It's nice to meet you. Is Pen short for Pencil?"

"Dad, are you serious right now?"

I let out a chuckle because I've never heard that one before. "It's short for Penelope. But I don't go by that."

"Penelope doesn't really suit you. I like Pencil," he says. His hair is dark—almost black like mine—but his eyes and nose are definitely the same as Blake's. "How was Blake's band practice?"

"It was awesome. They sound pretty sweet."

"Did they do 'Heartless'?" He starts humming the tune, and singing a couple of lines.

"Dad, you're making fun of me," Blake says. "Which is not cool."

"Blake!" Mrs. Austin yells from somewhere down the hall. "Laundry, now! It's not my job to put your things away.

Welcome to our home, Pen. Do you put away your own laundry?
I hope you do."

"I do," I reply.

Blake gives me this face like, *This is so messed up.*

"Pen can hang out with me," Mr. Austin says. "Do you want
to prepare the bell peppers?"

Blake says, "She's not going to do that."

"No, it's cool. I'm actually really good at it," I say. "I help
my mom make sauce all the time. I have to gut, like, seventy of
these at once."

"Really?" Blake gives me a funny look. "Okay then. I'll be
ten minutes, tops. Don't say anything weird, Dad."

I wash my hands. Mr. Austin calls me to the island, where
he puts a bowl of peppers in front of me and hands me a fancy-
looking knife. I push up my sleeves and get to work. The knife
is sharp as hell. I'm used to our dull ones with wooden handles.
It takes me five minutes to get all three red peppers cleaned out
and rinsed. Blake's dad places three zucchinis in front of me.

"Dice those up," he says. I get to work, thinking about how
this isn't really awkward as long as I've got vegetables to muti-
late. Blake's dad slices tomatoes and runs his knife along the
edge of each quarter in one quick motion, taking the thin layer
of skin right off. I wonder if he has any idea I was sucking face
with his daughter a few minutes ago and that I wish I was still
doing it.

"So," he says, "should I give you the same speech I gave the
other guys?"

"Um . . . I don't know—maybe?"

"Blake's my little girl. Should you break her heart—well, you've seen how good I am with a knife." He keeps his eyes on the carrot he's currently dicing into little cubes. When I don't reply, he looks up with a grin that makes it clear he's joking, but underneath the joking, there's a real warning.

I try not to grin. "I got it, sir."

He nods. "Now, would you like to know my spaghetti sauce secret?"

"Totally."

He pretends to whisper. "I use a jar of nacho salsa."

I catch his eye and nod, wondering what Blake's dad thinks of me, who he thinks I am. I think I could be anybody as long as it means I get to keep kissing Blake.

TWENTY-THREE

LATE THE NEXT MORNING, THE SOUND OF A TRUCK door banging shut outside my window calls my attention. I know that sound. The truck's in the driveway as usual, except the flatbed's packed with stuff that belongs in the basement. The black floor lamp, the full-length mirror, the little microwave, and the mattress and box spring.

I race downstairs to Johnny's place, and run into Dom and Naveed as they finish unhooking the TV and carry it toward the patio door.

"What the hell? What's going on?" I ask.

"Hey, Pen," Naveed says, and they both stop in their tracks. "Your brother's coming back down in a sec. He just made a trip up."

Dom and Naveed head outside with the TV, while I scope out the place. The bedroom's empty, and there's nothing hanging in the closet. Nothing at all. Not even the shirts he didn't like—the ones he left hanging there, clean and ready for me to pick through. The living room's barely hanging on now that the TV's gone. The Xbox, the games—they're gone, too.

"Hey, man," Johnny says as he parts the blinds to come inside.

"What are you doing? What is this?"

"Found a place on short notice, so you know . . ."

"You're moving out?"

"Yeah. Not far."

"You're moving and you didn't tell me?"

"You knew. Don't be bustin' my balls, Pen. You—"

"Does *Mãe* know? Does *Pai*?"

"What are you smoking, man? We were all there yesterday. It had to be done."

"What's wrong with you? You think you're too good for this place?"

He's just shaking his head, like he has something to say but he doesn't want to say it now. He heads for the bathroom, where he starts chucking stuff into a box. The clipper—how am I going to keep my hair short? Dom and Naveed reappear and they go for the couch. I watch them carry it out, just like they did with the TV. It's like all of a sudden, this isn't my life. I feel like punching them, even though they didn't cause this.

"Where are you moving to?" I ask, once Dom and Naveed are gone again.

"McKinley buildings. It helps to know the manager."

"You got an apartment already? For real?"

Johnny steps away from the cupboard to look at me. "Pen, man, come on. Don't get all bent outta shape. Just take a breath. I'll tell you what the deal is."

But I can't even listen.

"It's cool. I get it. I mean, fine. Take everything and go."

He pokes his head out of the bathroom and gives me this look like, *Quit being such a drama queen.*

"I'm taking my stuff," he says, bouncing the clipper in his hand. "I got something for you, okay?"

"Yeah, that's okay. You can keep it." I'll buy my own damn clipper. "See ya."

"Hang on, Pen. Stop being such a little hotheaded idiot," he says, but I'm already gone. I book it up the stairs. My mom's in the front hall. She holds a rosary and stares out the front bay window, at the guys loading the couch into Dom's truck.

"Don't pray, *Mãe*. Jesus didn't do this. You did. Why did you guys even have kids?" I say before rushing upstairs and slamming my bedroom door.

I find my phone and head for my closet, where I sit on the

floor and message Blake. She's being funny and sweet, sending me pictures of what she looks like waking up in the morning, her hair all insane, and the side of her face creased with pillow lines—and it still manages to be hot as hell. Johnny doesn't even try to text me, so I text him two letters, F and U.

TWENTY-FOUR

I DECIDE IF I IGNORE JOHNNY'S TEXTS FOR A COUple weeks, it'll send the right message. I got better things to do anyway. Hanging out with my brother all the time, getting him to drive me to school—that sounds like stuff a twelve-year-old does. Why would Blake want to date a twelve-year-old?

On the way to school one day, while Tristan drools against the bus window, I tell Colby that Johnny moved out. It's probably time I say something about it, because Johnny's been gone for over a week now. And maybe it'll give me an excuse for having been ignoring Colby, too. All I've felt like doing lately is hanging out with Blake, or talking to her on the phone, or texting her. Or watching YouTube—been doing a lot of that.

"Get outta here," Colby says. "He moved out?"

"Yup. Finally. As if I'd stay at home until I'm thirty."

"Yeah, seriously. Imagine being thirty and having to screw chicks in your parents' basement."

"Pathetic."

"I told you he needed to move the hell out and grow up," Colby says. "I was wondering what was up with you going MIA for two weekends in a row."

"Yeah, well, my mom's been crazy, making me clean out the whole basement. She wanted me to call you guys to come help move furniture down from the spare room, but I didn't think you and Tristan would be into doing that all weekend." I look away because I don't want to know if he bought that or not. I'm kind of suspecting I've gotten better at this lying thing, which is good, but it's also bad.

"That's what you did on the weekend? Both weekends?" he asks.

"Last weekend, I did that. The weekend before, I was helping Johnny pack," I say, pretending to check my phone like I got a text.

"Well, you missed a good one. We all drove to Toronto on Saturday, and we tried to get into this strip club. It was hilarious. They almost let Ike in 'cause of the beard," he says, and I laugh. Even when his face goes back to serious, I'm still forcing out the rest of my laugh. "So you know Ike's buddy, Jake, the one with the massive ear spacers?"

"Not really," I say.

"That's funny—because he's pretty sure he knows you."

"Huh?"

"Yeah. Apparently you and him hung out the other day. A couple weekends ago, actually. That's what he was telling me on Saturday."

"What are you talking about? I never hung out with that guy."

"Went to see some band play at the community hall?" Colby says, and when I glance at him, he snorts. "He told us about how he saw this queer dyke sitting with the hottest chicks there. I'm pretty sure there aren't that many queer dykes around here."

"It was after I helped Johnny with his stuff. I was there with Blake for a bit."

"Wrong," he says. "You were there with Olivia. That's who you were sitting with the whole time. I'm not making this stuff up. Jake was there, dude. He saw you."

"It wasn't like that."

No more playful nod of the head from him now. Just slits for eyes. "What's it like then?"

"She was sitting all by herself, so Blake was all 'Sit with Pen.' I mean, what was I supposed to do?" More lies. "I wasn't gonna tell you because I knew you'd get pissed, and for nothing."

"Why the hell was Olivia there in the first place if she wasn't with you?"

"Uh . . . I think she's dating the bass player."

I probably shouldn't have said that.

COLBY BARRELS THROUGH EVERYBODY, swipes some kid's baseball cap only to stick it on some random girl's head, knocks Trent's binder out of his hands, and tells Garrett to screw off—all this on his way to the lockers from the bus. I stand at my locker, watching for Olivia's head to appear somewhere, hoping she's puked her way out of coming to school today. When Colby types on his phone, I'm imagining all the dumb crap he could be sending to her.

I'm such an idiot. Screwed Olivia over just to save myself.

When Blake gets to school, it makes me feel like even more of an ass. She's deep in conversation with Robyn, and both of them have their hair super straight, like they made a deal to both go for the straightener today. It makes Blake look . . . softer, I guess? Like she'd be less likely to knee you in the balls than usual. I think she'd make an exception for me today.

So I run away to hide. I loop around the shop class hallway and come out by the end of the faculty parking lot. Then I hang by the side entrance, waiting to spot Olivia. Two minutes until the bell rings, still no Olivia.

A text comes from Blake: Where r u? Wanted 2 talk 2 u b4 class.

Me: sorry—late 2day—but i'll be staring @ u all through french class

Her: Ok. :) Can u stay after school with me & O? About the project. Meeting with Mr. Middleton.

Me: probably—u seen Olivia 2day?

Her: Yeah. A min ago. No idea where she went.

Oh, man.

First bell goes off. Back in the grade-eleven hallway, there are only a few people left scrambling or just taking their sweet time to get to class. Tristan's still at his locker, just waiting.

"Colby wanted me to wait for you," he says.

"Why?"

175

Second bell goes off. He shrugs. "We're late for class."

"I know that. Just go. I'll catch up."

He heads off toward French class with a sigh. Once I've got my books, I make a stop at the bathrooms, just in case.

She's there. At least I think it's her, by the sound of the cough I hear coming from the one occupied stall. It sounds like her. Maybe it's not.

I cough. Nothing.

So I clear my throat.

Wash my hands.

There's a sniffle from behind the door, like someone's blowing their nose. It could be her. It could be any girl in the world.

Clear my throat again . . .

Nothing.

So I go to leave, but then come back. It's like I'm a creeper right now. I pretend to kick the garbage can. "Oh, man. Stupid thing's always in the way."

"Pen?"

"Finally! Yeah, it's me."

"What's wrong?" she says.

"Uh . . . are you, like, done in there?"

The toilet flushes and then she comes out to wash her hands. It looks like she puked recently because her face is pale, her cheeks red, and she's kind of . . . sweaty-looking. Strands of her black hair are stuck to her forehead and cheeks.

"I did something stupid," I say.

She stares at me through the mirror, flicks water off her

hands, then turns around. She looks ready to fall, or cry. Or both. "You told him?"

My face is what falls because I hadn't even thought about how she'd think I told Colby she's knocked up. It makes me breathe a massive sigh. "No! Oh, man. No, I didn't tell him *that*."

"Well—what did you do?" she asks. "Am I in trouble?"

"This keeps getting better and better," Colby says from behind me. The *F* word goes through my head over and over, and Olivia's wide eyes are begging me to let her in on what's happening. Too late. I turn to Colby coming into view.

"What's up, Pen?" Colby asks. He crosses his arms and leans against the wall. "Hiding in the girls' bathrooms because you think I won't come in here?"

"You can't just walk in here like a—" Like a stalker, but I don't finish the sentence. "You're not allowed in here, dude."

"If you're allowed, then I figure I'm allowed, too," he says with a twisted little grin. He turns to Olivia. "How's your bass-playing boyfriend?"

"What?" Olivia asks, searching my face.

"Oh, was it a secret?" Colby asks. "It's not good to keep secrets."

"Colby, man," I tell him. "Just lay off."

He's ignoring me. "Don't be mad at Pen for telling me all about your older musician boyfriend. She's my bud, you know. It's her job to tell me everything. Everything."

"I don't have a boyfriend. I don't know what's going on here," she says.

"Don't lie," Colby tells her, after taking a few steps closer to her. We're like a triangle right now. "Lying is bad."

"I didn't," she says. "I don't know what you're talking about!"

"You move on pretty quickly, huh?" he tells her. It pisses me off so much that he said that. "Say one thing, do another. This is why I never trusted you. No matter what you said."

Colby's words actually seem to have hit her, like if it had been some special command in a game, it would've knocked a third of her health points down.

"I lied!" I say.

They both turn to look at me, but it doesn't matter that I said that. He just wanted to lay into her about something.

"I have to get to class," Olivia says, taking two steps back, keeping her eyes on me long enough to make it clear I'm the one she holds responsible for this. All I can do is suck in a breath and hold it while I watch her walk away.

"What the hell is your problem, huh?" he says to me. "Are you being this dumb on purpose or what?"

Some girl comes in, gives us a dirty look and leaves.

"You made this big deal about getting her off your back, and now you're the one who won't leave her alone," I say. "I lied about Olivia and the bass player because I thought it would get you to move on."

"She's *my* ex. I get to do what I want," he says. "If she thinks getting a new boyfriend will bother me, she's crazier than I thought. She'll still be calling me."

"She'll call you?" I say. "Or you'll call her."

"What do you care, huh?"

"I don't—"

"You do. Why do you care so much?" he says. "You're such a bad liar. You didn't even *ask* me if I wanted to come see that band play when *I* take you everywhere I go. Your whole basement-cleaning thing's probably bullshit. So were you hanging out with Olivia all of *this* weekend, too? You didn't want me getting in your way with her, right? Admit it, Pen. Admit you like her."

He makes my fists curl. He makes me clench my jaw. It's like he might as well hold a finger up to my arm and poke it, over and over. He won't stop.

"Just leave her alone," I tell him. "That's all I'm saying."

He makes this face, like I just said something funny. "Or what?"

"Just . . . stop. You just really need to lay off her," I say.

"You like her," he says. "Admit it!"

"Yeah, I like her," I say. "Just not like that."

"Like what then?"

"She's nice and funny. You should know that since you guys had a thing," I say. "Obviously you know that if you can't stay away from her."

"Oh, suck it, Pen. Stop talking like some douche with the feels." He runs the sink and flicks water around me, never actually touching me with it. "So you're gonna swoop in and take her, huh? Because you're such a badass."

"I'm not taking her," I say. Why does having a girl's back mean I have to have a crush on her? It makes me wonder if—"*You* like her, don't you. Like, really like her. That's why *you* care so much about this. That's why you're worse than usual."

This time he gets me with the water, in the face. It drips down my left cheek. "I care because you're trying to step on my territory, trying to show me up. Are you the nice guy now? Is that what your deal is? You're Pen the Nice Guy. Girls don't want the nice guy, dude. Girls laugh at the nice guy, especially when the nice guy is a girl with tits. Pretty nice tits, though. I'll give you that."

Water droplets fling onto the front of my shirt.

"You know what, Colby? *You* can suck it."

He grins at me. "You know just because you cut your hair doesn't mean you can be me, right? You can't even be in the same category as me. You're still just Pen, except I'm starting to not be able to stand you."

"Yeah, well, same here." My fist is up over my thigh, hovering in the air. Just in case. Just in case I grow some balls and decide to—

"What is going on in here?" It's some grade-nine teacher we usually see patrolling the hallways. He's looking at Colby mostly, because I'm off to the side. "What are you guys doing in the girls' bathrooms? And during class time? You think it's funny to come in here and prevent girls from using the facilities?"

Colby laughs.

"You think that's funny, huh?" he says, then he points to the exit. "Office. Now."

"Sir," Colby says, a thumb pointed over his shoulder at me. "That's a girl. It's Penelope."

The teacher's eyes are on me when I turn, and he recognizes me. Everyone eventually recognizes me, after they look a little more closely. "Well . . . regardless. Office. Both of you, for your late slips."

So we follow Mr. Jones or Johns—whatever his name is—to the office, where we get late slips that have to be signed by our parents.

COLBY AND I MAKE it back to French class for the last twenty minutes, interrupting Mrs. Wexler's reading. I head for my usual seat at the back, Colby not far behind me. I pull out my book while Mrs. Wexler carries on reading aloud. Blake twists in her seat to give me a confused glare. I give a barely noticeable shake of my head, hoping she'll understand that I'll fill her in later.

"You and I are gonna have to settle this," Colby says to me.

"Settle what? I have nothing to settle," I tell him. "I'm done with all this."

"*Mademoiselle* Oliveira, since you insist on chatting, why don't you carry on with *la lecture?*" Mrs. Wexler says, and I swear the way she says "mademoiselle," it's like she's rubbing it in. "*Nous sommes à la page cinquante-six.*"

People laugh at me now, because sometimes I get confused and pronounce words in my parents' Portuguese accent. A lot of French words are almost the same as Portuguese words. Beside me, Colby doesn't laugh at all.

TWENTY-FIVE

AFTER SCHOOL, BLAKE COMES TO MY LOCKER.
My mind is so full of Colby and Olivia, I have to split in two so
I can be normal with Blake. Sometimes I wonder if Blake and
I could ever end up being like a real couple, where I could tell
her stuff and she'd be on my side.

"I think Olivia ditched us!" Blake says, hoisting her bag
over her shoulder. "She's nowhere."

"Oh," I say. "Well, that sucks."

"It's not really a big deal, because she just wanted to talk
to Mr. Middleton about you guys having switched places, and
she said she had some notes, but we can get those later," Blake
says, while I fling things to the bottom of my locker. "I doubt
she has much. Every time we tried to pick a time to get together
to work, she had to cancel because she was sick."

"Oh, really?"

"She came over to my house one time, for not even an
hour." Blake leans closer to me. "During that hour, she was
sick and started crying."

"Maybe she can't eat gluten and it gives her bad heart-
burn," I say. "My aunt Joana gets that."

"Well, my dad has antacids, if that's all it was. She wouldn't

182

tell me. Just cried, and then left." Blake waits while I zip up my bag and slam my locker door. "You're friends with her, right?"

"No. Who said that?"

She gives me a funny look. "No one said it. You guys hang out together, so I just assumed you were friends."

"I mean . . . we know each other. She dated Colby in the summer."

"Oh." She fakes a gag. "That's a little . . . *not* righteous."

I drop my bag at my feet and face her. "You know you're, like, the only girl who doesn't like Colby?"

"I doubt that." She gives this little laugh, but then when she realizes I'm serious, her face freezes into this suspicious expression. "You're serious right now?"

"I guess I just don't get it."

"Get what?"

"Get why."

"Why what?" she asks, and she touches my arm when I reach up to palm my chin.

"Nothing," I say, staring at her fingers. "I'll call her and see what's up."

"Okay," she says. "We're meeting in room thirty-two."

While we walk, I text Olivia: need 2 talk 2 u

MR. MIDDLETON LOOKS GLAD to see me, saying it's about time I explore my interests. He probably figures I'm into photography. My interests are pretty much the hot blonde next to me, but photography might be okay, too. He goes over the project, and it starts making me crap my pants a little.

"In front of the whole school?" I say.

"Not just the whole school. The anniversary celebration is a cocktail party and our alumni, as well as many members of our community, are invited to attend," he explains.

"Oh, man . . ." I look at Blake. "I won't have to, like, talk in front of a mic, will I?"

Mr. Middleton shakes his head. "No. Each team will be set up around the auditorium, and you'll man your stations. We'll invite attendees to have a look at your diaries. And each project will be displayed for the audience throughout the evening."

"That sounds pretty important," I say. "And we have . . . six weeks left?"

"Just about," he says.

"That's loads of time," Blake says. "It'll be righteous. I'm not even worried about it at all."

After that, Mr. Middleton hands me a form to fill out, which basically gives me permission to use any of the A/V equipment I need—and I didn't even know this school had any A/V equipment. Then it's official. Blake and I are Team 3.

When Mr. Middleton leaves, Blake hangs back, letting the door close behind him. The classroom we're in is empty, and the windows face the deserted field out back. It makes me think dirty things. Blake grins at me like she can tell. Or like she was thinking the same.

"You want to go out Friday?" she says.

"Sure."

"I mean . . . like a date."

"In public?"

She nods like, *Now you're catching on.* "Yeah, in public."

She's asking me out. It should've been me who did it. It's okay, though. It's still good.

"Yeah," I say. "I definitely wanna go on a date with you."

"You better."

My phone vibrates in my pocket. Then Blake's right in front of me, leaning in. Her lips barely touch mine before they're gone, before I have to ask her to stop, in case someone was to catch us. I've been thinking about kissing her again ever since our last kiss, in the chapel room, two days ago. Now I wish we could do it some more, but she's already heading out into the hall.

I GET OFF THE bus in the old section of town, where the one-story houses are small but there are big trees everywhere. The streets look the same, and they're all named after trees, which I guess is appropriate. Olivia's house is on Poplar. The driveway is empty. It's a little brick house. The lawn is pretty healthy-looking, and the flower beds and bushes are ready for winter. It makes me wonder if Johnny does work here.

Before I knock, I call my house. Mom answers on the second ring. When I tell her I'm at the library working on a project, she makes this sound, like she doesn't buy it. So I tell her I have this big essay to write with Tristan.

"Ya, you do what you want," she says. "Like all the time."

I don't bother saying bye because she already hung up on me.

Olivia comes to the door, and on her feet are bunny slippers.

"Did you leave school because of this morning?" I ask.

She shrugs. "I didn't feel well."

She moves back to invite me inside. When we texted earlier, she didn't want to meet me at the coffee shop. I figured it was because she was pissed at me, but then she invited me over. The house is super clean. Hardwood floors, dark tiles, and stainless steel. Olivia goes through the kitchen. I slip my sneakers off and follow her. We head down a set of stairs, to what looks like a second family room in the basement. Olivia takes a seat in the armchair and grabs the mug with a tea bag string dangling from it. I take the loveseat.

"I'm sorry I said that to Colby," I say. "It was dumb."

"What did he do after I left?"

"Tore into me," I say. "I'm getting used to it by now."

"No, you're not," she says. "No one gets used to people being mean to them."

"He wasn't *mean*. He was just being an ass."

"What's the difference?"

"Colby's always been like that," I say, but then something catches my eye in the shelving unit that holds the old box TV. It's a mess, things piled one on top of the other. But I see the console clearly, sticking out from between other things. I've seen some of my gaming YouTubers review games for it, but I've never seen one for real. "Is that an Atari?"

Olivia looks to where I'm pointing. "Oh, probably."

"An Atari 2600," I say. "Wow. Whose console is that?"

"My uncle's. He left a lot of things here before he moved out. He used to crash here when he was between places."

"Does it work? Can we play?"

Olivia goes to the TV and starts pulling out things she thinks belong to the console. She opens a cupboard door and there's a stack of cartridges in there, along with a stack of CDs and a couple of board games. I find the AC adapter and a joystick controller. Olivia hands me an HDMI cable, and it makes me laugh.

"What?" she asks.

"That's about—I don't know, thirty-something years into the future for that thing," I say. She stuffs the cable back into the mess of things, then watches me hook it all up. Oh man, *Pitfall!*, *Pac-Man*—I've watched videos about all these games. "This TV is perfect. It's old, so the graphics will look better."

When I power the console, and *Pitfall!* starts, Olivia goes, "And that's supposed to be *good*? It looks like a four-year-old made it."

"It's from the seventies," I say.

So we sit on the carpet in front of the TV, and even though there's only one button and a joystick, I suck so bad.

"That doesn't look like fun," Olivia says.

"What are you talking about?" I say. "It's retro gaming. It's a piece of history."

She watches me try to make the character jump over things that roll at him, swing on ropes to avoid big holes in the ground.

"There. I just had to get the jumping down," I say.

I play for a while, and the further I get into this game, the more it makes me want to start collecting retro stuff. The emulator isn't the same as this—holding the real joystick in my hand.

"Pen?" Olivia asks. "Why did you come here?"

"I felt bad. I wanted to make sure you're all right."

My little dude falls into a hole. I put the controller down, flipping through the other games. *Combat* looks good—well, as good as these old games get.

"Pen, what is this?" she asks.

I push the game into the console. "*Combat.*"

"Not the game. This," she says, pointing at herself and then me. "Are you . . . trying to get back at Colby for something?"

"Why? Why are you asking that?"

"Because. I don't understand. You being nice to me—it's just getting you in trouble with Colby," she says. "Is it that you feel sorry for me because I said it was your fault that you didn't warn me about him before? Or is it that you're using this to get back at him?"

"What would I want to get back at him for?" I stare at the startup screen, not pressing any button. "He hasn't done anything to me."

"No?"

"What are you talking about right now? What's he saying about me?"

"Nothing."

"Nothing?" I say, shifting my weight so I can look at her. "Because whatever he says is lies. He twists things to make himself look a certain way."

"I know that," she says.

"He's a douche, okay?"

"I know, Pen," she says.

"So why do you keep hanging around, hoping he'll change for you?"

"Because when he's nice, it's like I forget how mean he is the rest of the time," she says. "You know what I'm talking about."

"No, I don't," I say. "It's not the same thing."

"How?"

"Because . . . I'm not just some girl, okay?"

Silence, and I stare at the TV screen.

"Neither am I," she finally says.

"Yeah, you are, okay? You're not his friend. You don't have history with him, and loyalty. You're some girl he hooked up with, and the minute it got too complicated, he turned into a jerk and bailed."

"I have to go to the bathroom," she says, and before she's reached the stairs, I can hear her bawling.

I did that. I acted like a jerk, and made her cry. What the hell is my problem?

TWENTY-SIX

UPSTAIRS, I FIGURE OUT THE BATHROOM IS THE
one door that's closed. It's right past the room I'm assuming
is Olivia's, because of the purple-everything inside. A couple
knocks on the bathroom door, and she opens it. Seeing her
with tears in her eyes is starting to feel regular. I wonder what
she was like, before Colby.

"Can we just not talk about him from now on?" I ask. "He
turns me into a jerk, and I'm not like that. I don't want to be
like that."

"How can we not talk about him? He's the one thing we
have in common. The only reason we're even hanging out right
now," she says. "You feel sorry for me."

"Yeah, I guess I do. Because all this sucks," I say, pointing to her stomach, and it's like I'm suddenly hit in the face
with reality: right now, this very second, there's a baby inside
Olivia's stomach. There's no forgetting about Colby for her,
because he's always there. "Are you going to have the baby?"

She shakes her head, but I'm sure a yes is going to come out
of her mouth. "No. I'm not."

She stands there in the doorway of the bathroom, staring

back at me. Her eyes are dry now, and when I look down at her stomach, I still can't see anything there. Did she lie? Was it a lie this entire time?

"Then what's going on?" I ask.

"I've been thinking about something for the last couple weeks," she says after a deep breath. "But now I have to stop thinking about it and actually do it."

"Do what?"

She walks past me, heading for the purple bedroom. She sits on the edge of the bed, and I stand just past the doorway, watching her. My heart won't stop freaking out and knocking against my ribs.

I have to ask. "Did you lie? Did you make it up just to try to keep him around?"

Her face tells me what I need to know. It's not a lie.

"I wish you were my friend, Pen," she says.

"Why?"

"Because then I could ask you to come with me, and you'd probably say yes," she says.

There's a little white chair tucked under this desk to my left. There's a sweater or something folded over the back of it. I pull the chair out and sit, careful not to knock the sweater off. Olivia's eyes are almost screaming at me to help her. No one's ever needed my help. Not for real.

"You're getting an abortion?" I say.

"Yes."

"Because of Colby?"

She shakes her head no.

"But—I mean, that's a big deal. What about, like, adoption? Or having it?"

"I thought about all that." She closes her eyes like she's giving herself a little refresher. "I just need someone to come with me to Crestonvale, wait for me, and ride home with me."

It sounds easy. Not a big deal at all. Except it's an abortion. There's no pressing Pause and going back to the last checkpoint once you realized you messed up.

"Did you, you know, talk to someone about it all?"

"I talked to a counselor at the clinic twice. She got me to read all this stuff. I did my homework for this." She looks lost for a minute. "I made an appointment. But I chickened out because I was by myself, and they said I need someone to take me home. I don't know what's going to happen, but what if it's bad and I can't even take the bus by myself? My mom will figure it out."

I'm just listening.

"It's already been almost eight weeks, and it has to be figured out before I get to twelve," she says. "I don't want to puke anymore."

"How's it been two months already? It just happened last week or something."

"I found out a couple weeks ago, but that means it had happened a little while before that."

I pull out my phone to scroll through the calendar app. It still doesn't make sense to me. Time's going too fast.

"Do you think it's even possible for me to know what's right and what's wrong?" she says.

"What do you mean?"

"What if I think I'm making the right decision, but it turns out to be a horrible mistake, and I realize I should've known better? My mom's always telling me people my age think they know everything, and then when they get older, they realize how stupid they were," she says. "What if I'm doing something stupid and I don't even know it?"

"Oh," I say. "Well, I think people always think those who are younger than them are dumb. My uncle thinks he's smarter than my dad, and my dad thinks he's smarter than my brother—who's to say who's right? And sure, our older selves are always going to look back and think our younger selves were idiots—but it doesn't mean anything." I think I'm freaking her out with my rambling. "Say your older self ended up regretting the decision you make today, well, what does it matter? She's not here right now. You are," I say. "I think maybe you shouldn't think about doing what's right, and maybe you should just do what feels *less* wrong."

"I just want it to be over, Pen. I want it to be done."

"Okay."

"I just don't want to go by myself," she says. "I'm always by myself. There's never anybody here."

"Don't cry, Olivia. I'll go with you. Don't worry."

AFTER THAT, OLIVIA MAKES us dinner. She pulls out a box of Kraft Dinner, and I could eat KD at every meal and be happy, so I give her a thumbs-up.

"You can have that Atari system, if you want," she says later, as she places a bowl of macaroni and cheese in front of me.

"What? Are you crazy? Won't your uncle be pissed?"

"He came back last month to pick up the rest of his stuff. He left that there, so I figure he doesn't want it."

"Shouldn't you ask him?"

"I want you to have it," she says, taking a seat across from me at the round kitchen table. "You seem to really love it. It's just shoved into our piles of junk. Take it."

"The games, too?"

"All of it."

"Wow. Johnny would . . ." But I don't finish the thought, because Johnny's gone. "That's awesome. It feels like a bribe, but I'll take it. Thanks."

When I grin, she lets a little grin of her own pull the corner of her mouth up. We eat our KD, and every once in a while, I look up to watch the way she eats. It makes me feel like a slob, so I try putting only a few pieces of pasta on my fork and chewing eighteen times before swallowing. It's exhausting as hell, so I go back to shoveling forkfuls in my mouth.

"We met with Mr. Middleton earlier," I say. "We have barely over a month to come up with a concept and shoot everything. I'm kind of freaking."

"I'm sorry I bailed on you guys," Olivia says, putting her fork down. "If you really get stuck, you can go with my idea. I told Blake about it before I quit."

"Really?" I say. "What was it?"

"The project is supposed to be about capturing what it's like to be a student at St. Peter's, right? Well, I'd been thinking about asking people for quotes about what it's like to go to this school," she says. "Combining their words with their pictures."

I let that sit for a moment, picturing what it would look like. I'd gotten as far as deciding black and white would probably make the pictures look artsy. Words might be good.

"That sounds pretty cool," I say. "But . . . who would actually want the truth plastered over their picture? They'd get laughed at."

"Well . . . ," Olivia says, then we both go quiet. "Maybe some people aren't ashamed of the truth."

"Doubt it." I point to her bowl. "Are you not gonna eat that?"

She shakes her head and pushes the bowl over my way. "Orange things have been grossing me out lately."

"Orange? Just . . . anything orange?"

"Juice, cheese, mangoes," she says. "Ugh, carrots are the worst."

"That's messed up," I say. "Orange is an important food color. Jalapeño Cheetos are orange. Me and Colby eat, like, two bags of those a week."

At the mention of his name, we both stop and look at each other. There's no way to *not* talk about him; he's everywhere.

"Pen?" she says. "How come you're friends with Colby?"

"I can't really remember right now," I say.

"Can I tell you something?" she asks. When I nod, she adds, "Because I don't think I was just some girl."

"Yeah, okay. Maybe not."

"The third time we hung out, he told me he loved me," she says.

"Colby said that?" It's like she'd need to point him out of a lineup for me to believe we're talking about the same dude. "Love?"

"He'd text me in the morning when he'd wake up to say good morning. For a month he was like that. Then the summer ended and school started. Things changed. I don't know how."

"That just sounds . . . like you're talking about some other dude."

"When I was worried about being late, I called him. He came to meet me and it was horrible. It was stupid, but I thought . . ." Olivia looks over and her face breaks. I never want to be the reason a girl's face breaks like that.

"You thought he'd step it up, stop being a douche, and man up," I say. That's what she thought—it's on her face. "So that's why you backtracked and told him you made a mistake."

"There was nobody but him around," she says. "I'm always by myself. But telling him was a bad idea. It just turned him into the biggest jerk."

"You're not the one who made him like that. He came out that way," I tell her. "And don't worry. I got your back. I mean it."

The thing is, girls can man up, too.

TWENTY-SEVEN

FRIDAY, TWO DAYS LATER, IS DATE NIGHT. I TOOK two showers, just in case I missed a spot. I saved my best fancy shirt for this—this black golf shirt Johnny had bought for me last summer. Over that, my white Portugal warm-up jacket. And my jeans are baggy as hell and ripped at the knees—my legs are shaved, which is probably the only girly thing I do. I scrubbed the white rubber of my skater shoes with alcohol to get rid of some of the scuff marks. As I step into them, my mom wanders over from the living room. "You no go out like this. You look like punk druggy."

"I know. But I like it." One last check of my pockets for phone, keys, and wallet and it's time. Mom's huffing and puffing behind me. I turn. "Can I go?"

"Why you no put on nice clothes? You think this nice? You look like you steal something. You wanna look like a boy, huh? You think the good nurse in the hospital look like boys?"

"I don't want to be a nurse."

"You no this, you no that. All the time, you say no." Then in Portuguese, she says she doesn't know what she did to God to be given kids like the ones she got.

"Maybe God's not listening to you," I say.

Her fist goes to her heart, and she faces me with a look of disgust. "Something wrong with you, Penelope. Something wrong with you, big-time."

"I know."

My mom wants me to dress pretty, to go to college to be a nurse, and to meet a nice man to be my husband. What if I want to dress sharp, go to college to study landscaping or plumbing, and meet a nice girl to be my wife? Shouldn't that technically be the same thing, only better because it's actually what I want?

I walk out, and she doesn't try to stop me.

CRESTONVALE HAS A NEWER movie theater with way more showtimes and way bigger screens than Castlehill. The theater's in the middle of a bunch of restaurants and night-spots, with little paths connecting everything and a gigantic parking lot surrounding it all. There's music blasting through outdoor speakers and neon lights splashing over every surface. Plus, the bus stops right at the entrance of the lot. Blake's standing below the center light post where we agreed to meet. I hang back, hidden by one of the big planters with evergreens growing inside.

The dessert place next door is packed. Johnny likes to take girls there for something sweet. I scan the people inside, doing a quick sweep of faces and bodies. I don't even know why. He's not in there.

My eyes fall back on Blake. I go to her, but I don't get too close.

"Sorry, were you waiting long? I should've left earlier," I say.

"Are you scared I'll bite your head off if you're late? I'm not *that* bad, am I?" When I make this face like, *Um, kinda*, she lightly smacks my arm. "I'm starving."

"Same."

While we walk to McDonald's, I make sure to keep at least three feet between us.

"Olivia told me about her idea for the photo project," I say.

"She did?"

"Yeah," I say. "Do you think maybe we should just go with that idea? I can't really think of anything else that's doable. I mean, all I could think of is to pixelate the image, but . . . then all that'd do is make it impossible to see any detail."

"I guess we could go with her idea," Blake says.

"Unless you have a better one?"

We cross between the arcade and a steak house. My phone goes off with the *Turtles* theme. It says "Home" on the display screen. I put it on Silent and let it fall back into my pocket.

"Was that Colby?" Blake asks.

"Nah. Probably my mom."

"Is Colby still freezing you out?" she asks.

"Guess so."

"All this over Olivia?" she says.

"I don't know anymore."

We hop the curb to McDonald's and reach the door. "But I thought you said you and Olivia *aren't* friends," she says. We're not going inside, because Blake is closer to the door than I am, and she makes no move to open it. "That's what you said before, right?"

"Yeah, she was just some girl," I say. "I thought that's all she was."

Blake's squinting like she's waiting for me to go on.

"Maybe we're sort of friends," I say.

Blake opens the door and heads for the counter, taking a spot in line. We order and wait. She doesn't try to take my hand or touch my shoulder or anything. I wish I could thank her for being cool in public, but it doesn't seem like something to talk about—especially if she's sitting there feeling grateful about the distance, too.

I pick a booth in the back corner. It's better this way because it's like no one else exists. She dips her fries in a mixture of ketchup and mayo.

"He was a prick to her," I say. "I wasn't cool with that, and now things are sort of messed up."

Blake nods. After a sigh, her features lighten and she says, "What if—for the photo project—we mixed up the truth and the photos?"

"Meaning?"

"What if we get people to give us anonymous quotes and then we match them up with pictures of other people," she says. "Wouldn't that be absolutely amazing? Think about it.

The more mismatched it would look, the better it would be."

"People might actually tell the truth." I point at her with a fry. "You and Olivia would've made a way better team."

She looks down. "Or maybe you and Olivia would've made a better team?"

"The only reason I'm on any team is because of you," I say. "If there's no you on the team, then there's no me."

She slides out of the booth, only to slide in next to me. Our shoulders are touching, and no one can see us from here. It's pretty awesome, especially when both our hands are in our laps and they move closer to the middle until mine can wrap around hers.

I don't eat too much because I'm kind of thinking the universe would be enough of a jerk to give me the runs on my first date.

AT THE MOVIE THEATER, we're waiting in line for tickets, and I act like the display of showtimes is super fascinating. There are so many dudes here, dudes who are so obviously checking out my girl. I don't know if I should act like a tough badass about it, lifting my leg to piss against Blake like Colby would do, or if I should spare us both the extra attention by sort of acting like I'm randomly standing near her. If someone yells anything stupid or asks me if I'm packing, I'll absorb it all. I'll tell anyone that Blake and I aren't together. I'll say whatever I have to so she doesn't get laughed at. Or I'll punch someone if I get mad enough.

"One for *Steel to Hell 3*," Blake tells the ticket booth person. "I can't believe I'm doing this. I don't like scary movies."

"Oh, wait," I say, because it's my job to pay for her, but I didn't bring enough money. "Uh . . . I would've paid for you."

"Why?" she says, handing the lady some cash.

"Because," I say, then I whisper, "it's a date. I didn't even buy your dinner."

"So? I can pay for myself. You pay for you."

And that's what I do, leaving me with just enough left over to afford six kernels of popcorn, so I grab a stack of napkins just for something to carry. Blake orders popcorn and a drink. There are only, like, twenty other people in the dark theater so far. We head for the back seats.

"Popcorn?" Blake asks, tipping the bag my way. She leans into me and puts her head on my shoulder.

More people enter the theater, but it's so dark I don't think anyone would look at us twice. Tonight I hope people assume I'm a dude. I hope they think I'm just some guy whose hand Blake's threaded hers into. The previews roll, starting with a stream of movie-theater commercials.

Blake flattens my hand against her thigh, keeping hers on top. Going to a movie for a date is the stupidest idea ever. All I can do is sit here in silence and eat my date's popcorn.

This movie is playing for everyone else but me tonight. Instead, I draw circles on the inside of Blake's wrist, and I know she likes it because her hand twitches. Sometimes she lifts her head to look at me, and I know I could kiss her and she'd let me. But I don't try, because there are a couple guys ahead of us, and at any second, they could decide to turn around and ruin everything. I can wait.

AFTER THE MOVIE, BLAKE and I take the bus back to Castlehill. My phone has a couple more missed calls from home. At the terminal, we're supposed to get on different buses heading to opposite ends of town.

"I don't want tonight to end," she says.

Tonight can't end. Not yet. We haven't even kissed at all.

"Me either. I don't want you to go." But it's cold, and it's almost midnight.

"Come back to my house," she says.

"I want to, you have no idea. But my parents—well, my mom—she's just . . ." I make a face like I'm being strangled. "She'd kill me. I know you don't get it, but my parents aren't like yours. Even if it's the weekend, I can't just—"

"I do get it, Pen. I guess I shouldn't always assume everyone's parents are like mine."

Her hair blows with the breeze and strands get stuck against her shiny lips. I reach up to brush them aside.

"Wait—hang on. What if you came back to my house? Would your parents let you?"

"They're not that cool," she says. "But they're sleeping right now, so . . ."

Next thing I know, we're on a bus headed to my neighborhood, and I have no idea how the hell I'm going to get into my own house without getting a nice dose of my mom's pissy eyebrows and a swat of a dish towel.

I WALK BLAKE TO the backyard first and let her in using my key. I tell her to wait for me, then I head back out and let myself into my house through the front. My parents aren't there. There's no sound, and their bedroom door is closed. I go to the living room. With the TV set to the music channel, I set the sleep timer for 120 minutes. Then it's down to the basement, where Blake's waiting.

"No one's up. We should be good here."

Blake scopes out the place. It's so ugly, and I hadn't thought to explain. Concrete floor, drywall, and no furniture except for a broken kitchen chair.

"Uh, give me a second. Want something to drink? There should be some stuff in the fridge. And the bathroom's over by the—" I was going to say TV, but then remembered everything's gone. I point instead.

In the storage room, which was supposed to become a second bedroom at some point, I dig out one of the extra blow-up mattresses for when the family visits. I bring that to Johnny's empty room, plus a heavy quilt and my old Superman desk lamp. Blake follows me inside. The mattress has an automatic pump, and it's inflated within a couple minutes. I spread the quilt over the mattress. "It's ugly but it's clean."

"We're squatting in your basement," she says. "This might win everything."

We end up on our stomachs, side by side, making shadow puppets on the wall.

"Mine look like shadow puppets of hands sucking at

204

making shadow puppets," I say.

She bursts out laughing, and I clamp my hand over her mouth. She puts her hands over mine, and there's something in her eyes that I can't stop staring at.

"Penelope!" My mom's voice comes from far away, but still. "Why you down there? Penelope?"

Oh, man.

TWENTY-EIGHT

I BEG BLAKE TO BE QUIET AND NOT MOVE, THEN I rush up the stairs, where my mom's poking her head out.

"What you doing down there?" she asks.

"I was just looking for my lamp. My Superman lamp."

She makes a face. "You come back, huh?"

"I didn't leave forever. I just went to the movies with the guys, because it's Friday night. It was a three-hour movie, so it finished late."

"You lie! I see Colby tonight. He not with you."

Oh, man. I feel the guilt on my face, but still. "Me and Tristan weren't with him. He was being a jerk, so we went to the movies without him."

She doesn't look satisfied. "I call you, three times."

"My phone died. I told you the battery sucks. It's an old

phone. I charged it earlier, but it dies fast."

She's fuming. I can tell by the look on her face and the way she can't keep her arms crossed but she continues trying. "You go to bed. We talk about this tomorrow. You *pai* is very mad."

"Okay."

It's making her even more mad that I'm just standing here, saying everything like there's an invisible shrug that goes with it. It's making me mad that I have to lie because that's all she'll let me do. No one ever tells the truth about anything.

"Go to bed now," she says.

"I'm just getting something to eat and I'm gonna watch TV for a bit."

"Go to bed!"

"All right! I will. But I'm hungry."

She tells me to watch the crumbs, and then says if I make a stain, I'll have to clean it—as if I'm some four-year-old who can't help but spill her drink all over the place. She heads back upstairs mumbling to herself.

When I get to the basement, Blake looks ready to bolt. "Relax. I'm pretty sure we're safe. She yelled at me, then she went to bed."

"Are you sure? I don't want you to get in trouble because of me."

"It's fine. She doesn't even come down here because she hates how steep the stairs are," I say. Besides, my ears are on alert now, so the second I hear anything, I'll smuggle Blake out and pretend I didn't feel like sleeping in my room.

So we get back on the mattress, and we keep our voices

really low. She bites her bottom lip when she pauses between sentences. She tells me about the scar on her chin, the one I never noticed until she was lying down next to me. "After that, there were no more cartwheels in the house. That's when my career as a gymnast died."

"Can I touch it?"

She lifts her chin and I put my index finger on the little dent. My eyes blur on her neck where I'm pretty sure I can see a flutter, and if that's her heart beating, then it's going as fast as mine. She rolls onto her back, so I shift a bit to look at the side of her face.

"Am I the first girl you've kissed?" I ask, watching her closely. If she's kidding herself into seeing me as a boy, my question should bring her back to reality. I hope she's into reality.

"Yeah," she says, with no hesitation. "What about you?"

"I've kissed three girls. The first one was when I was five and we were playing house and she made me the dad. The second was a couple years ago when Colby dared this girl to kiss me. And the third was last summer, and it was this girl Colby was dating."

"You kissed Colby's girlfriend?"

"It wasn't like that," I say. "I think she was trying to make Colby jealous, and he didn't even really like her."

"So, you didn't like her either?"

"Yeah, I liked her. But it wasn't about whether I liked her or not," I say.

"Was it Olivia?"

"No way," I say. "I don't think of her that way. Never have."

207

Blake nods, still looking at the ceiling. I can't tell what she's thinking by the look on her face. Anytime I pay attention to a girl, people figure I must be into her, that I must have a crush on her. I don't know how to explain the difference between liking Olivia and liking Blake, or how to explain that one couldn't turn into the other.

I guess this is why guys can't really be friends with girls without all the drama.

"I think of you that way, though. All the time," I say, and she smirks at the ceiling.

"Since when?"

"Since school started," I say, but that's not totally right. "And maybe I used to like watching you play volleyball last year, when your hair was brown and always in a ponytail."

Her eyes are closed, and her hand rests against mine.

"When did you know you wanted to kiss me?" I ask. "Kiss me for real."

"When you came into the bathroom that time I was killing time instead of being in class."

"For real? That far back?"

"Yeah."

"What? How?"

She turns to look at me. "Your lips. I was watching them when you talked and then, I don't know. I just had this feeling."

"What kind of feeling?"

She shifts onto her side, running her fingers through her hair to get it away from her face. "This feeling that if you'd come up to me and kissed me, I would've let you."

Everything feels more real, more there. I push up on my elbow, and she rolls back, her face right below mine. She presses up against me, and then she closes her eyes like she's getting sleepy. So I rock this kiss Sleeping Beauty–style. I know how to kiss her now. I know the way her lips and her tongue move.

I think about putting my hand up her shirt.

Well, maybe not up her shirt right away, but on her shirt and *then* up her shirt. I roll on top of her, and then she's curling her hands around my collar, running her fingers through my hair, and it's all good. It's good enough that I lift my hand three times, thinking maybe it'll make it over or under her shirt. But I chicken out each time. The fourth time, she takes my hand and shoves it up her top and I almost want to thank her for helping.

We're both lucky she's got balls.

TWENTY-NINE

I HEAR FOOTSTEPS ABOVE ME THAT RIP ME OUT of my dream, which doesn't work because above me should be the roof. And I'm rocking back and forth like someone's jumping on the bed next to me.

"Oh my god, Pen!" Blake whispers.

"Oh no. Oh shit!"

Blake goes for her phone. "No calls—yes! Thank you! It's

only eight. My parents must still be asleep."

"Mine aren't."

"Ew!"

"What?"

She covers her mouth. "Morning breath."

"Oh—" I cover my own mouth. "Sorry. Oh, that's nasty."

"Not you, me!"

"Well, me too."

"Ew. Let's stay far apart."

"Yeah, deal."

We scramble around the room because Blake lost her shirt last night, and that black bra—man, that was awesome. And I'm only in a muscle top and jeans, which isn't something I meant to happen in the daylight, because I think my boobs are bigger than Blake's.

"What do we do?" she asks, a hand still covering her mouth.

"I think there's toothpaste left in the bathroom from before Johnny moved out."

"How old is this toothpaste exactly?"

"New, don't worry. He moved out a couple weeks ago."

"Oh really?" she says. "Where did he go?"

"Somewhere. He took the damn Xbox, too." I shrug. "Follow me, and be super quiet."

There's toothpaste, deodorant, and toilet paper left in the cupboard. The hand soap is still there, along with a box of tissues. Blake and I use our fingers to brush, twice. Then I step out, figuring she probably has to pee because my own bladder is feeling a bit overinflated—although *I'm* used to it.

It's my mom up there, going from the kitchen to the laundry room. I wish today was church day, but that's tomorrow. Both my parents are going to park their butts on the main floor all day. And there's also the fact that I'm supposed to be getting yelled at about yesterday.

When Blake comes out, we head for Johnny's room again. Her face is free of the smudged black makeup. She looks like she could be in grade ten.

"I'll cab it home. Can I just go through the back again?"

"Yeah, but stay close to the house and run to the side just in case my mom's at the window—she's always spying on the neighbors."

"I can do that." She dials and asks for a cab, looking to me for the address. "Okay, ten minutes."

I take a deep breath, finally relaxing a little now that we've got a plan and our breaths aren't rotten. "Your hair is completely messed up when you wake up."

"Told you. Feel it—it's like straw." I reach up like I'm going to feel her hair for real when she stops and her eyes widen like she just remembered something. "Tonight—I forgot to tell you about tonight. Elliott's having people over. We're all going after band practice. Do you think you could come?"

"Tonight? Yeah—"

"Penelope!" Mom sounds like she's right on the other side of the door—she had to have snuck down here quietly. The doorknob is turning and I don't even have one second to glance at Blake. My mom's standing there in front of us, staring at the unmade bed.

"WHO ARE YOU?" MOM says to Blake. "I don't know you. Why you in my house?" Then she turns to me, and I swear her hands are working the dish towel like she wishes it was my neck. "What you do, Penelope? What wrong with you?"

"This is my friend Blake from school. We have a project for school."

"You know my daughter not a boy? You *mãe* and *pai* know you kissy-kissy with my girl?"

This is not happening.

"You should go," I tell Blake. "Ma, let Blake leave."

"I talk to the girl," Mom says, refusing to move from the door. "You *pai* know you come to my house? You *pai* know you like the punk druggy girls? Did my daughter lie? She tell you she's a boy? Penelope is not a boy."

Blake opens her mouth, but I cut her off before even a word comes out of her mouth. "Ma, move out of the way. Let her go home. Her dad doesn't care who she hangs out with."

"You bring girls here to my house now?" Mom points a finger at me.

"Oh, man. I can't believe this," I say to Blake. "I'm sorry. She's just—I don't know. I tried to tell you."

"You go home," Mom says to Blake. Then to me, "You in big trouble."

Finally, Mom's out of the way and heading back upstairs. Blake's watching me, waiting. I can't believe she just stood there and took all that crap without even making a weird face.

"I'm sorry. My mom is just—it's not about you."

"It's okay, Pen. I guess I see what you mean now, about your parents. Hey, Charlie's mom hates me, too. I'm used to it," she says with a little smile that makes me feel worse. "But I guess you won't be able to come tonight, huh?"

"I'm going to try."

She nods. "I should go catch my cab."

"Yeah, okay," I say.

I stay far from her, settling for a stupid two-finger wave when she walks out the back door. My mom wrecked this for me. Of all the things she's messed up for me, this is the worst. I can't do this anymore.

I TIPTOE UP THE stairs, pushing the basement door open just wide enough to pass through. Mom's waiting for me, glaring.

"Wha' you doing?"

"Nothing."

"No? You no do nothing?" she says. "I tell you what you do. You listen to me now."

Dad appears behind her, shaking his head like I did a bad, bad thing.

Mom says, "I don't want the girl in my house no more. You no see the girl outside. You no put clothes of the boys no more. No more. Finished." Then she says if she has to send me to Portugal to live with my third cousins for six months and learn to behave, she will.

I look at my dad. "Do you wanna yell at me, too? Do you wanna kick me out?"

"Penelope!" he shouts. "You stop!" In Portuguese, he says the way I'm going about things is not going to help me get out of trouble, that I need to stop and think.

"Think about what?"

"I don't know, I don't know," Mom says to herself, shaking her head. "This girl she's broken. I don't know what happened. I don't know how to fix."

"Ana," Dad says, a warning for her to stop as well.

I stare back at my mom, with nothing to say to her.

I stalk upstairs with the same words running through my head: *I'm done doing what they say. I'm done doing what they say.*

Done.

THIRTY

ALL DAY, I'M IN MY ROOM. THERE'S NO XBOX because it's at Johnny's new place. Some of my YouTubers uploaded new videos yesterday, so I start with 8Bit Destruction's. I think about playing my Atari for a bit, but then I end up watching a couple of *Let's Play* videos of *The Last of Us* because that game is so epic, it's almost like a movie anyway. Plus, Ellie is one of the most badass video game characters ever. She might be the only girl character I don't mind playing. Blake's in my head, and I'm too much of a pussy to send her a text. So I move on to the DLC *Left Behind*, which is like a prequel game that tells the story of how Ellie got bitten by a zombie. I start rewinding the scene where Ellie tells Riley not to go. I don't even have a PlayStation, but I know this game so well that it's almost like I've played through it in all difficulties.

Ellie is, like—I don't know, fourteen maybe—and she has more balls than I do. Her best friend, Riley, is about to take off to join the revolution, and Ellie doesn't want her to go. I watched one of the first *Let's Play* videos that came out for this a year or so ago, and the whole time I was thinking, *Whoa—is Ellie gonna kiss Riley? Are they gonna kiss?* There was all this buildup, but I didn't know if I was seeing things. Then Ellie kissed Riley. They kissed, and that never happens in games. It's always a guy and a girl. It's never two badass teenage girls in sneakers and jeans who are into each other just because.

Then they get bit by zombies and everything goes to hell. At least Blake didn't get bit by zombies. There are worse things than getting told off by someone's pissy mother. Like, it could be the actual end of the world, zombie-apocalypse style. That's what I think about when I replay that kiss scene, over and over.

When my phone beeps with a text, I nearly flip backward on my computer chair reaching for the phone on my bed. But it's not Blake. It's Tristan: Yo. Wanna hang 2nite? Crypts!!!

Me: grounded as hell 2nite dude—plus no xbox 2 play crypts

Him: Right. That sux.

I need to see Blake tonight. I'm going to make it happen.

LATER, WHEN IT'S DARK out, I tiptoe downstairs and wait by the front door for the right time to open it. The TV's on in the living room where my mom's watching, and my dad's passed out. I'm counting on his snoring to cover any noise I might make escaping. I pull the door open a crack and sneak out barefoot. I don't even put on my shoes and jacket until I know no one could see me from the windows.

Olivia picks up on the second ring.

"Did Elliott invite you to his place tonight?"

"Yes," she says. "But I told him I'm sick."

"Oh."

"Are you going?"

"Sort of," I say. "I mean, yeah. I'm going."

"I can't wait for everything to be over so I can just—you know?" She sighs. "I'm so sick of this shit."

"You just said shit."

"I know," she says. "It felt wrong."

I'm almost at the bus stop, but it doesn't come for another twenty minutes. "How come you never swear?"

"My mom swears all the time and, I don't know, I just always thought it made her look so trashy."

"Am I trashy? I swear a lot."

"No. You make swearing cool."

"Damn right, I do." I give a wide grin to nobody.

Olivia's quiet, then she goes, "Elliott's really nice."

She's always telling me that. "You're allowed to be into him, you know."

"I'm not into him. I don't even know him," she says. "He's just . . ."

I make my voice come out all girly. "Nice. He's *so* nice. He's, like, the nicest guy *ever*."

She laughs. "That was a little bit scary."

"I know, right? It's my idiot voice."

I sit on the curb and hold the phone between ear and shoulder.

TWENTY MINUTES ON THE bus and I'm at Elliott's. He lives in the nice new development behind the community center, where the houses are super skinny, super tall, and all stuck together. There isn't enough grass to make getting a lawn mower worth it, so Johnny says they probably just do it with scissors. There's music trying to force its way out the door, so I walk in because no one's going to hear a knock. I ditch my shoes but keep my jacket. There are people sprinkled throughout the upstairs and the basement. I recognize some from school, but most of them are from other schools.

Elliott's upstairs, surrounded by a group of guys, including Charlie. On the couch, Billy picks his electric guitar even though it's unplugged and the music's so loud. Elliott hitches his chin up at me. "What's up, man?"

"Thanks for the invite," I say.

"Yeah, no problem," he says. "I invited Olivia, too, but she said she's not feeling well."

"She puked in front of me the other day," I say.

Charlie laughs. "Yum."

I'm such an idiot. Why would I say that? I just didn't want Elliott to think Olivia's trying to ditch him.

"You guys know where Blake is?" I ask.

"Downstairs, showing off," Charlie says.

I nod at him and Elliott before heading off.

A couple girls standing in the kitchen look my way as I slip off my jacket. One looks curious, the other smiles. My response is to hook my thumb in my pocket like some cowboy and try to smile back, but the moment's passed, and I kind of wonder if she was just messing with me anyway.

A couple guys at the staircase move to let me pass. One of them says, "What's up, dude?" I ignore him because it almost sounds like he's trying to bait me. Like if I say "Nothing, man," he'll be all, "Are you packing, big boy?" Or maybe he's just being friendly. I can't tell, so I'd rather be safe than sorry.

There have to be at least thirty strangers in this house; it would be nice if one or two of them were queer in some way. I'd take a super-flaming gay dude even. Just someone else to stand out a little with me. And if there was another queer person here, then I could kind of assume the rest of these people aren't jerks. But it's just me. It's always just me.

Downstairs, a group of people are crowded around my girl, who is kicking some dude's butt at *Street Fighter*. And I mean, kicking a butt-load of butt. She's doing all the special moves. There's a big cheer every time the other guy's player wipes out. When he's finally KO'd, some other guy steps up, saying he'll kick Blake's butt for sure. She looks ready to go again, until she sees me and bounces up.

I told myself I'd know by the look in her eyes whether we're cool, or if she's suddenly spooked by the thought of me turning into a pissy European lady who hangs out in the kitchen making sauce and bread all day.

Whatever's going on in her head, her eyes are saying they want me. I should know, because she had that look all last night. Her hair's huge, her face is all black lines and wet-looking lips. It's not like I forgot what she looks like, but damn.

She reaches for my hand, then full-on presses herself against me. "You win everything for coming tonight."

I want to win her, that's all. That crap's not going to come out of my mouth, though, because I play it totally cool, squaring my shoulders and slipping an arm around her waist.

"I thought you weren't into button-mashing beat-'em-ups," I say.

"I'm not." She winks. "Doesn't mean I'm not righteous at them."

"That's a massive turn-on, you know that, right?" I meet her gaze.

"Uh-huh." She kisses me then, a little one like that time at school, and I just want to go somewhere, back to my basement.

She pulls me by the hand as my phone vibrates in my back pocket. It's Olivia.

"Colby's here!" she whispers.

"At your house? What the hell's he doing there? Don't let him—"

"Not at my house. At Elliott's. I shouldn't have come!"

"You're here?"

"In the bathroom. I took a taxi over after we got off the phone . . ." She goes quiet, and that's when I hear the voices upstairs get louder. Then the call ends.

"What's up?" Blake asks.

"Trouble, I think."

THIRTY-ONE

I GET TO THE TOP OF THE STAIRS, AND SURE enough, there's Colby and Garrett. They're surrounded by Ike, Tim, and Ray from grade twelve, and two other guys I don't recognize. They're taking up the whole entrance-foyer thing. Way at the back is Tristan, throwing dirty looks at me. I lied to him.

I'm guessing the door they're blocking to the right is the bathroom.

"What's up, Steve?" Garrett says to me. "Is this your girl-friend?"

"You guys were not invited here," Blake says.

One of the guys I've never seen before says, "I was. They're with me."

Colby's hands are in his pockets and he stands in the middle of the pack, a half grin on his face just for me.

"Hey, Blake. Some guy was just asking if you were

available," Garrett says through a crooked smile. "Don't worry. I told him you already have a boyfriend. Then I told him maybe you're a dyke. I wasn't sure what the deal was."

I open my mouth to tell him off, but Blake's already going. "Thanks. That means a lot. Oh," she says, "I guess your friends forgot to tell you this wasn't a Halloween party. No one else dressed up, so you can take off that creepy mask now."

"Whoa, relax. Why are you getting all bitchy? Is it your time of the month?" Garrett asks her.

"Dude, say whatever you want about me," I say, "but back the hell off her."

Garrett smacks Ike's arm, then he says, "All right, Pen. Relax. Can I just ask one more question?"

"No," Blake says. "But you should consider donating your organs to science. Like now."

"You say weird things," he tells her. Then to me: "Steve, your girlfriend's feisty!" He leans closer to me. "You must be packing a pretty huge one, huh? To be able to nail a girl like that."

"I'm getting Elliott. You guys are so out of here," Blake says.

I lean over to her and whisper, "Olivia's stuck in the bathroom. I gotta keep Colby away from her."

She heads upstairs to find Elliott. This whole scene is messed up, and Colby's just standing there watching it all go down, loving every second of it.

"It's not like I can see a package hanging there, but maybe you picked a small one to wear so people wouldn't be able to notice, right?" Garrett says, tipping his head to the side and staring at my crotch.

I look at Colby, shaking my head. He looks back like, *What—you got a problem?* I pull out my phone while Garrett runs his mouth and the others laugh, texting Olivia. *Stay there. Taking care of it.*

"What are you guys doing here?" I ask Colby. "Did you come just to mess with me?"

"Yeah, because you're that important, right?" he says, thumbs hooked in his pocket like I was doing earlier, except on him, it looks legit. "You gotta stop telling your mom you're hanging out with me, because you're not."

"Whoa, Steve's a big liar, lying to her mom. You got balls. I mean, that's good, right? You *want* balls and all," Garrett says.

My phone buzzes, but I ignore it. Olivia just has to wait. Nothing I can do until Elliott gets here.

"Dudes, why are we just standing here on the welcome mat?" Ike says, pushing toward the front. There's no way a guy in high school can grow a beard like that. He must've failed a lot. "I'm sweating my balls off here, and I ain't got time for that."

"All right, guys, you gotta go," Elliott says, suddenly behind me. He moves right through them, right for the bathroom door.

Colby's eyes fall on Olivia, being led out by Elliott, their hands clutched.

"Hey, Livie. How are you?" Colby says. Livie? She doesn't reply, just looks at her feet. "Hey, *Olivia*. How *are* you? Miss me?"

Olivia looks at me. I should be doing something.

"Can you guys just leave already?" Blake says. My phone vibrates, and it won't stop. It's a phone call.

"Jake, you can stay," Elliott tells one of the guys I don't know. He comes to stand before us like he's our shield, because he's the guy and we're three girls. I step up too, standing next to him. "The rest of you, out."

"Who are you? Are you the musician?" Colby asks Elliott, taking two steps until he's right in front of us.

"This is my house. Who the hell are *you*?" Elliott asks him. I reach blindly into my back pocket to shut off my phone. Colby's phone starts going off.

"Yo. man, we're just gonna come chill a bit, then leave, all righty, buddy?" the guy, Jake, says, and Ike sighs all exaggerated.

"Yeah, and for real, my man, you need to check your thermostat. It's hotter than Satan's crotch in here. My beard is frizzing," Ike says, running his fingers through it.

"Sorry, dudes. I don't know most of you, and for real, though, you're being douche bags, so turn around and head back the way you came, all right?" Elliott says.

Colby's phone goes off again. He pulls it out of his pocket but doesn't do anything with it. He stares at Olivia while Elliott and Jake negotiate. I just wish they'd all leave.

"Hey, Livie," Colby says, then he blows her a kiss when Elliott's not looking. "Come with me."

"Man, leave her alone. Just go," I tell him.

Garrett starts laughing and pointing at me. The two guys from grade twelve look bored and head out the door, followed by Ike, who's fanning his beard off. Tristan's finally visible from this angle. He nods his head to the beat of the music coming from upstairs. He shouldn't be hanging out with these guys.

"Tristan," I say, and he looks over with his blank face, which means he's pissed at me. "You can stay, if you want."

"Uh, I don't think so, Pen," Colby says. "Tristan's with me."

"You got a problem, man?" Elliott asks Colby.

"Yeah, I do. I got a—" Colby stops talking when his phone goes off again, and this time, he picks it up but doesn't say anything into it. Instead he yells at me: "What the hell! You need to stop telling your damn parents that you're hanging out with me, all right?" He stares at his phone now, like something catches his eye. He scrolls like he's totally forgotten what's going down right now.

I glance at Blake, and we both shrug.

Colby dials his phone and puts it against his ear, retreating toward the door, huddling down like he's trying to hear better. Something's up.

"Who's that?" I ask, but Colby's not listening to me. "Is it my mom?"

"All right, out. For real. Out of my house," Elliott tells the guys, pointing to the door. Jake shrugs and leaves, followed by Tristan and the rest of them. Garrett gives me the finger first with his right hand, then his left, but I'm staring at Colby with his phone to his ear.

Finally, he turns around and drops his phone into his pocket.

"You need to check your phone," he says to me.

"It's my mom?"

"Yeah," he says. "They're at the hospital. Something happened to your brother."

224

No it didn't. He's lying.

I pull out my cell phone and there are four missed calls from my house. Three voice mails. I dial my house but it just rings and rings.

"You see, that right there is loyalty," Colby says to no one.

"Why don't you take your loyalty and get out of my house?" Elliott says. He turns to me and goes, "You need a ride to the hospital?"

There's no answer when I dial Johnny's number. It's all messed up after that. I don't talk to anybody. Someone finds my shoes for me.

This doesn't feel real. It's like my stomach falls into my shoes, in a bad way.

THIRTY-TWO

FOR TWENTY MINUTES IN THE BACK OF ELLIOTT'S car, a silent Blake next to me, I think up reasons why Johnny would be in the hospital—all of them bad or terrible. I don't even know what he's been doing since he left. It's like he's not even my brother anymore. What if some crazy homeless dude wandered here from Toronto and stabbed Johnny? What if a drunk driver drove right into his truck?

What if he's dead?

Elliott pulls up next to a parked ambulance and drops me off at the ER doors. Blake doesn't ask to come with me, and I'm glad for it.

"I'll text you later" is all I say before pushing the car door closed.

THIS IS THE EMERGENCY room. There are people lined up, some holding a part of their body that hurts, some looking ready to fall over and die, and some rifling through their wallets and pulling out cards. There's a guy my age in handcuffs. The cop next to him yawns and crosses his arms.

I have no idea where to go.

There's a nurse behind a plastic window, but she's got that massive lineup of people to take care of. There are sliding doors that don't open when I stand in front of them. A sign says *Authorization Required Beyond This Point*. On the other side of the doors, there are lots of stretchers with people lying on them. Some look dead.

I can't call my parents because only my dad has a cell phone, and it's usually dead in the glove compartment. So I stand here, right in front of the doors, until finally, some doctor comes through and I sneak in.

It smells like butt. For real.

My eyes fall on a curtain next to a sink bolted to the wall. My mom sits on a chair. My dad's not there, but there's a stretcher and Johnny's sitting on it. He's holding a wad of something against his eyebrow and there's blood leaking down his arm—all over his shirt, too. He's all mangled.

226

At least he's alive.

"What happened?" I ask when I get to them.

Mom looks up at me with a head shake and a heavy sigh. She's still pissed at me, but I think right now she's more mad at Johnny.

"Just some stupid stuff," Johnny says, and that's when I notice he's talking all weird, like his tongue's not working. I don't look directly at him.

In Portuguese, I ask my mom what happened.

"Oh, you *irmão* is a big shot," she says, rolling her eyes. "Big big shot break his *cabeça*."

"Oh, please, man," he says, looking at me with one squinty eye. "It's a concussion."

It sounds like *cuncuthon*. "What's wrong with your tongue?"

"Bit down on it when I got knocked in the chin. Got some stitches. Waiting for them to fix the eyebrow," he says, lifting the wad of gauze from this huge gash that's spilling blood. Even his eyeball has blood in it. Some of the fingers of his right hand are taped together.

"Who'd you fight with?"

"Couple guys at the bar. Going around acting like douche bags," he says. "One of them swung at Naveed, man. Must not have seen me right next to him. And his buddy threw a bar stool at my face. Regretted it real quick, though."

"Ah you!" My mom gets up and makes like she's going to smack him. "You big shot, always in other business!" She mutters about Johnny being everyone's personal bodyguard, then she turns to me. "You, I no forget. You in big big trouble, too. You stay in the house." She walks away. I sit on the chair she was on. There's silence while I count the flecks in the tiles at my feet.

"You're in trouble, huh?" Johnny says. "What'd you do?"

"I breathed."

He lets out a chuckle and rolls his eyes—his one eye. When I turn my head away, he sighs. "It's not that big a deal, okay? These eyebrow cuts bleed so damn much. It looks worse than it is. Relax, man. *Calma*."

"I'm relaxed."

"Stop bouncing your leg like a maniac then."

I stop the leg, but then the other one starts going. Two cops walk over. They ask Johnny if he wants to make a statement. Johnny tells them no. "Nothing happened, you know?"

The one cop nods like he's not surprised. "Yeah, figured as much." Then he says if it ends up being worse than a concussion or if he changes his mind to call them back. There's just a bunch of silence between us, and some moaning coming from behind other curtains.

Finally, Johnny goes: "I'm gonna need my key back. Dom took the truck home for the night and he's got my keys."

"I don't have it." I'm not giving that key back—what if I want to sneak Blake over again or something? "*Pai* must have it."

"Why the hell does *Pai* have it?"

"Why the hell do you care?" I say. "Are you coming to the house to sleep in your empty bedroom or something?"

"Huh? No."

"Exactly. You don't live there anymore."

"Hey, man." He kind of laugh-winces at his tongue problems. "You're acting like a little idiot."

"*I* am? This is a question of loyalty."

"Loyalty? Pen, man, what the—" He gets distracted by a droplet of blood that lands on his knee. He fusses with the wad of paper, then directs his one eye back on me. "Apparently *you're* the one who cut me out."

I'm standing now, shoving my hands into my pockets and feeling all the things I've wanted to say to him bubble up inside me. But most of it stays inside. I give a pathetic shrug. "Well, look at it this way—now you don't have to pull fake knives on douche bags because of your stupid little sister. You're welcome."

"Man, you need to relax."

"I am relaxed! *You* need to relax. I gotta go."

He says something but I don't know what it is because I'm down the hall, and because he's talking like an idiot with that fat tongue. I wait outside the ER, taking a seat across the pissy dude in cuffs until my dad walks by and looks surprised to be running into me.

"Can you drive me home, please?"

"You *mãe*?"

"Johnny's not done. She's staying. But I want to go home."

He gestures toward the exit, getting his keys ready, and he doesn't say a word. Not even about my getting caught in the basement with a girl, or about sneaking out earlier. I turn off my phone.

THE NEXT DAY, MY phone's full of texts from Olivia and Blake when I turn it on. I text back to tell them it wasn't as bad as it might've seemed last night, that everything's cool. It's not cool, though. Because Johnny was acting like nothing was a big deal. Like that wasn't the first time I talked to him since he up and left two weeks ago. Like his face wasn't gushing blood the whole time. Like he had no idea I thought he was dead.

Downstairs, there's only the faint sound of the TV going. No banging and shuffling around the kitchen.

"Where's *Mãe*?" I ask my dad.

"She with João."

"At his place?"

He tells me the doctor wanted someone to watch my brother because of the concussion, to make sure he didn't end up with anything worse. Mom spent the night at Johnny's new place, and it pisses me right off. I mean, I don't even know which building he lives in. My parents throw him out the door, and now they're all hanging out at his place.

It's too early for this crap, so I go back to bed.

THIRTY-THREE

voices talking and laughing. It's almost dinnertime, but I'm still groggy. My house is full of Portuguese people. No one in my family ever discusses visiting beforehand. We all just show up at each other's homes whenever. It smells like sweet bread's been in the oven. I make a stop to the bathroom to brush my teeth and de-crustify my face, then I head down.

"Hey, Pen!" my cousin Constance says.

"Hi. What are all of you guys doing here?" They're about a week late for Thanksgiving—not that we even make a big deal about Thanksgiving. We're more about Christmas and Easter than anything.

"We heard about your brother's head—it sounded pretty serious when your mom called. So my mom said we should maybe visit, and then my dad said it was a great idea. I figured what the hell. Phil's working anyway." She fluffs her big black curls, then pats my head. "Johnny's not here, though. We didn't know he moved out!"

"Yeah. I thought my mom was over there."

"She's here, in the kitchen. Making bread."

Constance smiles and rubs my shoulder. I start in the

living room, where my uncle Adão, my aunt Joana, and my cousin Paulo are sitting with my dad. My cousin Marc's leaning over the arm of the couch, checking out the apps on the TV.

"Hey, Small One Johnny!" *Tio* Adão says to me. "You tough girl. What you do today?"

"Just . . . sleep."

I make the rounds, kissing everyone on the cheeks. My cousin Paulo is from my aunt Joana's side of the family, so we're not technically related, but he's always been around. He's close to my parents' age, which makes him a pretty old cousin.

"You eat?" *Tia* Joana asks.

"I'm not hungry yet."

In the kitchen, Constance is helping my mom peel potatoes. There's a big pot in the oven, and when Mom opens the oven door to check on it, the stench tells me it's pigs' feet stew. I hate pigs' feet. I don't think feet of any kind should be eaten, ever. My mom notices me making a face and scowls.

"What?" I say. "You know I don't like that."

"You think I forget you go out yesterday and no ask me? No ask you *pai*?" she says. Constance makes an uncomfortable face and drifts off. Mom points at the pot. "You wanna do what you wanna do? Why you no make you *comida*, huh?"

I thought with what happened to Johnny last night and today's surprise visit, my parents might've forgotten about all the stuff I did wrong yesterday.

"That's okay. I don't need to eat," I say.

"Stop, you. I make you *chee*-ken." She lifts the lid off a

casserole where breaded chicken is frying. Okay, that I can deal with.

"When are we eating? I gotta go take a shower."

"Soon," she says.

"Are you taking some of this to Johnny?"

She ignores me. I jog back up to my room and pick out some clothes, then head for the shower. Just as I finish gelling my hair, my mom yells, "Penelope! You come now!"

With my foot on the first step going down, I see Constance at the front door, doing cheek kisses with Colby.

"Come in, Colby! You have to stay for dinner," Constance says, pulling at Colby's leather jacket.

We exchange this look, Colby and I, and I don't know what's passing from his eyes to mine, but it feels weird so I look away.

"Yeah, okay. It smells awesome," Colby says, slipping his jacket off. "As usual."

"Oh good!" Constance pulls him by the sleeve and Colby nods at me on his way to the living room.

COLBY LIKES PIGS' FEET. Watching him chew on the meat is making me want to puke. We're all sitting around the dining room table, and there's a butt-load of food on it. Everyone squeezed over to allow me to sit beside my best friend, which sucks. I keep picturing myself smashing his face down into the bowl of mashed potatoes. My uncle's downing the beers and getting louder by the minute. He tells the same stories, and everyone laughs at the right places. Especially Colby.

"Hey, Koo*bee*," my uncle says. "What you do, huh?"

"Oh, you know." Colby gives a smirk and a shrug, then shoves a forkful of potatoes in his mouth. He cuts a wedge of corn bread to soak up the stew juice.

"Where Johnny, huh?" my uncle asks.

"He come later," my dad says. Then he says Johnny's always late but this time he's got an excuse. "He *cabeça* is broke."

"Koo*bee*, you want this?" My uncle Adão reaches across the table to offer Colby a bottle of beer. "This is family good time. We drink, we talk, we laugh. You drink this. The man all drink for the good time."

Colby reaches for the bottle and twists off the cap. No one thinks anything of this because that's how it is in my family: no one likes a drunk, but no one thinks it's dumb to keep bringing my uncle fresh beers, or to offer teenage guys a drink during family good times.

When dinner's over, Mom tells me to bring the dirty dishes to the sink and she'll deal with them. Colby brings the heavy stuff to the counter, then he makes a sideways peace sign and bounces it against his lips, meaning he wants to go out for a smoke. I shrug like, *Go, I don't care.* He tips his head and his face goes hard.

Loud enough for anyone around to hear, I say, "Ma, can I go out with Colby?"

"You watch out now," she says.

She was supposed to say no—I was *counting* on her saying no. But she said yes, and now I have to follow Colby.

234

WE HEAD OUT INTO the cold. Colby goes between my house and the neighbor's and gets his smokes. For a second, I wonder if by the end of this conversation Colby and I will have figured things out. If we'll have settled things enough to stop with the bull.

"Your uncle's awesome," Colby says.

"Yeah, no. Not really."

"He's hilarious."

"He's just a drunk who repeats the same stories over and over and tells everyone else what to do."

"Well, I think he's pretty badass, all right?"

"Yeah, I guess you would," I say. "What do you want?"

"Did you tell your little girlfriend about what happened?" he asks.

"What?"

"I just wanna know if you told her about what happened."

What's he talking about right now? Does he know that I know about Olivia?

"No. I didn't." I cross my arms so my hands won't shake.

He looks even more serious now. "Did you tell Olivia?"

"Tell Olivia what?"

His face bends under the WTF glare he gives me. "About us. You and me. What happened."

"Oh," I say, feeling a chill go through me. Not that again. "No. No way."

"You're lying."

We're all lying. We're all holding on to bits of the truth. About this, though, there's no lying on my end. "No! Why would I ever want to—no. Just no."

He lets go of the breath he'd been holding, and his eyes blink seconds too long. He believes me, and he's relieved. "Did you tell anyone?"

"No," I say. "Why would I want to talk about it again?"

"To mess with me."

"You're paranoid."

"I'm not gonna have everyone think I'm a fag just because you want to get back at me."

"Get back at you for what? For being a douche? It's not like I'm just finding out now what you're like."

"You think I haven't figured out Olivia's telling you things?" he says, and he looks pissed off about that most of all, like it's killing him. He whips his cigarette butt against the brick of my house and paces back and forth. "You think I don't know you have things you could be telling her, too—just to make sure I'm gone for good, huh? I know everything. I see everything. I saw you swoop in there."

"Because you left her hanging, okay? You took off, but you kept her hanging just enough so you could mess with her. Why? What's the point of doing that?"

"The point is, it's mine!" He glances at the street and lowers his voice. "It's my territory. I can do what I want with what's mine, you got that?"

It's like he really thinks his pissing on things means they're his—including people. "If you're going to be a douche

236

to people, they're going to leave. Might take them a while, but eventually they're going to grow some balls and tell you to suck it, Colby."

He snorts, and his pacing gets quicker before it stops altogether. Then he's nodding, shaking his head, nodding again—like he's making decisions. I'm just standing there, three feet away, waiting. Finally, he goes, "All right, let me tell you how it is: if you say anything, I'll come at you—"

"Colby, come on—"

"For real, this time. If you and Olivia try to get together with your lies and get in my way, I'll make you regret it so bad, you have no idea. I'm talking about rocking some real shit here. Everything I know about you, your parents can easily find out. One word from me and my dad cancels his business's contract with your brother."

He says anything he can think up when he's this desperate. But that's my brother's business. That's his reputation, and it's a big contract. I can't believe he'd even go there.

"Colby," I say, and my knees lock into place, my fingers curling into fists, "back off. Don't even try to mess with my brother right now."

"I'm serious, Pen. I'm not gonna have you running your mouth off about me. Telling people I'm some queer douche who likes dudes. I'm not gonna have you telling Olivia that about me. I'm not gonna have her think that!"

"I just told you I never told her. I never told anyone! You think you'd feel like a fag? How do you think I feel?"

It's like we're arguing about too many things at once. I

don't know where I end and where Olivia begins. I don't know what to defend myself against. A punch—a nice clean punch in the mouth would probably say all the right things.

"I'm just letting you know right now, okay? This is how it's gonna be: all this better stay dead. You don't tell Olivia anything, and you don't let her run her mouth off either. If not, shit might go down."

"Stop threatening me! Stop telling me what to do."

"What—are you going to run to your mommy? You gonna get Johnny? Where's he been, huh?" Colby flashes me a twisted grin. "Face it. You're on your own."

Ass—I just can't even.

"You got nothing, Pen," he says. "So you're gonna keep your mouth shut and not get in my way."

"I'll keep my mouth shut," I say, letting my hands spread out at my sides. "If you swear you'll leave Olivia and Blake alone."

"Just watch your back, all right?" He laughs, flicking his cigarette somewhere at my feet. Then I watch him stroll away, his back to me like he knows, without a doubt, that I'm no threat at all. I'm just a girl.

THIRTY-FOUR

MONDAY, COLBY AND HIS BUDDIES FIND ME AT school, swarm me without saying anything, then seconds later they take off. I should be glad they don't say anything, that they don't try shoving me around, but it's awkward as hell. I end up standing there, never looking any of them in the eye, and just waiting for it to end.

Tuesday, Blake and I are so busy with our project that it makes lunchtime easy to deal with. We go around asking people for their truth. Olivia usually holds the truth box, because it's not like we're going to let her spend her lunch period sitting in front of her locker.

"Why don't you just get back on the project?" Blake tells Olivia. "We could be a threesome."

Olivia's cheeks redden, which makes me laugh. What a prude.

"It's cool," I say. "Olivia can be our secret little helper. She's already all right with us taking all the credit for the work."

I give people these cue cards and Blake asks them to write down one sentence with a truth about their life as a high school student in our community. They fold the piece of paper and put it into the box. It's all anonymous, but a lot of people still say no. By the time lunch is close to ending, we have a total of thirteen truths. Olivia and I sit at a table to shove our lunches down our throats before the bell rings. Blake and Robyn took off early for art class because of some sculpting project.

I stare at the stuff on Olivia's fork. "What the hell are you eating?"

"It's a seven-grain salad."

"It's yellow and weird."

"Yes, I guess it is compared to a bun with fancy cheese."

I wave the sandwich in front of her face so she can get a good whiff of smelly Portuguese St. Jorge cheese. "If you promise not to puke, I'll give you half."

"Really?" She takes the piece I offer, then she pushes her container over to me. "Try it. I offer you the same deal."

"Uh, no. Well, yeah, okay," I say, taking her fork. "Aren't you afraid of my germs? Queer cooties and all."

"I've had worse cooties."

"Yeah, like what?"

She munches on the other half of my sandwich for a minute while I try her salad. I nod like, *It's not bad*, before handing her fork back. Then Olivia says, "Okay, this is gross, but the first guy I ever kissed, like with tongue—his name was Johan, and we were in grade eight—well, I found out, like, a month later that although he was super cute, he would also pick his nose." She takes this deep breath and closes her eyes. "He would pick it . . . and eat it."

"Oh, ha! That's totally nasty!"

"I know. It was a complete betrayal," she says, shaking her head.

The box of truths is sitting between us. I nod toward it. "I totally want to know what people wrote."

"Me too! But that's just curiosity. We can't give in or a cat will die," she says, stabbing her fork into her weird grain salad. "Have you two started taking the photos yet?"

"Not even a little bit."

She gives this look like, *Tsk tsk.* "Do you have any photography skills?"

"I'm not amazing or anything. I just press the button and hope it didn't go blurry."

"Well, I think that'll be enough. You can add effects and filters. Turn them black and white, and make them sort of blurry on purpose."

"Are you sure you don't want to come back? Mr. Middleton would let us be a group of three."

She shakes her head. "I don't think I can." She frowns. "Pen?"

"Yeah."

"I made an appointment," she says. "Thursday next week, after lunch."

"Oh." Then I see her face. "Oh, man. Okay. Got it."

"Yes?"

"Yeah, yeah. For sure. I got this."

I'd been wondering what was going on with that, but I sort of figure with this kind of thing, it's best if I don't talk about it unless she brings it up. Maybe in my mind, I was hoping the whole thing just went away. But it didn't. Not until next Thursday.

AFTER SCHOOL, I GET home to find two black T-shirts folded on my bed. They're not mine, and there are still tags hanging from the sleeves. Ever since Johnny left, finding clothes to wear has been a pain, especially when it comes to going out, because I don't want to be the dirtbag who rotates through the same three shirts all the time. So, two new T-shirts is a good thing. Black tees, too. I don't know what my mom's trying to say with this move.

I pick up the first one, flicking my wrists to unfold it.

My mom's message is printed all over the front of it. I throw both shirts over my arm and march downstairs. Mom's flipping through the newspaper in the living room.

"Why did you buy me this?"

"It's nice. You want the clothes." Then she says I should just be grateful to be getting anything after the way I've been acting these days.

"I don't wear stuff like that. You know that."

Mom puts the paper down next to her and gives me this long, up-and-down look. "This get worse, Penelope. I no like. You *pai* no like. You like the black, okay, I buy you the black. But this too much worse."

"You bought me T-shirts with Disney Princesses on them, Ma! There's glitter and pink."

"This too much. You not a boy. How you gonna get the nice

242

boyfriend?" Then she says Colby's not going to wait forever. "How you gonna get married?"

"Ma, please. That's nasty."

"You big girl now." She tells me I have to grow up and grow out of this tomboy stuff. This conversation would never have gone on this long if Johnny still lived here. I'd be smacking my foot on his ceiling right about now. "I try to be calm and wait. I try yell at you. Now I try talk to you like a big woman. We talk about real life."

"Real life." There are no other words inside me right now. Real life? What does my mom know about that? She's in the house most of the time.

"Maybe I did no good." The look on her face is sour, like it stings for her to say this part. "Maybe I no do good job with you when you small one. Maybe I no teach you to be nice girl. I wait, and I wait. I be calm." In Portuguese, she says she was hoping it would fix itself. "Maybe I give you too much."

The T-shirts are still in my hands, and it feels like I could shred them right now, like I could make Wolverine claws bust out from between my knuckles. "It's not about you," I tell her. "I decide."

"You no decide nothing!" she snaps. "You stop this. It puts too much the stress. Too much the fighting." She says Johnny's living his life now, and I need to start growing up, that life is easier when you do your best to be good.

"I *am* good. I'm only bad when I have to be."

She shakes her head and waves her arms like she won't have this. "This nice shirts, you ask you Koo*bee*. This is nice shirts. We go to store, we go see the lady with the makeup—"

"You don't get it, Ma. You don't get it," I say.

"I get it!"

"No, you don't. I decide. Me. I get to decide."

"This my house. I decide!" she says. "You a girl, Penelope. You be a girl now. You *mãe* decide. You gonna be a pretty girl."

Everything inside me feels tight and ready to bust.

"I'd rather be a guy than be a girl who wears those shirts," I say. "I'd rather be a guy than be a lady like you. I'm not a lady. I'm just whatever, Ma. I'm whatever. Leave me alone. I'm whatever!"

She's quiet for a second. Only for a second.

"You whatever? You wanna be whatever? You get outta *minha casa*!" She pushes to her feet and yanks the shirts out of my hands before storming off.

THIRTY-FIVE

THE WHOLE TIME I RIDE THE BUS TO THE MALL, I think about how insane all this was. I've never been threatened with getting kicked out of the house before. Wouldn't it be easier to just wear a wig and change my clothes? I could pretend Tristan's my boyfriend. I could buy a Barbie and put it on my shelf.

Why can't my mom see that I'm a good girl already?

When I get to the Gamer Depot, Blake is at the counter, flipping through a gamer mag, looking bored. I wander in, passing by the counter, acting like I'm just some shopper coming to browse on a Tuesday night.

She smacks the counter with both hands. "You win everything for surprising me at work! What are you doing here?"

"I was wondering what you're doing after work."

"Nothing. Feel like coming over?"

"Totally."

My phone starts ringing at the same time the store phone does. Blake answers the store call, while I pull my cell out. It's my house. I don't know what would be worse right now: answering or ignoring it. I decide to answer it, but to say nothing.

"Hello? Hello? Penelope? Wha' you do, huh? What?" It's my dad, using the voice he usually saves for Johnny. "You *mãe* cry. She cry too much because of you. Wha' you do, stupid girl?" Then he says I make a big mess and I take off, just like my brother.

"Uh, well . . . sorry" is all I say, then I hang up. Blake's watching me, fluffing her hair like she doesn't care which way it'll fall. "So when do you get off work?"

"Eight."

This super-tall skinny man walks in like he owns the place. He nods to Blake and goes, "Work, Blake. Look lively. Sell something."

"I'm trying really hard, but this customer is so cheap," she says, pointing at me.

My eyes go wide. The man shakes his head like Blake's impossible, then he walks right to the back, disappearing through an employee-only door.

"Thanks," I tell her.

"Mitch is cool."

"He's your boss?"

She nods.

"I need to get a job. A real job."

"Oh—oh!" Blake says. "Hang on a minute." She puts the store phone to her ear and dials. "Mitch! Can I talk to you for a second?" She hangs up and waves me away. "Go look at stuff. Come back when I signal you."

So I back step to the Xbox section, giving her my suspicious face. The tall Mitch guy comes out of the office and strolls over to Blake's counter. He leans on one elbow while she does most of the talking. A twenty-something dude wearing a Gamer Depot tee enters the store from the mall and goes to take a spot behind the counter, so Blake and Mitch move down to the other end. It takes a couple minutes, then the Mitch guy gives a nod before heading over my way. He gives me a hitch of the chin before going back through the door he came out of. Blake waves me over.

"Okay, I talked to him. If you're up to going back there and talking to him, he'll consider you for part time," Blake says.

"What? Work here?"

"Yeah."

"How'd you manage that?"

"I told him there are hardly any women in gaming, and by

hiring another girl, he's making a statement that girls are part of the gaming community and every bit as knowledgeable and skilled as dudes are," she says. "I'm pretty sure he's a feminist. So go back there and be righteous."

She pushes me over while I plant my feet down. "I don't even have a résumé!"

"It's no big deal. I told him about you. If it works out, then you can send him your résumé. He prefers talking to people anyway."

"I can't go in there. I'll stutter and say dumb stuff." I turn to meet her gaze.

She fixes my collar and zips up my hoodie. "Come on, Pen. Do you know how many people want to work here?"

I'm at the employee-only door, staring at it. Blake waits next to me. For a minute, I take a couple deep breaths and picture how I'm going to introduce myself—

Hey, I'm Pen.

Hello, I'm Pen.

Good afternoon, sir, I'm Pen Oliveira.

What's going on, Mitch, my man?

Before I can settle on something, Blake knocks on the door and takes off. The door opens.

"Well, hello there. You must be Pen," Mitch says.

"Hi, yeah, sorry."

"Why are you apologizing?"

"I don't know," I say.

He laughs and opens the door wider. "Come in."

It's a tiny office with no windows, a desk, boxes, and a big metal safe. Mitch takes the nice-looking chair and pulls out the smaller one, motioning for me to sit. So I do.

"Blake says you're looking for a few hours a week."

"Yeah—yes."

"Have you been employed before?"

"Not officially, but my brother has his own company—he's a handyman—and I've put in hours working for him for the last two years."

Mitch nods, pulling a leg up to rest his ankle over the other knee, which is totally how I want to be sitting right now, but instead I'm doing Olivia's proper-posture thing. My back hurts. "Blake says you're willing to kill to work at the Gamer Depot. I don't want you to murder anyone, though, are we clear?"

"Very," I say.

"So why do you want to work here?"

"Uh, well, I'm a gamer, so I think I could be useful for, like, questions. And also to sell things. And to, uh . . . look lively?"

He laughs. "You're a gamer, huh? Okay. Here's a little scenario: a little old lady comes in looking for *Mech-Soldier 3.0* for its solo offline campaign. What do you do?"

"I'd tell her she was screwed—uh, in a professional manner—because that game was only released for online gameplay."

"And what if the little old lady said she doesn't play multiplayer?"

"I'd tell her to try *War Zone 3*. It's not like she'll be able to have the whole robotic-mechanical armor, but the gameplay is similar because they're both shooters made by Shinewear, and, well, it's a really good game with a pretty decent offline campaign."

"Do you know the difference between a debit card and a credit card?"

"I think so."

"Do you know how to count?"

"Yes."

"How high?"

"Infinity. And there's a calculator app on my phone."

He squints like he's sizing me up. "What do you think of stealing?"

"I think it's evil."

He nods all serious, but there's a smile in his eyes waiting to take over his face. "Do you think the Gamer Depot is the greatest store in the world?"

"Totally."

"Are you prepared to abuse the employee discount?"

That makes me smile wide, because I hadn't even thought about that. "Yeah, for sure. It would be an honor."

"How do you feel about punctuality?"

"I like it. I'm down with being on time."

He makes a considering face, staring at me for a minute before reaching for a form and a pen. "Fill this out. You mind if I call your brother for a reference?"

"Nope," I say, but I wonder if Johnny will know how to do a reference call. Maybe I should warn him first, except I don't want to talk to him. I'll text him.

Mitch then tells me what he'll need to set up direct deposit for my paychecks, which I think means I got the job. Then he goes through one of the boxes and comes out with a blue Gamer Depot T-shirt.

"Something tells me you're into shirts three sizes too big," he says.

I nod. "Thank you. Very much."

"I suppose you'd like Blake to be your trainer?"

"That would be . . . cool."

He shakes his head. "That would be foolish. I can't do that, but nice try, kid. How about Sunday, noon to six-ish, with Elliott."

"Elliott with the dreads?"

"Is *that* his full name?" He smirks. "That would be the one."

"Cool."

"No screwing around. At the Gamer Depot, we work, we look lively, and we sell stuff."

"Got it."

He looks like the kind of dude who could've rocked a mustache and a top hat. "Any questions?"

"Thank you," I say. "Which I guess isn't a question . . ."

"Welcome to the team."

Just like that, I got a job. My parents are going to be pissed.

LATER, BLAKE AND I are reclined on the carpeted basement floor, side by side, with our legs resting over the couch. The TV's on the music channel and we're watching it upside down. I shouldn't be out this late, so it's a good thing I don't care about that anymore.

"I can't believe you got me a job," I say. "Should we act like we're just friends when we're there?"

"Why? *Are* we just friends?"

"No. Hell no. I just don't want it to cause problems."

"So what? You want to pretend we're only friends so no one will think I like girls?"

"But you don't . . . like girls."

"I do, though. I like you."

It makes me turn my head to look at her. "People will wonder why you don't have a boyfriend instead. A dude with a beard."

She pulls her legs up and swivels around until she's sitting. I do the same, and we're both cross-legged on the floor and facing each other. "Why do you think I like you?"

I crinkle my forehead, filing through the possibilities. Then I shrug.

She scowls. "Why do you like *me* then?"

"Because you're sweet, but you're tough. And you're funny. And you're a gamer, plus you know your stuff. And you don't fall for bull. And you're always upbeat and ready to kick butt."

She smiles and puts two fingers on my arm. But as soon as I smile back, she shakes it off. "But it can't all be personality, right? It's about looks, too. It's always about looks." At that, I make a face and she holds up a finger. "It's not shallow to admit it's all about looks, because it is. You can't have the hots for someone that you don't think is hot—doesn't work."

I tip my head to the side, thinking about blind people all of a sudden, wondering how it could possibly be about looks for them. I snap out of it, then finally nod. "Okay, fine."

"So you think I'm hot," she says.

"You're hot as hell. Your clothes, your face, your hair, your eyes—your eyes drive me nuts—and, well, your, um." I point at her chest. "Those. I really like them—"

She covers my mouth with her hand. "Stop!"

"It's true," I mutter from behind her fingers.

"Okay, so you think it's not about looks on my end?" At my shrug, she sighs and scoots over to be right in front of me, no space between our legs. "Your hair? Yes, hot. Your clothes? Uh-huh—that silver chain is righteous, by the way. The way you smell, that men's cologne? Oh my god, yes." She curls her fingers around my shirt collar, and it makes me get chills. "The way you act, the way you walk—well, just everything."

"Everything?"

She nods while she keeps fussing with my collar. "I guess for me, it's that I like guys, but . . . I like when girls are being guys even more. Maybe that doesn't make sense, but I don't care."

My fingers tingle with the need to just grab her. "What do we do now?"

"We make out hard-core, and for a long time. Right now, right here."

"See, that's another thing I like about you: your balls. I hope I grow a pair as big as yours one day."

"It'll never happen," she says, pretending to cup two watermelons in front of her crotch. "Look how big these are, Pen. *Huge.*"

Everything she said—it was so much. I shouldn't be asking for more, but . . .

"Blake?" I say, looking at the ceiling instead of her face. "Say I had a question to ask you and I was—"

"Is this where you take an hour to ask me to be your girlfriend?" she says. I hold my hands out like, *How did you know?* "I'm impatient, okay? I know you like me. And I like you. So, yes. The answer is yes."

"Okay," I say through a massive sigh. "Okay, awesome. I got a girlfriend and a job in the same day. I'm on a roll."

I am on a roll. I just hope it's not the crash-and-burn kind.

THIRTY-SIX

ON SUNDAY, I LEARN THE LAYOUT OF THE STORE, and then I start my training on the register. Elliott's super chill about it, but when the store phone rings, he catches me off guard by picking it up and passing it to me. I go "Hello?" then remember it's not my cell so I rush into "Thank you for calling the Gamer Depot. How can I help you?" He laughs the whole time, but then says I did all right.

On Tuesday, I get home from school to find Garrett's rusted van parked at the curb and all the guys hanging out in Colby's garage. The noises coming from their end are the same as the ones I hear at the mall, at the pizza place, at Walmart even. I dart up to my room. Blake's meeting me at the library in a couple hours. She was all, "We cannot work at my house because you know what'll happen." She's right, because what would happen is we'd either play video games all day, or we'd fool around all day. So I said, "No. I swear it won't be like that. We'll work." But I was lying, and she knew it.

So now I fix my hair, and spritz my cologne. The *Turtles* theme starts playing. I hop over my bed to find my cell.

"Hi," Olivia says. She sounds funny. There's a woman yelling stuff in the background. "Um. Are you busy today?"

"Is that your mom? Sounds like she's losing it."

"She is. She . . . does that. I was wondering—if you're not busy—if you'd want to, um, rescue me from this?"

"Blake and I are going to the library in a couple hours to work on the project," I say, slipping into my jeans. Her mom goes off about "lazy ladies" and "not in my house." That kind of stuff makes me not be able to wait until I own a house so I can go off about what can and can't be done in it. "Man, she sounds pissed. Listen, why don't you come to the library with us?"

"I don't want to mess up your date," she says.

"It's the library, Olivia."

Her mom launches into something that sounds like "work all week" and "Jin thinks he can just" and then Olivia goes, "Okay, yes. I will meet you at the library. Now?"

"Uh . . . yeah, why not. I'm pretty much ready anyway."

We hang up, and I go to my closet for a shirt. Something's not right.

Stuff is missing. Some of my stuff is missing.

I THROW ON MY black-and-red tee, except it's not what I wanted to wear tonight. The shirt I want—Johnny's old gray one with the chain design—isn't here anymore. Neither is the white tee, or the yellow-black one. But the worst part is the white shoe box that's not on the shelf anymore—my Ninja Turtles figures. I grab my phone and my bag, then head downstairs, where Mom is watching TV and knitting dishcloths.

"Where's my stuff, Ma?" I'm trying not to sound angry. I'm trying so hard.

"I take João clothes to João."

"They were mine. He gave them to me."

She shrugs, not looking at me. "I don't know. João say he want clothes, I get João clothes."

"He told you to come take them from my closet?"

Another shrug; she turns up the Italian cooking show.

"Where are my Turtles?"

"I don't know, the turtle."

"My Ninja Turtles, in the box. Where are they?"

"I clean up. Too much the stuff. You no play with toys. You big girl. I give to *Tia* Val."

"What?" On purpose—this is all on purpose. "*Mãe*, what did you do with them?"

She stays silent, pretending to pay deep attention to the show. I head for the basement, taking the stairs like some idiot asking for a broken leg, and I barge into the storage room. Still stacked on top of the cabinet are the two blond Barbies and the doll that pisses and craps itself. I pick the stack up and fly back upstairs, telling myself not to lose it over toys, telling myself to be cool.

"I want my Turtles back. Where are they?"

"You no talk to me like that. I no listen," she says, not acknowledging the stuff in my hands. "No *respeito*, no listen."

I go to the kitchen, where a bunch of stuff is packed in boxes, like she went through some random late-October cleaning spree. There's a bunch of useless house stuff in there, an old telephone that should really go into the garbage, mason jars, and at the side, my box of Turtles. I check inside, just to make sure they're all still there. Then I shove the doll and the Barbies into Mom's boxes. In the living room, she's still pretending to be super interested in this lady plucking shrimps out of their shells.

There are so many things I want to say. All a waste because we don't speak the same damn language, and she doesn't know how to listen anyway.

"*You* don't have *respeito*, Ma!" At that, she looks up at me and drops her knitting. "You stole my stuff—my Turtles. You went into my room and stole my things."

My mom doesn't like me, that's just the reality.

She thinks everything about me is being done deliberately to screw with her, to make her look like a bad mother or something. It's the reverse: she's the one screwing with me on purpose, trying her best to make me look like the worst daughter ever.

"No *respeito*," I say.

I shove the box into my bag, and it won't zip up. My mom and her shocked expression are behind me.

WAITING AROUND FOR BLAKE, Olivia and I hang out at one of the library desks, looking through some encyclopedia about the French Revolution in the 1700s.

"Why do you keep checking your phone?" Olivia asks. "It's not . . . him, is it?"

"Nah." I shrug, putting my phone away. I sent Blake a text to warn her Olivia was going to be here, but now I'm wondering if I should've asked before inviting her.

The idea of having to go home later—it just sucks.

"Pen," Olivia says, and she's using her serious voice. "Thursday's in two days. Two days."

"Yeah. But after that, you won't be counting down to anything anymore."

She rubs her eyes. "You won't either, I guess."

"I'll be counting down to my first paycheck, then I'll be taking that sucker to the flea market so I can get an NES," I say, and she stares back like she's not following. "I'm going to make you try *Super Mario 2*. It's way better than the Atari—trust me."

All of a sudden, she's slipping into my arms, and I'm not the huggy type unless it's romantic, so I kind of sit there with my arms out and my eyes wide. But then I figure it's rude to not at least do the arm thing when there's a hug involved, so I put an arm around her shoulders.

"If my girlfriend sees this, we're going to be in trouble," I mutter.

"Pen?" she says from somewhere too close to my neck. "Why is your bag so big?"

"That sounds like a creepy pickup line." I glance around to make sure Blake's not here yet. "It better not be."

"Your bag," she says, pulling away from me and picking up my schoolbag by one of the straps.

"Oh, because I had to take my Turtles with me."

"You have turtles in there?"

"Yeah."

"Can I see?"

I pull out the box and take its lid off.

"Oh, they're not real turtles." She sounds relieved.

"What the hell? You think I'd be walking around with live turtles in my backpack?"

Her eyebrows go all pissy. "*You're* the one who said she had turtles in her bag."

"*Ninja* Turtles, with a capital T." I wave Leonardo around. "Action figures."

She picks Donatello up, my favorite Turtle. "He's so cute."

"Uh . . . no. These are not *cute*. These are badass."

"What do you do with them exactly?" She holds Donatello up like he's useless.

"What do you mean?"

"Well, with dolls, you can brush their hair, change their outfits, have parties. You can fix them up on dates, and they can sleep in the same bed together," she says. "Those don't really do anything."

"You're crazy! Okay, take a couple of them. But not that

one," I say, reaching for Donatello. "He's mine. But take Raph. Most people think Raphael's the best one anyway."

"Okay. Can I also have the rat?"

"Sure. But he's so not just a rat." I hand her the figure. "His name is Splinter, and he's a wise old dude. Now we gotta get some books. Heavy ones."

"Why?"

"We're going to build a fort."

"We're sixteen years old, Pen."

"So?" I place the figures back into the box, then I point to the encyclopedia. "Do you really feel like reading more of this book?"

"No," she says, pushing to her feet.

We get to work, but soon the librarian shoots us annoyed glares, so we take our stuff over to the back of the fiction section where she can't see. We build this thing that doesn't really end up looking like anything but an awkward stack of books, but it still works.

"What are you guys doing?" Blake says.

I pop my head up from behind the tower of paperbacks. "Oh, hey. Hi. Uh . . . Olivia made me."

"As if she'd believe I play with action figures. Turtle-y ones, too," Olivia says, while I'm trying to figure out how Blake's taking our twosome having turned into a threesome. "I'm trying to build a kitchen and bedrooms but Pen won't let me."

"That's because the Ninja Turtles order pizza and they live in a sewer," Blake says, dumping her bag on the ground and finding her way over to me.

"We're meant to be," I say.

Blake smiles so wide, it makes me want to take a picture of that and make it the only photo in our project. She kneels next to me and puts her arm around my shoulders. I wish I could tell her I missed her.

"That's disgusting," Olivia says. When Blake and I turn to stare at her, Olivia goes, "Oh, no, not that! I meant living in sewers."

Blake pulls out the box of quotes and we spread them out on the floor.

"Olivia?" Blake says. "I think you're pretty much back on Team Three. Face it. This is our project now."

"I don't know, you guys." Olivia sighs.

"Come on," I say. "I have no idea how Blake and I are supposed to get this all done and ready for the school anniversary."

Blake nods. "Yeah, and the guys and I are rehearsing three times a week until the Battle of the Bands, so we could definitely use your help, Olivia."

"I'll think about it," Olivia says, totally not convinced. "I have to go to the bathroom."

Blake and I watch her walk away, then I say, "She had to get out of her house. I guess I should've asked you first if it was okay."

"It's fine," Blake says. "Really. But . . . what's the matter with her? Is she sick?"

I stare at Donatello in my hands, but he's no help.

"This whole thing is suspicious," she says, untangling herself from me. "I don't like being the only one who has no idea what's going on."

"I can't really—" My face feels hot, and my eyes won't look up. "It's not my place to tell." That makes it sound worse. "Okay, look, Colby really messed her up, and I feel bad."

"You feel bad?"

"Yeah, because he makes messes and never sticks around to clean them up," I say. "Olivia's going to be fine."

"But you can't tell me what's going on."

"No." I feel like such a jerk right now. "You're probably mad now, because it looks bad—I know it looks bad. But it's Olivia's mess and . . . I guess I'm just hanging around her a lot while it gets cleaned up, just to make sure she's all right, you know?"

"Well, what if I could help, too?"

"You *can* help. Just be nice to her," I say. "She'll be fine."

Two more days and everything should be cool again.

THIRTY-SEVEN

THURSDAY COMES AND AT LUNCH OLIVIA DOES nothing because she's not supposed to eat or drink before the appointment. Blake wants to meet up for lunch so I have to lie and tell her Olivia and I are walking over to where her mom works so she can lend us a tripod. I end my text with: <3 like it'll make up for the lie.

This is what they say at the clinic: They say Olivia will be there for the rest of the afternoon. They say the procedure will only take a few minutes, but there's paperwork to fill out, and blood to draw, and she has to talk to someone before and after. She shouldn't drive herself home, but she doesn't have a license anyway. They say it's good she brought someone to help her get home, and that she'll be fine to go to school tomorrow. Some cramping is all she should expect afterward.

There's a decent waiting room with a TV playing talk shows and a stack of lady magazines I'd never flip through. My phone is the only thing here that can keep me from thinking to death, but I don't want to overdo the data usage because with the way things have been, I don't know how long my parents are going to keep paying the bill. But now that I have a job, I should probably start paying for it myself anyway.

What if Olivia is lying there wishing I'd barge in and stop her? What if she was hoping I'd tell her she could do it, have a baby? Maybe she'd be able to handle it. Maybe I should've said more stuff. Maybe Colby should be here instead of me.

Oh, man.

I walk over to the desk, where there's a lady typing at a computer. "Excuse me? Could I talk to my friend Olivia? She went in about an hour ago."

"I'm sorry. You have to wait out here. Is there something you want me to tell her?"

"Uh—let's say she changed her mind, would she be allowed to leave?"

"Of course. She's going to be speaking with one of our counselors regardless."

"Okay."

The lady gives me a smile, then goes back to her computer.

"But, um, can I ask another question?" I say. "Do girls who get this done end up regretting it a lot of the time?"

"I think it's different for everyone, and we can't know it in advance. I do know that with the fluctuation of hormones, women can feel sad or down. It usually gets back to normal once the hormone levels adjust."

My neck is sweating into my collar. "Oh, man. Will it be bad?"

"Are you all right?" the lady asks. "Do you want to talk to somebody?"

"It's okay. Thanks."

I grab my phone and head outside for air.

THIRTY-EIGHT

THE TRUCK CIRCLES TWICE AROUND THE LOT, TOO heavy on the gas. Then someone pulls out of a space, and Johnny takes it. He marches up to the entrance where I'm standing. He lights up a cigarette before reaching the curb. Two puffs later, he's looking down at me where I'm crouched against the wall.

"What the hell did you get yourself into, man?" he asks.

"I don't know," I say. "Could you call the school about me missing this afternoon? I can't have Ma on my back for something else."

He crouches next to me. "What's going on?"

"Olivia," I start. Then I tell him everything even though I haven't said anything real to him in weeks. Even though he stole back his clothes, took the Xbox, took everything away. I tell him about Olivia having decided to make this appointment. About how her mother doesn't know—that no one knows but me. I tell him Olivia's in there right now. What I don't say is that Colby, my ex–best friend, is wrapped up in this. "They told me she could feel sad and depressed afterward. She's already scared she'll feel like a different person. And her stomach's going to hurt. I don't know what to do with that."

"That's some big stuff you've got going on."

"Yeah."

"What have you been up to these days? Some guy called me for a job reference for you. Everything's different," he says, and he has the nerve to sound sort of annoyed.

"I've just been doing my thing. That's what you've been doing too, huh?"

He looks like he's going to say something, like tell me to screw off, but instead, he rubs his face, takes a drag of his cigarette, and goes, "So what's your plan then, with Olivia?"

"I have no idea."

"You were just gonna take the bus back to her place and that would be it?"

"Yeah."

He shrugs. "So why can't you still do that?"

"I'm freaking out because I'm worried she'll regret getting it done and blame me."

"Why would she do that?"

"Because maybe she didn't really want to do it."

He shakes his head and exhales smoke all over both of us. "Well, listen, man, that's her problem."

"What?" It's too bright out today for this. I shield my eyes with a cold hand. "That's rude, Johnny."

"It's not rude. It's the truth," he says. "It's a big decision, and you know, she might end up regretting it—who knows? But, it's her decision to make, you know what I'm saying? I mean, you ditched school to come here—that's pretty stand-up of you." He pats my head like I'm a dog. "You did good."

"What if she goes nuts over it?" In the pavement, I can almost see what a crazy Olivia would look like. "Maybe at the very least, I should be kicking the guy's ass."

"You could," Johnny says. "Or you could just make sure you don't ever act like that."

"Or maybe *you* could kick his ass."

"I could. But I'm not dumb enough to fight with a kid your age." Johnny pulls his phone out and taps my knee with it. "And who knows, maybe his dad's one of my clients."

My face goes numb, and I'm sure there's guilt all over it. But Johnny's pushing to his feet and says, "Just wait and see what happens when she's done, okay? Then you can worry about what to do. You want a smoke?"

"Nah."

"Good. You're not allowed to smoke. It's bad for you."

So he pulls out a fresh one and makes a point of holding it to his side, like it'll keep the smoke from reaching me.

WHEN OLIVIA COMES OUT, I'm back in the waiting room, in the same seat I started out in. She looks sort of blank. She's not crying. Her arms are loose around her waist, and her eyes find me. Still blank.

"Hi," I say.

"Hi."

We walk out into the hallway. It's weird. There's silence and for once, I want to talk.

"Sorry it took so long," she says.

"It's cool."

We get to the elevator. I'm the button presser. Olivia checks her phone, but makes a face like she regrets doing it. I wonder if there's a text from Elliott on there. I wonder if her mom's tried to call her. Or Colby even. I wonder so many things.

We walk past the pharmacy and the exit gets closer and closer.

"So, um . . . I called my brother."

"What?"

It's hard to tell if she's pissed about it because she's so mellow and almost sleepy-looking.

"He's outside, in his truck, waiting for us," I say.

266

"Why did you call him?"

"Because I turned back into a pussy for a minute, I guess. But he's cool, so don't worry. He can drive us back." Old people in walkers shuffle past us on their way to the elevators. Nobody goes into the deserted eyeglasses shop. Faint music plays overhead. Olivia looks thoughtful.

"Well, that's nice of him," she says. "I really don't feel like being on the bus."

In the parking lot, Johnny waits in the truck. He starts the engine when we walk up.

"Where to?" he asks Olivia.

She gives directions to her house, and Johnny puts on some of his classic rock, but not too loud. Olivia sits in the back, me next to her. Nothing is said while we drive home. Nothing is said when we pull up to Olivia's little house. The truck idles on the curb, and still nothing is said. Olivia stares at her house but doesn't make a move.

"Is your mom home?" I ask.

"No. Not until late tonight."

I push open my door. I catch Johnny's gaze through the mirror. "Thanks for the ride."

His eyes narrow like he's about to say something, but I hop out of the truck. It's a bit of a jump from the truck to the ground, so I rush over to the other side to take Olivia's bag.

"So that's it then?" Johnny says, looking down at me from his open window.

"Yup," I say. "That's it."

"Thank you," Olivia says.

He nods a couple times, then takes off, the tires screech-
ing. Guess I shouldn't be surprised he'd basically peel it out of
here.

"He's really good-looking," she says. "You're like a younger
version of him, except for your—"

"Boobs?"

"Well, I was going to say hair. His is long."

We start the walk up Olivia's long driveway. She's super
careful with each step and one of her arms is always against
her stomach.

"My drunk uncle calls me Small One Johnny. Everyone
thinks I'm some cheap Johnny knockoff with boobs."

She makes a sad face. "So you're pretty mad at him, huh."

"Nah. We're just both doing our own thing," I say. "So . . .
how's it going?"

"My stomach . . ."

"Yeah, well, you should probably sit down for a while or
something. And Tylenol," I say. "I bet Tylenol would help. It
helps with everything."

"You're missing the whole afternoon," Olivia says.

"That's okay. I don't really like school."

When we get to the side door, she unlocks it and then we
take our shoes off and head to the basement. Olivia curls up on
the couch, hugging a pillow against her belly. She looks out of
it. I sit down in a big chair across from her.

"You're probably tired," I say.

"I'm kind of dizzy," she says. "But it's better now that I'm
sitting. I'm not tired."

"Are you okay?"

"Yes." She smiles, but then her eyebrows shift and that's when I realize she's bawling. "I'm not even sad. I think I'm just being a baby."

"Whoa, Olivia, man." I get up, moving close enough to pat her shoulder. "I think you're leaking hormones all over your couch."

She tries for a little laugh and gets the hiccups. She wipes at her face with the backs of her hands. "I thought I'd feel guilty about today. But I don't. Do you think I will later?"

"You know . . . those hormones—"

"I mean after all that. Do you think I'm supposed to feel bad?" She's hanging on to my face with her eyes, just waiting. Waiting for me to make it better.

"I think so," I say, and her face shifts to make it clear she expected a different answer. "I mean, it depends about what. You don't have to feel bad for having done it, but I think you might end up feeling bad about something, anything. Like feeling bad you could never tell your mom, or feeling bad you didn't get the pill, or feeling bad for liking Colby, or . . . anything really." Man, I hope this is coming out right. "I think it's okay for you to feel like crap about this, but I don't think you're supposed to . . . die of guilt every day just because. You're not a bad person for having gone to the clinic today. You're still a nice girl."

She wipes a couple of tears that spill from the outer corners of her eyes. She covers her face, then breathes in deep. "How do you know, though?"

"Because. I saw this video on YouTube of this girl who

videotaped her visit to the clinic—not the actual thing, just from the neck up." I cover my face, because it's embarrassing to admit I sat there and YouTubed this stuff. "The girl said stuff about how girls are taught to think they're supposed to feel like bad people for getting that done. So she made this video, and way after the fact, she still doesn't regret her decision. She feels better. You should just feel better now. It's over."

She's smiling and covers it with the pillow. "You watched videos?"

"It wasn't like that! I was doing research," I say. "I'm on YouTube a lot. Stop looking at me."

"You know," she says. "If you were a boy, I'd probably fall in love with you."

I think it shocks us both. My cheeks feel hot.

"You're not, though, are you?" I ask. She shakes her head, and all I can see are her forehead and eyes peeking over the pillow. "Because I don't think I could handle *another* girl drooling over me. It's just too much, you know?"

She grins a little. "I know you're here because I asked, but still—you're a nice person, Pen."

It makes my face get hot. "I'm not just here 'cause you asked. That makes you sound like a charity case or something."

She shrugs. "You know what I mean."

"Look—yeah, I only started talking to you because of all the puking and the Colby drama," I say. "But that was then. It's not like that now."

"Well, then, what's it like?"

"Now . . ." I let out a breath and meet her gaze. "Now we're just hanging out."

She nods and goes to add something but a door upstairs closes.

I freeze. Olivia's eyes go wide, and I hold out my hands like, *WTF*? She shakes her head and stares at the ceiling, where we can hear soft footsteps. There's no exit down here that I can see. It's all tiny windows I'd never fit through.

"The dishwasher is still full!" a woman yells. "Olivia!"

"She was supposed to be working late." Olivia tries to get up and wobbles in place, a hand moving to cup her forehead.

"Don't try to stand," I whisper.

The footsteps get closer until they're on the stairs behind me. Olivia's mom is an Asian lady who looks like she's not that much older than Johnny. She's in some fancy suit, her arms crossed. "I guess we're having people over tonight, then. Thank you for letting me know, Olivia."

"This is my friend Pen from school. She came over because I, um . . . because—"

"She got sick in fourth period because of that pot pie thing at lunch. I told her not to eat it." It's all feeling like a rambling mess. "So I took the bus back with her. I think it's a twenty-four-hour thing. Unless it's really bad food poisoning, but I doubt it because she's not puking anymore."

"Well, perhaps eating a pastry filled with god-knows-what wasn't such a good idea," Olivia's mom says, looking sort of crusty and confused. "Thank you for bringing Olivia home. That's very nice of you."

"No problem," I say, even though it's pretty obvious the woman is more suspicious than she is thankful. She stares at Olivia like she's trying to figure out what kind of shape she's in. Olivia's pale and sleepy-looking, so it works. "All right, well . . . guess I'll see you tomorrow then?"

Olivia nods, keeping that pillow against her waist. "Thank you."

"Nice to meet you, Mrs. . . . . Olivia's mom."

"Same to you," she says with a tight smile.

I sweep by her and head up the stairs to take my shoes and escape out the side door. There's a text from Blake when I check my phone: So . . . guess 2day wasn't really about a tripod . . .

Oh, man.

I get as far as hitting Reply when I see Colby standing on the sidewalk, looking right at me.

THIRTY-NINE

HE FLICKS HIS SMOKE AWAY WHEN I GET TO THE sidewalk. When I lead off to the left, he follows. We're not going to act like dumb idiots in front of Olivia's house. Once her house can't be seen from where we are, I stop.

"What are you doing here?" I ask.

"I followed you. Both of you." He waits for me to react, but all I got is my stiff face. "You left school together. You went to . . . Crestonvale."

"You followed us since school?"

"I was around."

He's always around in his fake way of never actually being there. It pisses me off, because everything's already over.

"What's the matter with you, dude? Do you stalk her, too?"

He's in my face now. "You crossed a line, Pen. You crossed a shitload of lines. I can't even believe you'd go there."

"There's no line, Colby." Around us, the little houses are decorated with Halloween stuff. The sky is already darkening now that it's past five. "Do you even know where we were today? Do you know?"

He's just shaking his head over and over. "I know that if you hadn't swooped in, then—"

"If I hadn't *swooped* in or whatever, then she'd still be screwed, okay? Because you left it all up to her."

"She was *my* girlfriend," he says. "All she had to do—"

"No, dude. Don't even act like she was your girlfriend. If she had been, then it wouldn't have played out this way," I say. "She was just some girl."

"She said she made a mistake," he says. "She said it wasn't really happening."

"She said that because you didn't really give her a choice. And don't worry," I say. "It's *not* happening."

He rubs his palms against the sides of his head, and looks at the ground between us. "What the hell, Pen?"

273

I could probably tell him about it. He might even listen because there's a bit of desperation in his voice now—just a tiny bit. But he doesn't deserve to know.

"Leave her alone. For real. She doesn't need your crap anymore. It's done." I move back a step, but then I'm right in his face again. "And you know what? You didn't have to deal with any of it. So don't *ever* tell me I'm useless or that I don't have any loyalty."

"Get out of my face," he says.

"You get out of *my* face. I'm so sick of everyone's pussy moves, just taking off and leaving everyone else hanging," I say, and it's almost a yell. "It's gonna bite you in the ass again one day, except I might not be there to deal with it."

The look in his eyes changes. They're icy blue, frozen. I take a couple steps back.

"You think you're doing me a favor?" He points a finger at me. "You think I owe you anything? All of this is *because* of you." When I say nothing, he continues, "All of this is because you thought cutting your hair would . . ."

"Would what? What did I think it would do?" I say.

All of a sudden, I realize my bag's not with me. Colby seems to be thinking about how to finish his sentence, while I feel my pockets to see what I have on me. Phone—that's it. I had it when I left school, and it was with me all the way here so . . . In the truck, on the floor next to my feet—damn.

"You know what? I don't even care anymore," Colby says.

"Neither do I."

"No. You don't get it," he says. "I literally don't give a shit

274

what happens to you anymore. You're on your own."

"Fine."

How many times is he going to tell me he's done with me? He walks past me, headed to where I guess the bus stop must be. Not like I can go that way now, because then we'd end up following each other home.

THE MCKINLEY BUILDINGS ARE this set of three high rises, and Johnny lives in the middle one. I had to suck it up and call him to ask. When he comes to the door, he says, "I still don't get why you wouldn't just let me come bring you your bag, man."

"I can handle taking the bus by myself across town to pick up my stuff."

He snorts and goes, "You wanna come in, or what?"

"I don't know."

Johnny leaves the door open and wanders away, like he's so sure I'm going to just come hang out. The place smells like his cologne, and also like fried onions. I take off my shoes and wander a little farther inside. The entrance area opens up to a walk-through kitchen at the left, or straight to where Johnny's set up his computer and sound system, with his punching bag and workout bench next to that. On the opposite side is the living room. Johnny's on the couch now, scrolling through his phone, then bringing it up to his ear like he's checking his voice mail. There's a sliding door that goes to a balcony. Between the workout bench and the sliding door is a short hallway. The first door is skinny, so I figure it's a closet or something. To the right is the bathroom. There are two more doors: one's closed, and the other is open a crack. Johnny's bedroom stuff is arranged inside.

Even though the couch is dented from my butt, it feels weird just sitting in my spot and acting like this is no big deal. The Xbox is set up like usual, but the TV looks bigger here.

"You're such a prick," I say to Johnny's reflection in the TV. "With your damn calendar hanging there, and your . . . white paint!"

He looks over and pulls his cell away from his ear. "What did you say?"

"I said you're a prick."

"I'm not a prick, man. Get over yourself."

"I am over myself, you know?" I say, feeling myself almost bouncing in place. "I'm just saying . . . nice place."

He snorts and then gives this heavy sigh. "Thanks. I like it."

I hate that I can't just go sit somewhere, or open a cupboard, or even take a leak in this place because it's some strange apartment. It would be nice if my brain would think of things to yell at him that wouldn't make me sound like a pissy little douche. I just want to call him a prick again.

"Did you think I was gonna live at the house forever?" he asks.

"No," I say. "Obviously. I'm not an idiot."

"I don't know," he says. "You've been acting like one."

"It's a question of loyalty. And respect, too," I say, waiting for him to show he feels like a jerk. But he's just squinting at me like when he gets smoke in his eyes. "You made *Mãe* get your old clothes from my closet. I mean, who does that? A prick, that's who. No one would argue with me on that one."

He gets up and goes to the kitchen, then comes back holding a bottle of beer. "How's your friend doing?"

"She's fine."

That's all I say, so he nods a couple times before saying, "I'm going for a smoke." He slips a cigarette in his mouth, then goes out on the balcony. For a moment, I just stand there wondering what I should do. Blake hasn't texted me since earlier, at Olivia's, and with every minute that passes and I don't respond, it looks worse and worse. Olivia hasn't texted me and now I'm wondering if it's because something bad happened.

So I slide the balcony door and step out. There are a couple of plastic chairs out here and nothing else.

"You didn't even finish the job out back. The little tiles are still leaning up against the house," I say. "*Mãe's* pissed."

"She is, huh?"

"Yeah. Because you just abandoned everything."

Johnny rolls his eyes, and maybe he thought I wouldn't be able to see that. "You're pissed at me. I get it, Pen."

"Okay." I want to know what he's going to do about it.

Johnny puts the beer bottle on the ground between our chairs and he focuses on his smoke. "*Pai* raised my rent last summer to almost what I pay for here. It would've been dumb to stay."

"You paid rent to live at home?"

"I didn't ask for the clothes, all right?" he says, leaning back on two wobbly plastic chair legs. "I know Ma's been telling

277

you stuff. That's why you didn't text me back or take the key."

"What key?"

"The key with the note I left." He rights the chair and turns to me with his serious face. "When I moved, I came back and left an envelope on your bed."

"I didn't get a key," I say. "There was no envelope."

He sighs like he should've known better.

"She took them," I say. "She came into my room and took my stuff. Why does she get to do stuff like that and get away with it? Do you know what she did? She took my Turtles and put them in a box to give them away without telling me. My Turtles, man."

"All right, Pen. Relax," he says, dropping his cigarette butt into another beer bottle tucked closer to the wall on the ground. "If you go up against *Mãe* and *Pai*, you're gonna find yourself knee-deep in shit with no one to pull you back out. Sometimes you gotta wait to make your move, you know?" It sounds like he's talking to himself. "You can't always be a hot-head and go rushing in all pissed off, you know?"

It reminds me of Blake's way of gaming, about learning all you can before you go up against evil—but we're button-mashers in my family. We get mad and we hit something. Johnny knows that.

"Says the guy who breaks people's faces at the bar for his friends," I say. "Being pissed off is the only way to get anything done. It's the only way anyone listens."

"You wanna know something I learned? Getting pissed off at something and doing something about it is good, but in between that, you gotta calm down and think things through. Otherwise, it's just a shit-show." He pulls out another smoke but only tucks it behind his ear, then stands. "Come."

I follow him inside. He goes to the last door down the little hallway, the one that's closed, and pushes it open. It's just a bedroom with a sheet-less single bed and a boring dresser.

"Who lives here?" I ask. "Oh man, not Jenna? Please tell me you didn't move in with her."

"Hey, why the hell would I move in with a girl and have her sleep in a different bedroom with a garage-sale bed?" Johnny says, then he flicks my forehead. "Whose room do you think this is, huh?"

"I don't know . . . Dom's?"

We both know half of Dom's legs would hang off that bed. I take another look around the room. The little bed creaks when I sit on it. Johnny crosses his arms and leans against the open door.

"Someone died in this bed, didn't they?" I say, my lips spreading with a giddy grin. "Is the mattress bloodstained under the bottom sheet?"

"Watching horror movies warped your brain."

"It's like the mattress Julia crawled out of hell from in *Hellraiser II*." I bounce on it. "*Mãe* would never be down with this."

"She's not down with a lot of things."

"Why? What's the matter with her?" I say.

"She thinks she's doing you a favor." He shrugs. "*Mãe* and *Pai* are from a different world."

"What kind of world?"

279

"The kind of world where people got one way of doing things, and that's it. The kind of world where it's the parents' job to keep their kids in line. Then when stuff happens, they think they're proven right, and they get even worse."

"What stuff's proven them right?"

Johnny stares back, and even though our gazes are aimed at one another, he's not seeing me. He gets that way when he's thinking.

"Sometimes I think *Pai* isn't as bad, but then he always ends up doing the same thing she does and backing her up," I say.

"That's because she's always talking in his ear," Johnny says, making his hand flap open and shut like a mouth against his ear. Then his face goes hard. "Even if he's better, it's not by much."

"I wish they spoke better English, or that I spoke better Portuguese," I say.

"I'm gonna talk to them, tell them to relax." He points a finger at me. "And you—don't go do anything stupid just to make them mad enough to screw things up even more."

"Me? You're the one who loses it!"

He rubs the scar on his eyebrow and nods. "All right, fine, man. You watch yourself, and I'll watch myself."

"Deal."

"You want something to eat? I was gonna make some hot dogs," Johnny says while he heads back down the hall.

"Yeah. I'm kind of starving, actually."

FORTY

IT'S LATE WHEN JOHNNY DROPS ME OFF, AND I
still haven't texted Blake back. The moon is up, and I stare at it
while the phone rings in my ear until Blake answers.

"So . . . today wasn't about a tripod," I say.

"Okay."

"I wouldn't lie to you unless it was to keep someone else's
secret." That sounds a lot worse to my ears than it did in my
head for some reason. "I mean . . . oh, man."

"I don't really know what to say." Blake sounds weirded
out. I wish I could just tell her what's up. "Because I don't know
what's going on."

"I know."

"You said Olivia would be fine."

"She is. I just . . ." How can I make it okay with Blake
without telling her everything? "I should've just told you
something was going on instead of making up some tripod
bull. I'm a douche."

"So Olivia's making you keep a secret?"

That annoys me, the way she says it. Why do I have to be
stuck between two things all the time?

"She's not making me do anything." I mean for it to sound

serious, not harsh, but I guess it really depends on how Blake wants to hear it. "The Olivia stuff is separate. It's not about you—and I know that sounds rude or whatever. It's just . . . well, I got friends and I gotta have their backs. That's all this is."

She's slow to respond. "That's really all this is?"

"What else would it be?"

"Sometimes it's righteous to be the hero and rescue the princess, you know?"

I sit on the edge of my bed, sighing.

"Say I was a hero," I say. "Olivia could be a princess, but she wouldn't be *my* princess."

"Who would your princess be?"

"I don't think she'd be a princess, actually. She'd be a badass vigilante bounty hunter with a unique ability. And we'd be on the same team, and I'd have my own ability. So when we'd go into battle, we'd kick so much ass, it would be nuts. All the weapons and treasure would be ours."

"We should totally play *Borderlands* co-op." Her voice has a smile in it. The fact that she knew what I was talking about without my having to explain it is awesome. "All of them. That would so win everything. What DLC do you have?"

So we talk about that for a while. I lie on the bed and stare at the ceiling. While Blake speaks, I put the phone on speaker so my texts are accessible, hoping I'll be quick enough so Blake won't notice. I type How's it going? and press Send to Olivia.

"Pen?" Blake says. I'm sure I'm busted until she goes, "I don't want to be jealous of Olivia."

"You saying that makes no sense to me—what could you

possibly be jealous of? You're Blake."

She lets out a little sarcastic laugh. "What does that even mean?"

"It means you're it. You're at the top."

"The top of what?"

"You know what I mean." I shift onto my side. "You have to know what I mean. What are you worried about?"

"Guys like the cute, nice girls who need to be rescued."

"Yeah, well . . . ," I say. "Girls like the tough douche bags with beards."

We're quiet a minute, and it's starting to feel awkward. But then she goes, "I wish I could've seen you tonight."

"Same," I say, picturing her face, and my lips spread into a grin.

My phone does a beep, and I do something I haven't done since I was, like, thirteen: I tell Blake my mom's calling me just so I can end the call. But it's only because Olivia's texted back, and I have to see what's up.

After we get off the phone, I pull up my texting window with Blake and I type: say u wanted 2 b a nice cute grl—& say u wanted me 2 rescue u—u'd still b @ the top—k?

Now I pull up the window for Olivia. Her text: I'm OK. Tired but can't sleep.

Me: u could watch a movie

Her: Not really in the mood.

Me: yeah—makes sense

Her: What are you up to?

Me: saw my bro 2nite—went 2 his place

283

Her: Really? That's great!

So I text her about that for a while. Her replies are almost instant, and she's typing these long messages—that tells me she's in the mood to talk—maybe not about what happened, but at least about something.

Blake texts back: It's weird that I didn't really know u until this year.

Me: i know

Just below my Olivia text window is Colby's. The last text is one he sent me after Elliott's party: Loyalty.

I delete the entire text conversation, all four hundred and twelve texts we'd sent each other since school started.

Then I go back to flipping between Olivia's and Blake's texts.

FORTY-ONE

THE NEXT MONDAY, HALLOWEEN HAPPENS. WHILE kids ring our bell and force my mom to get up every thirty seconds, I'm at work with Blake. It's our first shift together, and I manage to get this old guy to buy a brand-new PlayStation console. At the checkout, he says, "Nice costume, kid. I went and saw the first *TMNT* movie when it came out in 1990."

"That must've been epic," I say. "What do you think of the new ones?"

He sighs like that's a loaded question. "People want to complain whenever someone tries to mess with the past. They want to get excited for the new, but they can't let go of the way things used to be," he says, handing me his credit card. "I was excited to see it grow, become a thing for the new generation. And you know what? Even as a loyal fan since the original comics, I wasn't disappointed. They preserved the Turtle essence."

This guy is smart. I wish he'd talk some more about this stuff. "Me and my brother went and saw the first one. I was literally sitting on the edge of my seat, I was so into it."

There's this knowing smile on his lips like he totally feels me. The sale goes through, and I hand him his card and receipt. He says, "I don't need a bag. Take care, kid."

I hand him the box, and he walks away.

"You just geeked out with a guy who's probably older than my dad," Blake says after the man leaves.

"What are you talking about? That guy was badass," I say. "Geeking out is badass. And Turtles are badass as hell."

She reaches for my hand below the counter and I squeeze hers for a second. Every time I touch her, it's dangerous. Especially when we're in public. Sometimes I feel like I could kiss her right here and not give a crap about people walking in, about getting fired, about anything at all.

"I'm going to go put the returns away, okay?" she says, grabbing the basket of things people have brought back or decided not to buy once they got to the register.

"You're going to leave me all alone up here?" I say.

"If anyone comes to checkout and it's too complicated, just call me over."

When Blake is wandering the aisles to put stuff back on the shelves, I reach for my phone under the counter. Olivia's still not quite right. She calls it "feeling blah."

The last thing I said was: just wait it out

Her: I'm tired but I can't sleep.

I want to ask her if she regrets it, the abortion. Maybe that's why she's feeling blah. But if she says she does regret it, then what?

Me: u think maybe u should talk 2 some1???

Her: About what?

Me: how u feel & stuff . . .

Blake gives me a thumbs-up from the computer-game aisle, and I give her one back. A customer walks in, but he heads right over to the toy and collectible section, so I go back to my phone, making sure it stays under the counter. Mitch isn't so much into employees standing around texting.

Her: I feel OK. It's just the sleeping thing.

Me: think maybe it's the hormone thing?

Her: Maybe.

Sometimes I wonder if I'm totally sucking at this friend thing. If Blake was in my shoes, what would she be telling Olivia? I keep telling her to just wait it out, but part of me wants to tell her to snap out of it, man up a little. Just dust yourself off and move on. My guy friends would get it, but I know it would sound mean as hell when said to a girl.

Me: just . . . wait it out i guess

I'm pretty sure that whatever I give her is a hell of a lot better than what she'd be getting from Colby. Johnny says just being there is enough, so that's what I'm doing.

BLAKE AND I GET a pass to leave early from second period on Friday to set up for the photo shoot. The school camera we borrowed is fully charged and the memory card is empty. We have a couple of wide rectangular signs—that Robyn and Blake painted white for us in art class—and each person is going to hold one facing the camera straight on. Once all the photos are taken, we're going to use the school's editing program to place quotes on the sign in each picture. We already have three people waiting to get pictures taken by the time the lunch bell rings.

"What if we get more than twenty people wanting to pose?" I ask.

"We'll take them all. We'll get more quotes if we need to," Blake says. "And we are so putting our own pics in there. It'll be righteous."

"Yeah—I'll pass."

"Olivia?" Blake says, and I turn to see Olivia wandering over from the science hallway. It blows my mind that she hasn't skipped school at all. "You're having your picture taken, right?"

She shakes her head no.

"You guys suck!" Blake says. "How about your truths? We all have to be in there somewhere."

"We are," I say. "We're taking the pics, editing them, and writing all the text slides."

Blake rolls her eyes and heads for the spotlights we borrowed from the drama department. We've got three areas set up: in front of the library; in front of the massive mural that's an ugly mash-up of the school mascot, the school colors, and religious things; and in front of the first set of grade-twelve lockers, right around the corner from the mural.

"Hey," Blake says, so Olivia and I look over at her. "I was talking with the guys and we think you two should totally organize a photo shoot for the band."

"You don't even know if we can take a decent photo yet," I say.

"It's all about the lighting anyway," Blake says. "We're going to make a Facebook page for when the Battle of the Bands happens, so real band photos would rock. What do you think?"

"Can you guys afford to hire us?" Olivia asks. When Blake's face freezes awkwardly, Olivia laughs. "I'm kidding. I think a photo shoot would be pretty cool. Will you give us photographer credit?"

"Of course," Blake says.

Olivia searches my gaze to see what I think of the idea. "I'm in."

When first lunch starts, crowds of people head by our stations and they want to know what we're up to. Olivia is here to help people pose, while I fix the lighting. Blake and I decided we'd split the actual shooting between us and see whose pictures end up looking the best.

At first, it feels awkward, acting like some photographer. But then it becomes like a job, and we get into it. The caf starts to empty out next to us as lunch ends. Blake takes off to get done up for her turn in front of the camera.

"How's it going?" I ask Olivia while she flips through all the shots we've taken today. Those three words must come out of my mouth—or my fingers—three times a day. She's probably so tired of hearing them, but I can't stop asking. Her answer is a smile.

"My turn," Blake says, swaggering over in the school skirt I never see her wear, fishnets, black boots that go up to her knees, and this cropped leather-looking jacket thing. She looks like some biker dude's girl. She looks like my girl. "I made my hair super big. Make me look absolutely amazing, people."

"This will not be hard," I say, hooking my finger with hers. "Damn."

"Wait!" She heads for one of the empty cafeteria tables. "Do me here."

I fumble with the camera. "Uh—"

"Please don't be gross," Olivia says. "We're professionals."

Blake ignores us and steps right up on the table. "Pass me a sign." Olivia hands me one, then she drags the lighting equipment over. Blake's legs are spread apart and she holds the sign at waist level. She does this head-banging move to make her hair go nuts, and she looks down to where I'm sort of crouching, deciding to shoot her from below. Her face looks badass, like she's some demon slayer or something.

I take, like, seven shots.

"So?" she asks, hopping off the table.

"Hot," Olivia says.

I nod. "Yeah, what she said."

"Nice." We do the finger-hooking thing, then she goes, "Okay, I have to go change back. I'll be quick!"

Blake disappears around the corner.

"Hey, guys," Tristan says as he wanders over. "Can I be in your project?"

"Sure, dude," I say. "Take a sign."

Tristan takes a board from Olivia then follows me to the spot in front of the library. He goes right into one of his I'm-gonna-try-looking-up-through-my-long-bangs poses. Tristan's like a statue under my aim, and I'm ready to snap some shots.

"The hell are you doing, Tristan?" Colby's coming from my right.

"I wanted to get my picture taken," Tristan says.

"Yeah? You some kind of model now? Let's go. Garrett's waiting for us," Colby says. Then he turns to me. "Nice try, Pen. Tristan's one of us, so therefore he can't be one of you—no matter how girly his jeans are."

"Come on, Colby. This is getting old," Tristan says with a heavy shake of the head before turning around and going off on his own.

"What?" Colby says to me, coming a step closer. Now there are maybe five steps between us. "You got something to say?"

"Nope."

290

"Nothing?"

"No. Oh, well, yeah," I say. "You wanna be in our project?"

He lets out a chuckle, but his brow gets heavy. "Screw off, Pen."

So I hold up the camera. It's so quick and I've snapped a photo of him standing there, arms out, feet wide apart, and head to the side.

"Oh damn—I better watch my ass. You just took a picture of me," he says. "You're lame, Pen. I don't know how I ever looked past how lame you are."

I give him no reaction before turning around and heading back to where Olivia's waiting. She turns her back to Colby, too, as I sidle up to her.

"You're not putting him in the project, are you?" she asks.

"I'm just messing with him," I say.

She doesn't look impressed. "Maybe you shouldn't do that."

I know that. Part of me wishes Blake wasn't my girlfriend, and Olivia wasn't my friend, so that I could get back at him without worrying he'll go after them. In my mind, I've done all kinds of things to him—talked shit about him at school, told his parents stuff he'd never want them to know, showed up at his house with the guys in Blake's band to take Colby and his buddies on—but most of the time, it's just him and me and I finally tell him everything. Maybe I tell it all with one quote plastered over his smug face.

"You should delete the photo," Olivia says.

"Yeah. I should."

LATER, MOM STOPS ME as I head down the stairs to catch the bus for my shift in an hour. It smells like the white cookies she makes that I like, these hard, dry things I have to dunk in milk to be able to eat.

"Where you go?"

"I have to get to work," I say, which is how I decide to announce I've got a real job.

"Work? Where work?"

"I work at the mall, at a store. I'm trying to save money."

"You save the money? Why you need to save the money? You do schoolwork." She tells me she won't have me screwing up school by having a job.

"I can handle it. I *am* handling it."

Johnny still hasn't told me when he plans on talking to our parents, so I have to watch myself. Every day I want to tell her I've been at Johnny's; that her little plan didn't work for long. Instead, I'm riding the pissy aftereffects of her trying to steal my toys.

"You no work like that," she says, pointing to my clothes, one of the shirts I brought home with me from Johnny's, and these black dress pants I used to save for special occasions.

"We all dress like that. We have a uniform shirt anyway."

"You no dress like that at you work!" She says I'm embarrassing myself in front of professional people, strangers. "You go change!"

"My manager gave me the job when I looked like this. Anyway—it's not like it matters what you think." I throw on my jacket and slip into my skater shoes. "I gotta go. I don't want to be late."

"I call you father, Penelope. I call him, we talk, then you, *Mãe e Pai* talk. We talk all tomorrow."

Tomorrow I still won't be listening.

AT WORK, I RING in six sales in a row. I only mess up twice. Once by hitting "cash" instead of "debit," which makes the register pop open into my stomach when I reach over for the PIN pad. The other time is when I accidentally override the price of something and end up giving a customer a thirty-dollar game for half off.

"Mitch will have to report that to mall security," Elliott says. "It'll go on your mall-employee record, but only for seven years."

"What? For real?"

"Nope. What the hell is a mall-employee record?" Elliott says, cracking a grin. "I just made it up. Sounds legit, doesn't it?"

"Will I get in trouble, though?"

"My second shift here, I charged this woman a thousand dollars on her credit card and neither of us noticed until it went through and she was looking at her bill as she was walking away. She accused me of trying to rip her off," Elliott says. "I'm still here."

"I'm going to pay better attention on the next one."

Mitch sweeps past us, and for a second I think I'm about to get in trouble, but he just tells us to work, look lively, and sell stuff, then he's on his way out of the store.

"So listen," Elliott says. "You think I should back off from Olivia?"

"What do you mean?"

He pulls out a wad of transaction receipts and starts sorting them into piles. "I can't figure out if she's into it or not. She's sort of—I don't know—hot and cold or something?"

"Yeah, well," I say, but that's where it stops because there's nothing to say. I can't give him advice about how to get with some girl I know, because that girl's my friend and I don't want some other dude messing with her. "Olivia's nice, and she's sweet or whatever—"

"I know. That's why I like her."

"Good. So maybe if she's not rushing into anything, she's still worth sticking around for, you know?"

"Yeah," he says. "Got it." He puts the receipt piles back into the register. "That guy who showed up at my house—that friend of yours—is he going to be a problem?"

"Not for her," I say, although there's no way for me to be sure of that.

Elliott nods. It looks like he's going to say something else but the store phone rings.

THAT NIGHT, WHEN IT'S super late, Blake sings something soft into my ear, through our phone connection. I don't know what it is, but it's pretty. She tries to stop but I convince her to keep going. Pretty soon I'm closing my eyes knowing she'll be pissed at me for falling asleep on her again, but I can't help it. Her voice makes me all mellow when it's late and—

Something hits my bedroom window with a massive crack sound.

Then there are three more cracks.

I bounce up in bed, dropping my phone. "What the hell!"

It's like someone's smacking a hand against my bedroom window, except there can't be anyone there unless they can scale a brick wall. Through the curtain, the moon shines and round shadows appear. I pick up my phone, hearing Blake calling my name.

"I think someone just egged my window!" I tell her.

"Can you see who it is?"

"Hang on."

I pad over, parting the curtain just a bit. An egg cracks right at face level against the glass, making me jump back. I look again, and there they are past the blur of egg guts, standing in the bushes. Garrett, Tim, Ray, that Jake guy, and Colby. Ike and Tristan aren't with them. Garrett waves at me, then winds up to throw another egg while Ray holds the carton out for him. Garrett whips two more eggs at my window, and Colby smokes, watching it go down. He won't look directly at me, even though he's the one I'm staring at. My heart beats so hard, but I think it's mostly from getting startled awake by egg gunshots. Tim pulls out his phone and aims to take a picture. I close the curtains just as my bedroom door bursts open.

"What!" Mom rushes inside and goes for the window. "Duarte!"

Dad's yelling from somewhere down the hall or maybe downstairs already. Blake's forgotten at the other end of my cell phone which I leave on the bed while I run down. How did they even hear the eggs? My dad must've been up with indigestion or something.

Dad goes out in shoes and pajamas. I follow. Of course the guys are gone by then. The empty carton of eggs lies in the grass. My dad's silent but heaving like he's about to have a heart attack. He backs up and stares at my bedroom window. There are splashes of egg guts all over it.

"Who do this?" he asks too loud. I don't want the neighbors to wake up, to see how pathetic this is.

"I don't know."

"You no lie! Who?"

I back up then head into the house, hoping he'll follow so we can at least be loud inside. Mom's at the bottom of the stairs, holding the phone like she's waiting for the signal to call the cops. It's just eggs, not a drive-by. Still, this is bad. I don't have the kind of parents who tolerate any bull that happens after the sun goes down.

Dad comes in shouting about how I know who did it and I'm not telling. Mom marches around the front hall, nodding like she's been proven right about something. Dad goes off about how eggs eat at the paint and now the windowsill's going to be wrecked.

"You see?" my mom says. "I tell you. You go out look like this, you ask for bad things. I tell you stop it! I tell you! When you be a boy, boys come be boys with you!" Then she tells my dad she's had it, that he needs to put his foot down because no one listens to her.

296

"I don't throw eggs at houses! I'm not the one who made the mess. I was at work and then I came home. That's all I know."

"I call police," Dad says. He wants to file a report.

"It's just eggs, *Pai!*"

"This my house!" he shouts, taking the cordless from Mom.

It's everyone's house but mine.

Mom drifts off to go sit by her Mary statue, probably to complain about me in prayer, and Dad changes his mind about the phone. He does this thing I hate, motioning for me to follow him with this pissy finger-curling motion, like I'm a seven-year-old about to get in trouble for leaving my toys out. He grabs his jacket, so I grab mine, then we're back outside. He punches the combination to the garage door and it goes up. He comes back out with the hose, holding the end of it like a gun. It's almost three in the morning, and Dad shoots water at my bedroom window. The sound breaks the night and now I'm sure the neighbors will come see what's up. After a moment, my dad hands me the hose and says, "You stay here. You clean. You no come inside until everything everywhere is *limpo!*" He leaves me out here.

Fifteen minutes later, I've managed to wash off most of the egg, leaving a couple smudges and streaks that are probably frozen. By the time I roll the hose back up in the garage, I'm shivering and my nose is leaking.

In my room, my Blake phone call is long gone, replaced by five texts from her wondering what's happening. I dial, but not her.

"What happened?" Johnny says, sounding panicked through a sleepy haze.

"Colby egged my window. *Mãe* and *Pai* are awake and freaking on me."

"Pen, man. What's been going on?"

I didn't get to fill him in on everything. This Colby stuff, though, I thought was handled already. What I want to tell Johnny is that everything's blowing up around me. That Mom thinks I caused this by looking like a punk druggy dude, that she's two seconds away from enrolling me in a makeup class and forcing me to wear a wig. That Dad will back her up now because I've caused enough trouble to pull him away from his TV and out of his sleep. And I feel like the only way I can keep everything from falling apart in my life is by making sure Olivia doesn't fall apart—and those things don't even go together.

"I sort of realized Colby's an ass," I tell Johnny. "And now the egg's all frozen and it won't come off, but *Pai* says it'll ruin the windowsill."

Johnny sighs and makes sounds like he's getting up. "Listen, are you gonna be able to handle yourself with Colby?"

"Yeah." No.

"Because I can't ignore this kind of stuff for too long. If you can't deal with Colby, I will."

"No," I say. "I'll figure it out."

Sitting here in the silence means I'm stuck thinking about what the guys did, which ends up making me feel like more and more of a douche. Pretty soon the darkness inside me stirs—the darkness that's always hanging out in my gut but never gets me anywhere. I'm just mad as hell with no one to throw my anger at.

So I text Colby: u better watch yrself, douche—i'll take u down—i swear—i don't care what happens 2 u anymore

FORTY-TWO

MOM WAKES ME UP AT TEN THE NEXT MORNING by yelling my name over and over from wherever she is downstairs. I shuffle down barefoot where Mom throws a flowered apron at me.

"Busy busy," she says. "Chop chop."

She heads for the kitchen. When I get there, a bunch of cleaning products are lined up on the counter. Today is the day I learn how to clean an oven. She tells me to put on the apron, but I don't want to. She gave me the one with the spring flowers while she's wearing my dad's barbecue apron, the black one with an image of a stack of hot dogs on a plate. I know it's just an apron, but it's like she gets off on making me feel like crap. I won't put it on.

I help her scrub the grime off the grill, off the inner walls of the oven. Then we pull out the stove burners and soak them, replacing the little foil plates that catch all the spills. After that, it's laundry, where she teaches me how to fold a bottom sheet. She makes me try twice but it's all messed-up-looking.

I do all she asks, and I don't say anything about it.

She won't get a reaction from me anymore.

"Ma, I gotta leave for work by two," I tell her, which is in an hour. I don't have to work, but it sounds more legit than having plans with my friends.

She does this annoyed sigh, pouring Pine-Sol into the mop bucket.

"I'm serious. I have to leave in an hour. I have to get ready soon."

"What you want? You want the money? I give you the money. I buy you the clothes. I buy you the telephone."

"I want to work and make my own money."

"Why? Why you need the money?"

"Because."

She tells me she and Dad talked and they're in agreement: I don't need to be working. My only job is to do well in school. "You *pai* he got the money for school. You do homework, *Pai e Mãe* pay for the nurse school."

"I don't wanna be a nurse. Is it *you* who wants to be a nurse?" The look she gives me—it's like I dared to say something she wasn't expecting. "I have to go now."

She lets the mop fall into the bucket, hot water splashing around it. I've seen this look on her face a butt-load of times before. She's fed up to the point of crying. So I turn around and leave, because I'm starting to think that maybe I'm reaching that point, too.

AFTER MY SHOWER, I find my baggy jeans and my red tee. Over that, I try on this new silky black button-down Mom had bought for Johnny, but it's too tight around his biceps. It's short-sleeved so my leather wristband shows. I put my silver chain on—the one Blake likes. In the mirror, I start to think maybe I'd look cool with a lip piercing, or a pierced labret. I can picture black lines etched up and down my arms, no colors like in Johnny's tattoos, just tribal designs or something. I can see my hair going even a bit shorter, buzzed close to the scalp with a shorter fauxhawk. I can see so many things about me that I'd like to play around with.

People should just be allowed to look in the mirror and see all kinds of possibilities. Everyone should be able to feel nice when they look in the mirror. They should at least be able to see themselves reflected in there, even if they look all weird.

In the mirror, I see myself standing there and I think I'm all right. I think there's no other way I could look, or should look. My mom must be blind if she thinks her vision of me would look normal. It wouldn't. I know it wouldn't.

I start pulling off my chain, my wristband, my belt. I put it all in a bag, then I head for my parents' bedroom.

I TAKE THE STAIRS with this feeling that I could die before reaching the bottom. My mom's heels are maybe a fifth of the height of Blake's, but man, they're still massive stilts that make it impossible for me to walk the way I usually do. And this skirt keeps trying to get caught under my left foot. The

301

skirt is navy blue and I had to tuck it into my boxers because it would've fallen right to the floor otherwise. The blouse is one Mom's never worn before; it's the only one that was close to my size. It's shiny white, with small buttons that are covered in the same material as the shirt. My boobs are there, just being all girly about it. On my ears are gold round earrings my mom must've worn before I was born, or maybe never. There's this burgundy stuff on my lips, and I colored between the lines. I couldn't put anything on my eyes because it made them water when I got too close.

I'm the lady from the perfume counter at the mall.

I reach the bottom of the stairs still upright. The shoes clack against the linoleum. I head for the living room, where I know my mom will be scowling at the TV.

"I'm going to work now, Ma."

She doesn't want to glance at me, but she has to. Then she has to look at it. This costume she's been so desperate for me to wear. It's all right here, covering me up. I don't want to fight anymore, because I don't even know what kind of fight this is.

There's no relief on her face. "You laugh at me."

"I'm not laughing," I say.

I'm in drag right now. I'm a homo right now. This is worse than a Halloween costume because it's not funny.

Mom's chin quivers, and she puts a hand against her heart.

She's looking at me with all kinds of bad feelings in her eyes, which is no different from the way she usually gazes at me; the only difference is that now I'm looking at myself the same way.

"I look nice, just like you wanted, right?" I say. "So can I go to work now?"

My eyes sting, but I don't quit looking right at her. Not even when her face goes hard.

"Get outta here," my mom says.

So I leave.

IN THE TRUCK, JOHNNY'S mouth hangs open. "What the hell, Pen? I'm gonna have nightmares about this."

"Me too."

"What's going on?"

"Nothing." I put on my seat belt, fixing the skirt so I can let my legs hang loose. "Can we sneak in through the back door of your building or something? I need to take a shower and start over."

"You're playing a dangerous game, little sister."

"I'm not the one who picked the game."

"I can't look at you, man." He drives and keeps stealing glances at me. "You look like *Tia* Jacinta."

"Well, that's just great. I look like an old lady."

While we drive, I scroll through my cell but I keep going back to that text I sent Colby, which he never replied to. But he got it, there's no doubt about that. Lying in the dark, I felt so sure that I could beat the crap out of him. But right now, my head's somewhere else. I just never want to deal with Colby again. He could fade away, and that would be fine by me.

I have new friends, and Johnny and I are cool again. I feel all right. I'm still me.

303

I send Colby another text: u leave me & my friends alone, I leave u and yr friends alone—we don't have 2 talk—we don't even have 2 look @ each other—i'm over it—truce & walk away

I don't get a reply.

FORTY-THREE

AFTER OUR MINI LUNCH MEETING WITH THE REST of the photo reps on Monday, Blake and I realize we're way behind most of the others—and we have no excuse, because we're the only ones with a third, silent partner. It almost makes me wish Tristan was on our team, because that guy just gets things done—which is why Colby's always partnering up with him during group assignments.

"We can do this, right?" I ask Blake when we head off to eat lunch in the fifteen minutes left before the bell rings.

"Absolutely. We're going to focus and plow through it."

"You say that like it's so simple."

"It is," she says. "We'll just get together on nights we're not scheduled at work and I don't have practice. Or maybe you could come watch practice and we could work on things after the guys leave."

I give her an awkward look. "Uh . . . I really doubt my mom's going to be cool with me going out every night. Trying to get out of the house for work is already a pain in the ass."

She stares back at me like I must be exaggerating. It's not like I'm being held hostage, but Blake doesn't get that the crap my mom dishes out—the looks, the sighs, the nagging, the threats—is sometimes just not worth dealing with every day.

"What if we work on it at school a lot?" I offer. "Maybe at lunch, and we can ask Mr. Middleton if we can get a pass to get out early a couple times. And maybe we can stick around here after school on nights I have to go to work? The mall is closer to here than it is to my house anyway." Plus, it'll save me from having to go home before work.

Blake squeezes my forearm. "Okay. Let's do that."

So for the next few days, every minute at school or after school is spent finishing up our photos and sorting our slide show.

Almost every minute. Some of my minutes are spent looking over my shoulder, making sure I know where Colby is at all times. In class, he's with Garrett. At lunch, he takes off with his buddies. In between classes, when we cross paths, his slit-eyed expression is all he's got for me. He got my text, I'm sure of it. So this is our truce. This is us walking away.

On Wednesday, Blake, Olivia, and I are in the computer lab at lunch. The photos are black and white because it makes the quotes pop more. In each picture, a student stands arms out, holding up a cardboard sign with a quote pasted onto it. In each of them, the quote doesn't go with the person holding it. You see a face, a body, and you don't even realize you're assuming things about what you're seeing. Then you take in the words of the quote, but they go against what you'd assume for what your eyes are seeing.

"Am I the only one who's going to be in our project?" Blake asks Olivia and me.

We're still trying to figure out how to add the quotes on the white signs. I'm doing the mouse-clicking, while Blake leans over to point at the screen. Olivia sits next to me, watching us go.

"You should at least put your truths in there. Something! This diary is going to be epic. I mean, do you guys realize that in two weeks, the mayor of Castlehill will be seeing these photos? We have a chance to really say something. They want the truth about what it's like to be a high school student? Well, they're going to get it—the amazingly messy, ridiculous, shocking truth," Blake says. "You guys have to be a part of it. You have to put yourselves out there."

Olivia meets my gaze, and it's obvious she's thinking what I'm thinking. Neither of us is interested in calling attention to ourselves. Blake's badass; she's used to putting herself out there, and that's a big part of what makes her so damn hot. Not all of us are like that.

"So?" Blake says, smiling like she expects Olivia and me to throw a fist in the air after her passionate rant.

"We'll think about it," I say.

Blake sighs. "Well, I tried." She puts her finger on the computer screen. "That font is righteous. Let's keep it."

Robyn comes in with this pissy expression. "You said you'd be ten minutes!"

"I know. I'm coming!" Blake says, before leaning super close to me. But she stops before our faces touch. Her perfume's like a cloud around my head. My fingers curl around her shirt and I pull a little.

"You're the hottest girl in the world," I whisper in her ear. "I wish I could—"

"Can we go already!" Robyn shouts.

So I kiss Blake, right on the lips. I kiss her until I forget where I am. When she pulls away, her face is flushed and she rakes her fingers through her hair. I watch her go. When I get back to the computer screen, Olivia's frozen in her seat, shoulders hunched.

"Sorry about that," I say.

"You guys are so cute!" she says, then she pushes my chair with her feet and I go rolling into the aisle. At the same time, she moves to take control of the computer. "My turn."

The picture of Blake is one of the few we have left to design. Her sign says, *I think all the guys on the basketball team are jerks. Even me.*

"Look at her," I say, running my hand against Blake's photo up on the monitor. "Would you go gay for her?"

"I'd go gay for Elliott," Olivia says.

"That makes no sense at all."

"Your question was stupid," she says.

"Hey, guys," Tristan says. He collapses into a chair and rolls his way over to us.

"What's up?" I say.

"Not much," he says. "That's a cool pic. Blake looks legit."

It makes me smile.

"You wanna play *Crypts* later? Feels like we haven't played that shizz in forever," he says.

"Yeah, it *has* been a while," I say.

"Do you game, too?" he asks Olivia.

"Not at all," she says.

"Pen's pretty legit. Have you seen her play?" Tristan says.

"I did give her this old Atari system and watched her play some of that," Olivia says. "It wasn't much fun."

Tristan smacks my arm. "You have an Atari? She gave you one? That's the shizz."

"Yeah. All these games, too," I tell him.

After a bit of silence while we watch Olivia prepare the next photo, cropping the edges and going through filters, Tristan hitches his chin up at me. "So you gonna invite me over to check out your new stuff or what?"

"Well, I just figured—you know, with Colby and all . . ."

"Figured what?" he asks.

"He's not going to let you be friends with me," I say, after a long pause. Olivia continues clicking away, not reacting to the conversation going on around her. "You know that, dude."

"I'm not Colby's peon," he says.

"His what?"

"I might look like a spineless Colby minion, but I'm a free man," Tristan says.

He says that now, but he'd know that's bull the second he'd try walking away from Colby. Tristan can either be a minion, or he can leave the guys to hang out with a bunch of girls, and make an enemy of Colby in the process. Colby and his buddies wouldn't hesitate to mess with him. The fact that I'm a girl is probably the only reason I'm not getting my ass kicked.

"You *do* remember you and me were friends first, right?" Tristan says.

"Yeah, I know."

Olivia leans her head back against the chair and starts rolling back and forth. Tristan and I copy what she's doing, and pretty soon we're all zoned out, twirling around in our rolly chairs, staring up at the ceiling.

BY FRIDAY, WE'VE FINISHED up the thirty-five pictures that will be part of our diary. Before we send them to print for the album, we're testing them out with a mini screening at lunch. Blake and I sign out a projector and take it to an empty classroom. Robyn comes along. Olivia shows up with a bag of popcorn, which we pass around.

"How's it going?" I ask her.

She smiles and throws a popcorn kernel at my face. I flick one back and miss her completely.

Pictures go up, one after the other, and it kind of blows my mind that we could've put something like that together. It doesn't *just* look like some high school project. It sure as hell doesn't look like something I'd be a part of. This looks legit, like a real series of photos you might read about online or see hanging in an art gallery. It looks like something to be proud of, something you'd

309

want to show your parents. It's epic, just like Blake said. My face or my truth might not be in it, but I'm still all over this project. I wonder what Johnny will think about it.

At the end Blake says, "This will win everything. I'm sure of it."

Olivia says, "It's not a contest. They're just going to pick the best ones—"

"That's how Blake talks," I tell Olivia. "No one's actually winning anything."

Blake leans against me and says, "But for real, you're going to win everything. And you get the prize."

"Oh, god," Robyn says. "Gross. Don't be gross."

I put my lips against Blake's ear to tell her I want the prize.

After we pack everything up and head off in different directions to find our lockers, I walk by Tristan. He puts his hand up like he's about to wave but gives up, and his gaze falls to the ground.

"Hey," I say, and he stops. "If you wanted to come by my brother's place later, I'm having some people over."

"Oh yeah?" he says. "Can I bring Trent? We were gonna hit the bookstore tonight. Maybe we could come by after?"

"Yeah, sure."

"Legit!"

"I'll text you the address," I say. "And don't tell Colby, all right?"

He gives me a thumbs-up. "Yeah, no worries, Pen."

We bump fists, and then he takes off for his locker. At the same time, I pull out my phone and text him Johnny's address.

WHEN THE LAST BELL goes off, I stop at my locker before meeting up with Blake and Olivia. We walk through school like this: Blake on my right, fingers hooked together, and Olivia to my left. We head for the lobby, talking about Blake's show coming up at the end of December.

My eyes land on Colby and Garrett, hanging out by the girls' locker rooms, just as Tim and Ray head over. It looks right, Colby surrounded by his people. Not so much because guys should stick with guys, but because pricks should stick with pricks.

There's a look between us, and his mouth curls in a smirk.

I ignore it, but Colby's gaze moves to Olivia, and he raises an eyebrow, nodding like he's hitting on her. Olivia's eyes are closed and she shakes her head slowly.

"Don't react," I tell her. "That's what he wants. You know that."

"Are you kidding?" Blake says, then she gives Colby the finger. Garrett starts laughing and holds both his middle fingers out. "That guy needs to be taken down a peg."

I push her hand down. "Blake, seriously. You don't know—"

"Yeah, I do. You think these guys aren't calling me fat, or slut, or bitch every other day? You think I just put my head down and let it happen?" Blake says. "I mean—the guy told people I have crabs, for shit's sake."

Olivia's still looking down.

"Look," Blake says to Olivia. "I don't know what the deal is with you and him—Pen's been pretty good at keeping it all very

311

secret—but it's obvious you and Colby have bad history. Aren't you sick of it yet? Aren't you sick of walking around afraid you'll run into him in the halls, that he'll say something stupid?"

I'm about to open my mouth when Olivia goes, "Yes."

"Don't you guys think that maybe it's time Colby felt like shit for a change?" Blake says.

The three of us glance over at him. He leans against the wall, a foot up against it. The look on his face makes it pretty obvious he's loving the fact that we're paying attention to him.

"Yeah," I say. "It's time."

"So . . . let's get him then," Blake says.

FORTY-FOUR

BLAKE THINKS SHE CAN DO ANYTHING—AND SO far, it's not like that's ever been proven wrong. She stands there with this confident, no-one-can-mess-with-me glare, and Olivia's gaze is glued to her.

"What do you want to do to him? How do you want to get back at him?" Blake asks Olivia. "And don't pretend you haven't thought about it a million times."

Olivia's voice is even, and her eyes are on Colby. "Pen took a picture of him."

Blake waits for her to go on, her brow scrunching up like

312

she doesn't follow. But it's like I already know what Olivia's going to say.

"You didn't delete it, did you," Olivia says to me.

"No."

She looks Colby's way again, but he's talking to Garrett about something, like she's not worth his time anymore—again.

I fill Blake in. "I took a picture of him one of the days we were shooting for the project."

Blake nods with an evil smirk. "Absolutely amazing. We are so putting it up there. What quote should we brand him with?"

"Can you send me the photo?" Olivia says to me. Her eyes stop me, flaming with this crazy intensity, and I think maybe this is her manning up right in front of me.

"Okay," I say.

It's not sitting right with me, this plan. It feels shady, this idea of humiliating him. But Blake's right: it's time Colby got back some of what he dishes out.

Tristan's with the guys now. Garrett puts him in a head-lock, messing up his hair. Tristan laughs and looks at the ground, like anyone's supposed to buy he's having a good time hanging out with his buddies. Free man, my ass.

"Let's go wait out front," Blake says. She touches my arm when I don't follow her lead toward the doors.

"Tristan's so pathetic," I say, pointing at the guys. "Why doesn't he just walk away?"

We all look at the guys, at Tristan in the middle. Just standing there.

"So call him over," Blake says. When I give her my you-don't-understand face, she says, "What? If he's your friend, call him over."

"It would just make things worse. He'd have to choose between me and Colby."

"That won't be a hard choice to make. Anyone can tell he doesn't like Colby," Blake says. "He's one of us. He's probably just been hanging out with them because he's not sure you want him around."

"That's what he was telling you, back in the computer lab. You guys were friends first, before Colby came along," Olivia says. "You got that, right?"

Blake and Olivia watch me while I watch Tristan.

"You guys go ahead," I tell Blake. "I'll catch up."

Blake hooks her finger in mine and says, "Go be righteous, babe."

"What!" I let go of her hand and throw mine up. "I was gonna call you babe. You beat me to it."

"You snooze, you lose," she says.

I watch the two of them wander through the lobby, headed for the doors. Over by the girls' change room, the guys are talking, messing around.

I take a couple steps in their direction. They're still at least twenty-five steps away.

"Tristan," I shout. They all look over, even Tristan. I hitch my chin up. "You coming?"

His mouth spreads into a wide grin. He moves between Garrett and Tim, smoothing the dress shirt over his skinny chest, flinging his bangs into place. Then he turns to the guys, snaps his fingers into guns and, although I can't see his face, I picture him winking at them.

Then he heads my way.

SO NOW IT'S TRISTAN and me, just walking away.

"Okay, so Trent is totally down for tonight," Tristan says, like this is just us running into each other in the hall between classes. "I don't have to bring alcohol, do I?"

"Nah, dude. This is just a very chill affair," I say. "No booze."

The pounding of feet against tile rushes toward us. My body tenses up. I knew it was coming.

"Wait up, girls," Garrett yells, just as Tristan and I are about to reach the doors.

Tristan stops in his tracks. I smack his arm. "Keep walking! Come on, dude, man up."

Blake's watching from the curb. She taps Olivia on the arm, gesturing for her to pay attention. That's when I glance behind me, seeing the guys making their way over. Colby pushes through them. "Get your ass over here, Tristan."

"Uh . . . ," Tristan says, waiting next to me. "You're not gonna decide tomorrow that we're not friends anymore, right? You're not gonna do that again?"

"I didn't—never mind." I take a breath and put a hand up. "Do you want to hang out with those guys or not?"

Tristan shakes his head, then pretends to dust off his shoulders. "All right. All right. Let's get out of here."

So I push through the door, Tristan behind me. Blake and

Olivia crowd around us, and we walk away as a group.

"Pen!" Garrett yells my name a couple times. Then he goes, "Steve! STEVEN OLIVEIRA!"

"Ignore him," Blake says. "He's bound to get distracted by a bright light soon."

Tristan laughs. "Bright light. Legit, that's legit."

"Hey, Steve! Penelope! Just one question!" Garrett says. They've followed us out the door.

"I don't care," I throw over my shoulder. "No one wants to hear your stupid questions."

"Just one!" Garrett says.

Olivia screeches to a stop and whips around. "What! What is your problem?"

We've all stopped and backed up to stand with Olivia on the curb, right around the spot we were the day she lost it on me after missing her bus. Garrett holds his hands up like a shield. The rest of the guys are pounding over, Colby at the front.

"Was it good?" Garrett asks Olivia.

"Was what good?" Olivia asks, and I wish she hadn't.

"When Colby fucked you," Garrett says to her.

I'm ready to lunge for him, but then Colby's shouting from behind him, "Garrett—don't you talk to her."

Garrett makes this big show of acting like he's just realizing some mistake he made. "Oh, wait, sorry. Not you." He turns to me, even points a finger at me, and now that's where everyone's attention is. "I meant you, Pen. Was it good when Colby tapped that? Did it make you feel heterosexually straight? Did you feel like a woman?"

Someone pushes Garrett. He stumbles but recovers quick. I'm like a missile with Colby as a target before I even realize I'm the one who pushed Garrett because he was in the way. The girls are yelling my name. Colby veers right, circling the outside of the library, just jogging his ass away from this mess.

They're laughing at me—I don't know who. The laughter and the shouts are pushing me forward. He's not getting away with this one.

I'm gonna get him.

FORTY-FIVE

OUT BY THE SOCCER FIELD, COLBY STANDS WITH a cigarette between his lips, like he's waiting for me. He was my friend—that's all I can think of while I rush over to him—he was my friend and I have no idea why anymore.

"Why did you do it?" I say. "Huh? Why?"

He lights the smoke and inhales. "Like you weren't gonna tell? I just beat you to it."

I turn to look back to the front of the school where Blake, Olivia, and Tristan are still standing around with Colby's douche friends. Mrs. McCallion is there, and for a second I think it's all over, that she's going to see Colby and me and call this off. But her head never pulls up to gaze at us across the field.

"You told because you thought I was going to? I texted you about a truce. I walked away. I left you alone."

"And you trying to take Tristan—what was that?"

"You don't even like Tristan that much. And me and him were friends years before you came along."

"You think you can just take things when they belong to other people," Colby says. "You needed to be taught a lesson."

"I didn't steal anyone from you," I say, my feet pounding the half-dead grass. "They're people you threw away. You don't even really want them."

"Who says? Who says I didn't want her? She was mine," he says, pointing at me with his cigarette. "Stop talking out of your ass, Pen. And don't act like you weren't holding that crap over me, making your little fag comments and threats. You think you can just mess with me and nothing's gonna happen?"

"You're the one who's messing with me!" Now I'm yelling.

"You're going around acting like you're some tough dyke trying to show me up. You're obsessed with me, trying to be me. You're not me. You'll never be me. Physically impossible. She'll never be into you."

I hold my head up like, *Huh?* "So you lie and tell Garrett you and I did it?" I aim a finger at him. "You're the biggest liar of us all."

There's a twisted grin, a couple drags of his cigarette, and the whole time he stares at me. He knows I hate being stared at. "Are you gonna cry? Because I hate it when girls do that."

"Fine, tell people you got in my pants. If that's how desperate you are, go ahead. I'm just glad Olivia was smart enough to tell you to screw off. She never wanted you around." At that, he flings the cigarette at my feet and takes two steps closer to me, his fist bouncing at his side before he backs up again. His jaw's working like crazy. "That's the worst part of all this, isn't it. You couldn't get me. You couldn't get Blake. You couldn't hang on to Tristan, even. But Olivia—well, you *love* her; I know you do. So what do you do? You mess it all up because you can't stop acting like a total psycho for five minutes."

It's all just falling out of me. I can barely stop to refill my lungs.

"It makes no sense—no fucking sense, Pen. You're nothing," he yells, his fists curling, his whole body going rigid. "You're just . . . nothing—how the hell does it make any sense that everyone likes *you* better?"

There are no more words for a moment—only for a moment.

That's what this is about?

"You don't get to act jealous and blame this all on me!" He thought I'd cave, hearing him say that. He thought I'd back off. "You did this. You go around acting like you're this big moral dude who has this code, except you're just some guy who needs a bunch of—of *peons* worshipping you so you'll feel badass. Nobody likes you because you're not worth liking. That's what we all end up realizing, sooner or later."

And he cracks me one, right in the mouth.

FORTY-SIX

MY JAW FEELS LIKE IT'S SEPARATED FROM MY skull—but it only hurts for a moment, because the next one, I'm throwing myself on him. He collapses to the ground under my weight, and my hands claw at his jacket while I'm spitting in his face. It's all red, streaking across his hair and cheek.

"Get off me!" he yells.

His collar's in my hands now, and I'm pulling him up, slamming his shoulders and head into the grass. He thrashes under me, but I weigh more than he does. I go for his collar again, but he shoves me to the side. He gets up, dusting off his jacket, giving me enough time to scramble to my feet and shove him from behind.

"You're gonna run away now? You pathetic piece of shit," I say.

He lands in the dirt, yelling, "Dude, I swear to god I will fuck you up if you don't get off me!"

"Yeah? Try it, then. Go ahead." I hold my hands out like an invitation. "Get up."

I kick at his feet, sending bits of dirt and grass flying onto him.

"Stop it! Stop it, Pen!" It's Olivia, and it takes me a second to realize she's telling *me* to stop—not him.

"Don't tell me to stop," I yell at her, even though she's, like, two feet away. "You of all people shouldn't be telling me to stop, all right? You should be standing right here with me."

"Your face, Pen—there's blood," she says, reaching for me.

"I don't give a crap if there's blood. He's right there, Olivia." I point at him as he drags himself off the ground. "Tell him off. This is better than some quote on a picture, okay? This is you manning up and telling him to go to hell."

She stands there, looking at the ground in front of him—not at him. "This isn't about me."

"Are you nuts? So much of this is about you—you have no idea. Just tell him," I say, pointing at Colby.

Now Olivia takes a few steps back.

"Olivia's not a psycho bitch like you are, Pen," Colby says.

I body slam him, but he's ready for it, planting his feet on the ground. "Okay, all right!" he yells. "Back off!"

Suddenly, Blake's in front of me. "Pen, you have to stop."

"What's with you people? You were all for this five minutes ago, Blake! I stop when I say I'm done, all right? You guys need to get out of my face. This is between me and him—and I'm not fucking done with him." It doesn't sound like me yelling; it sounds like Johnny when he's so amped up, he doesn't know what's going on anymore.

I don't know what's going on anymore.

"Listen. To. Me." Blake's hands are on my arms. "You need to calm the hell down, right now. You're going to get yourself arrested, Pen. He's not worth that."

"What are you talking about?" I shout.

I whirl around to see the blue and red lights flashing, the police cruiser pulling into the school lot.

My stomach flips, but then it gets worse when I see Johnny charging through the field.

FORTY-SEVEN

"DID I JUST SEE YOU PUNCH MY SISTER, MAN? DID I just see that, Colby?" Johnny yells, his arms out at his sides, his whole back curved like he's about to trigger some overdrive move on Colby.

"It's okay," I tell Johnny, intercepting him before he can reach Colby. I put a hand on his chest. "Relax. Everything's okay. Don't get involved—please, man."

"Let me see," he says, lifting my chin with a finger. His head shakes from side to side the more he stares at my mouth, and that's when it starts to hurt. "It's not good, Pen."

"We were settling our shit," Colby says. "It's her problem if she can't handle it. She's the one going around acting like she's a dude. I warned her." Colby wipes his face with his sleeve. "You were begging me to treat you like a dude, and now that I have, you're gonna pull the girl crap?"

"I never pulled anything!" I yell.

"She can't have it both ways!" Colby yells, and it's desperate. He's looking at Olivia like he thinks she'll be on his side. "She can't!"

Colby's boys are all clustered to the left now, some looking at the ground, Garrett scratching his head.

Tristan goes: "You had it coming, Colby. You thought no one was gonna call you on it. It's a peon uprising, you got that? You've been defeated."

"You're such a moron, Tristan—what language are you speaking right now?" Colby says. "You guys don't get to call me a woman-beater when she's been going around trying to become a dude, so don't even go there." It's like Colby's speaking to everyone and no one now. "She provoked me. This is how guys settle things. This is what she wanted!"

I spit blood into the grass, but more keeps filling up my mouth.

"That's my sister, man. You're lucky I'm not breaking your face right now," Johnny says. "Man, I wanna break your face. Say something. Please."

"She asked for it!" Colby says.

"Just forget it, Johnny. Please!" I say. "It's over now."

"She asked for it so you hit her?" Blake says. "You sound exactly like all the other ass-bags who hit girls—"

"No!" I shout. "It's not about that! You all need to stop making it about that boy/girl crap—it's not about that! Don't say it should've gone differently just because I'm a girl, okay? I don't need to be defended—I can take it."

They're all watching me, like they're waiting for more of an

323

explanation. I can't untangle this stuff, or get rid of the confusion. Guys shouldn't hit girls—that's true. But this is different. We're on the same level now, him and me—and he's right: it's what I asked for. I don't know how to make sense of it with words.

"Listen, man. You might be able to take it, but it doesn't work that way. You gotta be careful. You don't know the kind of messed-up situation you can get into," Johnny says.

"Yeah, I do, Johnny." I face him, trying to let my eyes make it clear how much I know how seriously messed up things can get—that I know exactly what he's thinking about right now.

"And on that note," Mr. Middleton says, putting a hand on my shoulder, "I say we end this right now."

Two cops are marching over, and so is Mrs. McCallion. For some reason I can't stop staring at her high heels spiking into the soft ground with every step. The cops are coming to arrest me, and I can't stop thinking about how it never occurred to me that heels would do that.

FORTY-EIGHT

MRS. McCALLION IS ASKING EVERYONE WHAT IS going on. The cops come over to plant themselves on the edge of the area we're all standing around in. Johnny moves forward, putting himself in front of me so I have to look over his shoulder to see the cops.

"We got a call about a fight going on," one of the officers says—he's short and skinny, but he looks mean as hell. Olivia's staring at the ground, which makes it pretty clear, she's the one who called them.

"It's assault," Tristan says.

Garrett says, "Yeah! Assault with a deadly Pen."

"Are you saying a pen was used as a weapon?" the other cop—a woman with shoulders as square as Johnny's—says, turning to face Garrett. He closes his mouth and shakes his head no. "Well, then I suggest you keep your mouth shut and wipe that look off your face."

For a second, I'm not sure this is even real anymore.

"We need to speak to each of you," the guy officer says. "Now who was involved in the fight?"

"Oh, man," I whisper to Johnny, then I step out from behind him with a hand up. "I was."

The lady cop points at Johnny. "What about you, sir?"

"No," I say. "He just got here. He has nothing to do with this. He was just coming to pick me up from school."

She nods and sweeps the group of us with her gaze. "Who else was involved?"

Colby's standing at the far end by himself, arms crossed. He steps forward.

"All right—you guys want to tell us what's going on here?" the woman officer says.

"We lost our cool," I say, and my words are all muffled because my jaw throbs. It makes my eyes water. It feels like if I move my mouth any more, the thing will unhinge and fall to the ground. With my tongue, I can feel a gash on the inside of my bottom lip.

"You might need to have that looked at," she says. "Were you hit in the head? Did you—"

"No. I'm fine."

"Who hit you?"

Here we go—a girl got hit by a guy—that's all anyone's going to see.

I point at Colby. "He hit me, but I provoked the crap out of him, okay? I don't care that technically I'm a girl and he's a guy. We've been fighting for weeks, and it came to this. I can handle myself."

Blake hands me a wad of tissues. I shove it between my lip and bottom teeth, but the tissue just breaks apart and sticks to the inside of my mouth, so now I'm picking out little bits of bloody tissue.

It'd be nice if I could duck for cover and be healed a couple seconds later, like in *War Zone*—is it weird that I'm thinking this right now?

The cops are speaking with Colby now.

"You should go rinse out your mouth, Pen," Mr. Middleton says. He inspects my face. "That's a lot of blood. You might need stitches."

"It's not that bad. I'm fine."

After the cops get what they need from everyone, Mr. Middleton tells us all to calm down. "Those of you who are not directly involved need to head home now. School is over."

Johnny gives Olivia the keys to go wait in the truck. I can't bring myself to look at her. It's hard to know what she might be thinking, but I yelled at her, and she let Colby off the hook—and she called the cops on us. We're probably both annoyed with each other right now.

Blake comes over to me. She bites her lip and won't look me in the eyes. "I'm sorry—I think I egged you on before and made it worse."

"It was always going to come to this with me and him."

She doesn't look convinced. "Call me as soon as you can, okay?"

"I didn't mean to yell at you. I was just so amped up."

"I know. Just call me later, okay?" She touches my cheek. "And get your face fixed."

Now it's just me, my brother, Colby, and the teachers. Plus, the cops, who do not look impressed by any of this.

"You guys think it's cool, getting into fistfights?" the man officer says to me.

"No," I say.

The cops look annoyed now. "You guys need to grow up. Find other ways to settle your disagreements."

The woman officer says, "Are you guys going to go home to post about your little fight online? Tell your friends how you wasted our time when there are real crimes we could be dealing with?"

"No," Colby and I say at the same time.

"You know, we picked up a guy last year who threw one punch—one punch—and the guy he hit went down," the man officer says. "A blood vessel in his brain popped and he was dead just like that. One punch over a game of pool, and one guy's dead while the other got convicted of manslaughter."

At that, I look over at Johnny, shaking my head. This is the kind of dumb situation he could end up in, always jumping in there to defend everyone. I don't want him to hit some guy in the wrong spot and end up going away for manslaughter. Knowing how to defend yourself is good—I want to know how to fight—but I also want to be able to deal with things before they build until something has to break. Before my brother has to fix it all for me, getting in trouble in the process.

The cops tell Mrs. McCallion that the school will be left in charge of addressing what happened. The mean-looking cop points a finger at me, then Colby. "I really hope I won't have to see you two again. Learn to walk away."

"Mrs. McCallion is going to want to see Pen and Colby in her office," Mr. Middleton says to Johnny. Then to me and Colby: "Your parents will be called."

"THERE'S ZERO TOLERANCE FOR fighting," Mrs. McCallion says. "This is an automatic ten-day suspension."

"But school is over," I say.

"Doesn't matter, Pen," Mr. Middleton says.

I'm not even surprised. Mrs. McCallion hands out three-day suspensions just for uniform violations.

"Just deal with it, Pen," Johnny says, patting my shoulder. "You did something, and now you gotta accept what comes at you because of it. I'll go drive Olivia home."

I nod, hanging my head forward as Colby and I follow Mr. Middleton back to school, while Johnny heads back to Olivia. When Mr. Middleton isn't looking, Johnny makes a *V* with his fingers, pointing to his own eyes, then pointing at Colby to let him know he's going to be watching. Mrs. McCallion keeps saying she's so disappointed in us. "And less than two weeks from our twenty-fifth anniversary! Never, in all my years . . ."

After I rinse my mouth a few times with icy water, Colby and I sit in the office waiting area, on opposite sides of the room, not looking at each other. The secretary brings me an ice pack for my jaw and a wet cloth for Colby's blood-streaked face. Fifteen minutes later, Mrs. McCallion tells us Colby's dad is on his way, and so are my parents. I already know Colby's dad won't have anything to say about this. He'll let him stay home, play video games, and get drunk for two weeks. Colby'll get off with nothing. I'm the one who's about to get my butt kicked, Portuguese-mom style.

MRS. McCALLION COMES TO get Colby because his dad gets here first. When he sees me, Mr. Jensen shakes his head at me like he doesn't know what happened, but he's disappointed. I keep my face blank.

Colby and his dad are in there a good fifteen minutes, while I wait for my own parents with nothing to do but scroll through my phone.

People have written a couple things about what went down on Facebook. Mostly that Colby punched a girl. A couple girls wrote that my brother's hot. Garrett posted a picture of Colby's blood- and dirt-crusted face.

My mouth finally stopped bleeding, but my jaw feels heavy as it throbs to the beat of my heart.

Colby comes out first, his face set in anger. He and his dad sweep past me without saying a word. Mrs. McCallion calls me over with that same pissy little finger curl my dad does. She doesn't sit at her desk, but heads for this round table by the large window off to the side. As soon as I take a seat there, the door opens and my mom walks in, followed by Johnny—who must've come back here right after taking Olivia home.

I stare at my feet because Mom's eyebrows look like they might unstick from her face and come whack me in the head. She's alone, so I guess Johnny went to pick her up. That or she had to take a cab over, which she hates doing. She takes a seat at the table, across from me. Johnny goes to stand by a bookshelf, off to the side. He gives me a look that says, *Take it and deal with it.*

Mrs. McCallion places that notebook she always has with her down on the table. "This is pretty disappointing, I have to say. I'm sure the officers made it clear that the way you and Colby chose to handle your problems was not okay."

"I didn't have much of a choice—"

Mrs. McCallion holds a hand up. I glance at my mom, at her eyes narrowed and lips pressed thin. Johnny stares at the principal like he doesn't trust her.

"You've changed quite a bit in the last couple of months, haven't you, Penelope," she says.

"Yeah," I say. "I guess so."

"Maybe this is a good opportunity for you to reflect on the changes you've made. Is this how you want to spend the rest of your time here at St. Peter's? Think about that," Mrs. McCallion says. She doesn't seem to want an actual answer. "So that's a ten-day suspension. And I'm seriously considering not allowing you to attend the school anniversary celebration."

"But, I'm on Team Three," I say. "We worked hard on our project. It's all ready to go."

Johnny has no expression, but his temples bulge.

"Penelope, the rules are clear and if you won't live by them, then it's my duty to provide you with consequences." She gives me this stern glare.

"Fine," I say.

"You know we value student diversity here at St. Peter's, but this is still a Catholic school. I can see that you're going through something—" She points at my head. "We've allowed you your freedom to express yourself, but you have to understand, Penelope. It's our responsibility to preserve the values we promote at this school. We have to respect the other students and their families."

"Wait—what?" I ask. When I search Johnny's face, all I get is a massive sigh from him, like he expected this.

"I get it, you know. Girls don't always need to be proper young ladies—that's not what I'm saying here," Mrs. McCallion says. "Why not think about channeling some of this aggression into sports? Have you thought about trying out for our ringette team?"

Ringette is girl hockey. Sliding a rubber ring around using a stick, with no body contact allowed.

"Ringette—Ma, come on," Johnny says. But Mom does nothing.

"Wow," I say. "Girl hockey. Yeah, totally. I never thought of that."

"Let's not get immature about this," Mrs. McCallion says.

"Ma—you gonna let this happen again?" Johnny says.

"You shut up you mouth, João!" Mom says, holding a finger up at him. To me, she says, "This *you* fault. I tell you no act like the punk druggy. I tell you be nice girl or bad things happen. Now look! *Mãe* is right, you wrong. *Mãe* right before, *Mãe* right again."

"Before," I say, but that's all that will come out. This isn't the place to get into it, with the principal staring at me.

"You," Mom says to Johnny. She says she's had it with him interfering and leading me down this dark path or something.

"All right, now. I can appreciate that you all have things to settle outside of this," the principal says. She explains to my mom that suspension isn't a vacation, that I'm responsible for keeping up with my schoolwork by accessing it through the school website. "And Penelope? I'm sorry, but after the way our talk has gone, I think it would be best if you didn't attend the school anniversary."

"If I wear the skirt, and if I join ringette, can I come to the school anniversary?" I say, totally not able to take the edge out of my tone.

Johnny covers his face with his hand. Mom obviously didn't realize what I said was snarky and rude, but Mrs. McCallion stares me down with her sour smile. "Like I said, Penelope, you might want to reflect—"

The door whips open.

"Duarte?" my mom says.

My dad points a finger at the principal. "You kick my daughter outside?"

Mrs. McCallion shakes her head like, *Oh dear.* "Mr. Oliveira, please. Let's have a seat and discuss this—"

"No, no. You listen to *me.* I come to this country to give my *crianças* the good life. I work in the factory—you know the factory?" he says, still standing by the door in his heavy jacket. Sweat beads on his forehead, right under his gray hairline. "You no throw out the good girl because she look like the tough girl and play with boys. I go to church. I have *respeito.* You no tell my good girl she's a bad girl. Colby, he's a bad boy. He got no *respeito.* He throw eggs at my house!"

"Mr. Oliveira, the rules are clear. Both Penelope and Colby are suspended." Mrs. McCallion holds a hand out, like she wants my dad to sit. "Why don't I explain it in simpler terms for you?"

Oh, wrong thing to say. Johnny and I both hold a hand up to palm our foreheads.

"You think I need the big English words? I understand. My son tell me on the telephone. I no stupid Portuguese man. You think I'm stupid man, huh?" he says, and the principal closes her eyes. To Mom, Dad says, "Ana, *vamos.*"

Mom and I rise and follow Dad out the door, Johnny behind us. He heads for his truck, while I stay with my parents. There's only silence, but I keep glancing at Dad, wondering if he finally gets it.

FORTY-NINE

WHEN WE GET HOME, MY MOM THROWS HER hands up and goes right for the Virgin Mary, praying for the strength to not smack her kids over the head with a frying pan. We all end up in the hallway, standing around where we won't be too close to each other.

Everything unfolds in Portuguese, because my parents are doing all the talking.

Mom says this is over as of right now.

Dad says this is bringing shame on the family.

Johnny laughs, and I bet it's because Dad's acting like we're some Portuguese Mafia family whose reputation actually matters.

Mom goes on about Johnny needing to back off and live his own life. Each time she's listened to his advice, he turned out to be wrong. She says letting me do my own thing only leads to my doing stupid things.

I say nothing.

At this point, Mom disappears and then comes back with a bag of ice wrapped in a dish towel that she hands to me. I put it against my chin.

Dad carries on, saying it's not just one person's fault that this happened; it's everyone's fault.

Mom jumps back in, saying it's not her fault. She did her best but I won't listen. I mocked her by putting on her clothes to deliberately look stupid.

Johnny wants to know why everyone is talking about clothes. Who cares about clothes. They should be talking about the real stuff.

Dad tells Johnny to shut up.

I say nothing.

Mom says clothes matter because that's what people see. I must think this is all a big punk druggy joke. Girls can't decide they're not girls anymore.

I laugh because that's the funniest thing: I never decided I wasn't a girl anymore. That was everyone else assuming.

"What? Why you laugh, huh?" Mom asks.

"Nothing," I say.

Mom says I should've learned my lesson by now.

Dad tells me I shouldn't be laughing right now; my parents can't take the stress.

Mom looks up, asking the ceiling why I couldn't just be going around smoking cigarettes and sneaking boys up to my room like a normal girl.

I say nothing.

Johnny asks my parents what decade they're from.

Dad states the year he was born and asks what that has to do with anything.

Mom says Johnny needs to shut up right now.

Now Dad is the one whining at the ceiling, going off about

335

how getting dragged to school to deal with this shameful business is not acceptable. Getting suspended from school is not acceptable.

Mom puts her hands out in front of her while her face hardens. Then she says there are new rules for me to obey: No more job. No more boy clothes. No more girls over at the house. No more boys over at the house. No more short hair.

"Not gonna happen," Johnny says. "Nah, man."

Dad tells Johnny to shut up.

"Give me the key," I tell Mom.

Mom throws Johnny a pissy glare and turns her nose up at me. I take a couple steps left, getting closer to Johnny. Dad furrows his brow like he has no idea what's going on.

"Where's my key, Ma?" I wince with each word. My jaw feels huge. "You stole it, right?"

Now her evil look is on Johnny.

"Forget it, Pen," he says. "I can get another key."

"Duarte!" Mom says, stomping her foot like a kid.

"João, you get outta here," Dad says. "You stay at you house now." He says it would be better if Johnny stays away until we figure out how to get back on track.

Dad goes to walk away, back to the living room.

"Nah," Johnny says, stopping Dad in his tracks. "Not gonna happen. I'm taking Pen with me. You tried it your way again, and it's all messed up."

I look over at him, trying to see in his face, but he's having a stare-off with Dad.

"What you say to me?" Dad's puffing out his chest. In

Portuguese, he asks if Johnny just dared threaten to kidnap his daughter again.

"Pen, go downstairs," Johnny says.

"No way," I say.

"I'm not kidding around," Johnny says. "Go."

"You just said you were taking me with—"

"Go!" he yells, startling the crap out of me, making my eyes sting.

I stomp over to the basement door, slamming it closed behind me. But I park my butt at the top, bashing my feet against the stair to make it seem like I'm going down. I hold my chin with one hand, and the skin there is hot and swollen.

"Where is the *respeito*?" Dad says. Every word is clear, because they're right on the other side of the door. Why bother sending me away? They know we can hear everything through the walls in this house. Dad continues, "I never hear this from nobody in my life! No one talk to me like you talk to me, João. Nobody!"

"I can take it, the way you guys are," Johnny says. "In one ear, out the other. But I told you to let the kid breathe."

Back to Portuguese. Dad says the way they raise their kid is none of Johnny's business.

Johnny says this family likes to forget the important stuff. "I don't. I forget nothing."

"Stop talking," Mom says. *"Cala a boca."*

Then things quiet down. They've moved back to the living room, and they're muttering in Portuguese. I open the door a crack, just in time to hear my dad go, *"Respeito,* João."

337

That word. That goddamn word.

"What does that word even mean? What is *respeito*?" I yell from the hallway, cutting through their whispers. When I get to the living room, Mom's holding a picture of me at five years old—this picture of me wearing the one dress I liked, because it was Ninja-Turtle green.

The three of them stare at me.

I aim my words at Dad. "Everything you said at school about me—you didn't mean any of it. You just didn't want to look bad in front of strangers."

He holds his hands out like he's some helpless old man.

"This isn't respect. None of this is respect," I shout in a way I've never shouted at my parents before. No one interrupts me. "It's all just a bunch of rules. As long as I clean my room, and say *Pai bença* and *Mãe bença*, and wear the clothes you like, and don't embarrass you in front of other people, then you get your *respeito* and who cares what's really going on, right? Who cares how Johnny and me feel, right?"

Nothing. Dad sits in his recliner and covers his ears like I'm assaulting his hearing. Mom's frozen holding that picture of me.

"I have respect, okay? I have a butt-load of respect." I point at Johnny next to me. "For him." When I turn to Johnny, I wish I hadn't. His eyes are watery. Everything in me dissolves. "And you made him go away. You made him leave on purpose so I'd be by myself."

Oh, man—my voice is shaking.

"That's so mean," I say in the most pathetic voice ever.

My eyes get blurry. Johnny's hand lands on my shoulder, and now it's over. I'm leaking tears.

"I don't like you guys. I keep trying, but you make it impossible." Why is my voice so high-pitched when I cry? I rub at my leaky nose. "I can't respect people I don't like—people who don't like *me*. When everyone was picking on me at school when I was little, it was Johnny who came with his buddies to check on me. Johnny bought me my Turtles. Johnny took me to the movies. Johnny gave me his clothes. Johnny let me play hockey outside with him. Johnny cut my hair. Johnny—"

Now I have the hiccups.

"I didn't have to ask him for that stuff. He just did it," I say. "That's *respeito*."

"All right, man," Johnny says. He swipes at a lower lid—because he doesn't have to make a girly mess of this crying thing. "Chin up, take a breath."

Mom storms out of the living room. It goes quiet, and then Dad gets up to follow her. Then it's just me and Johnny standing in the middle of the room. But I'm not done.

I'm not done yet.

From the kitchen doorway, I tell my parents what I've wanted to tell them since I was eight years old.

"Remember grade two? Remember when Victor and his friends trapped me in the change rooms and wouldn't let me leave? Remember that?" My head hates dragging that memory back up to the surface. It's full of those messed-up feelings— the kind of feelings that I was full of that night with Colby. "We all remember it. Those kids wanted to know if I was a boy or a

339

girl. They wouldn't let me leave until I proved what I was."

"Pen," Johnny says. There's an edge to his voice. I know he thought I'd blocked out that day, or just let it fade until it wasn't real anymore. I know that's what he thinks about every time something messed up happens to me, every time someone gives me a look, or laughs at me.

"Do you know what those kids wanted me to do?" I say. Every word tastes like puke on my tongue.

"Pen, come on," Johnny says. "Let's go outside, all right?"

"No—I have stuff to tell them. I have—"

"I can't listen to this! I don't wanna hear about this again." Johnny's voice is a loud rumble, and for a second I think he's going to punch the wall. But just like that he lets the tension out. "Come on. Let's just go, all right?"

Mom's got that look in her eyes again—she's not defeated yet. "When you small one, the stupid *crianças* they no understand why you look like that, why you be like that, okay? They don't understand. They stupid *crianças*, okay? That's why you stop making hard! If you stop making hard, people stop doing bad things to you. Look—it happen again today!"

I run my hand against the back of my head, letting the prickly feeling of my buzzed hair numb my fingers. "You're blaming me again, Ma! I didn't do anything to Victor. He almost made me pull my pants down in front of his friends." If the teacher hadn't walked into the change rooms that day . . .

"Do you remember what you said?"

Mom's crying now.

"You said I should've tried harder to be a good girl."

She's swaying like her legs won't be able to hold her up. Dad rubs her back and shakes his head.

"Stop crying, Ma! I have everything to say." I'm done holding on to this stuff just so I won't make her feel bad. She makes me feel bad all the time, and she doesn't seem bothered by it. She's more than twice my age—she should know better. "Victor wouldn't leave me alone after that. He kept following me home and yelling stuff at me, calling me a boy-girl. You didn't listen. *He* listened." I point to Johnny again. "He fixed it. And what did you do? You kicked him out for it!

"You making Johnny go away—how could you do that? And you did it twice," I tell Mom. "That's the meanest thing you could ever do to me. *O pai ea mãe sabe que*—you knew he was the only one who had my back. That's my brother, *and* my parent, *and* my friend—you must really hate who I am to do that to me. For real, man."

I'm not going to cry again. Chin up, take a breath.

Dad's face—it's like he wants to be sorry for it all but he's not allowed to. He just rubs Mom's back faster, while she buries her face into Dad's chest.

"You *irmão* he go there and tell everybody he fight—" Dad starts over in Portuguese, saying Johnny made us look like savages, showing up at school with his bandanna, threatening little kids, following them after school, getting the police called to our house. "And now he do it again! It's no good."

"What you want, huh?" Mom says, sniffling. "Why you do this to me? Everyone laugh at me since you small one. They laugh at me, *Oh look at the little boy Penelope*. My *mãe* was a bad

bad lady. She no like me, no buy me nice dresses, always say *Ana not a pretty girl*. When you came, I tell everyone this is my little *princesa*. I gonna have the pretty *princesa*. But you no like nothing I do. You no like me." She hugs the framed picture to her chest, like the kid in that picture is dead. "What you want? What you want?"

"Nothing," I say. My hands aren't shaking anymore. It's like I could go to sleep right now, and I'd probably sleep for a day. "I don't want anything. I'm just telling you all this because that way you'll understand why I'm leaving."

Just like that, Johnny and I are outside, hopping into the truck, and taking off.

FIFTY

BEING SUSPENDED IS ONE OF THOSE THINGS that's good and bad at the same time. I don't want to leave my friends alone at school, not knowing what Colby's friends could be doing to mess with them—but I'm also kind of glad to not be there.

I thought it would be weird suddenly being at Johnny's apartment, but it just feels like his place, normal.

On Monday, Johnny gets home from work and collapses face-first into the couch. I'm scrubbing the crap out of the stove top because I let the water boil over when I made Kraft Dinner and it turned crusty brown everywhere. Finally, Johnny says, "I'm starving."

"I made two boxes of KD," I say.

"Again? I'm a carnivore, man. Can you make us steaks or something?"

"Yeah, right," I say. "But I cut up hot dogs into the macaroni this time."

"All right." He sits up. "Hey—did you know they don't call it KD in the States?"

"They don't have Kraft Dinner in the US?"

"Well, yeah, they do. But they call it macaroni and cheese," he says.

"That's the most original name ever."

"Well, if you think about it—what the hell is a Kraft Dinner? Dinner is supposed to mean mac and cheese in a box?"

I nod like, *Totally.* "How'd you hear about that?"

"Dom found this list of foods that are different between Canada and the US. I'll send it to you. It's weird as hell," he says.

"Totally send that to me. I wanna show Blake."

He pulls out his phone. "So what are you doing tonight?"

"Well, after this, we're hitting the weights. I think I'm ready to start with the ten-pounds. Five-pound weights are sort of pathetic," I say.

"You gotta start at the beginning. But pretty soon you'll be lifting forty like I do."

I hand him a big bowl of KD/macaroni and cheese and take a seat in my usual spot on the couch with my own bowl. "Me and Tristan are playing *Crypts* later, too."

"How about we skip the weights tonight? We got some place to go," he says, chewing with his mouth open. "*Pai* says it's okay for you to go pick up some of your stuff."

"Maybe next week."

"You know that crap Ma said to you . . . ," he says, sighing like he's not sure how to finish the sentence.

"Don't worry about it. It's not like I care."

"It's bull, all that *princesa* stuff."

"Yeah," I say, twirling the fork in my bowl. "Was *Avó* Fernanda that bad?"

"That's what Ma's always said," Johnny says. Neither of us met our mom's mother. She died a long time ago. "Who knows. Apparently she was a bitter old lady. They wanted to bring her over from Portugal—bought her round-trip flights a couple times—and she didn't wanna visit. But bitter old lady or not, it doesn't mean our own mom has an excuse to turn into the same thing."

"Yeah."

Still—I can't help but wonder what kind of mother my mom would've been, had she ended up with a *princesa* for a daughter.

"All right, well, if you won't go to the house," Johnny says, "we're gonna have to hit the dollar store, because my body wash is expensive and you're wasting it all."

"Fine."

"You talk to Olivia yet?"

I shake my head, pulling my phone out to check for missed texts. Not that I've texted her yet either.

ON WEDNESDAY, FIVE DAYS after that crazy showdown at school, I get a notification that my cell phone account's been suspended. Johnny calls the company to get it reactivated under his name, getting me a new number in the process. He makes me sign a made-up contract that says I'll pay the bill every month myself. "Not a day late or I'm throwing the phone into the toilet."

"I think that's a pretty fair deal."

I talk to Blake a couple times a day. She fills me in on what people are saying about me at school. Some are saying I punched Colby, which they seem to think makes me badass. Others are saying I backed Colby in a corner, trapping him into punching me and getting in trouble for it, that this is the kind of things girls do to get guys in trouble, because girls have too much power these days. Some are saying I should just never come back to St. Peter's because I should be at a public school anyway, since Catholic schools are for religious people, and I'm not allowed to be religious when I'm so queer.

"Now don't let this go to your head," Blake says. "But there are these three grade-nine girls who have been writing 'Team Pen' on their hands with black marker."

"What! No way."

"Totally," she says. "My girlfriend is a badass stud with a fan club."

I laugh. It sort of *does* make me feel a little badass that these girls think of me that way, even if they're little grade-nine kids.

"Have you called Olivia yet?" Blake asks.

"Almost."

"Do it. This is getting old," Blake says.

"She called the cops on me. I could've gotten arrested."

There's silence on the other end, then a sigh. "I called."

"What—why?"

"Because," she says. "I thought it might've gone to hell."

"You thought I was going to get my ass kicked?"

"I thought you might've broken his neck. You looked a tad psychotic when you went after him," she says. Before I can respond, she goes, "So no more excuses. Call Olivia."

"It's not like she called me, either!"

"Yeah, except you're the one who has a new number now, so she can't even call you if she wanted to."

"Oh. Right," I say. "Is she still planning on using Colby's picture?"

"I don't know. I tried asking her about it but she brushed me off, saying she was still thinking about everything."

"What do *you* think she should do?" I still haven't sent her the photo, and now I'm wondering if I'd be dumb to do so.

"I'm not sure anymore," Blake says. "She told me a bit about what happened between them." My heart jolts while I wait to find out if Olivia told Blake about the abortion. "He sounds like a manipulative stalker—basically the worst boyfriend ever. I'm sure there's a lot more to it, because that's nothing to be all secretive about."

"Blake . . ."

"I'm not trying to guilt you into telling me," she says, and it

346

sounds legit. "If Olivia wants to tell me someday, then she will. I just know that he must've done something awful—and if it's that awful, then he probably deserves that photo revenge. It's probably a way milder revenge than he deserves."

"Yeah. It would be." Now I'm the one sighing. "I can't believe you called the cops on me."

"Believe it, and now get over it."

After my phone call with Blake, I think about all the video games I could be playing right now. It feels like I've been separated from the Xbox for so long, and now that *Rusted*'s out—I bought it with my own money, and my twenty-percent employee discount—there's a lot of gaming I could do.

But I shove my phone and wallet into my coat pockets and head for the bus stop instead.

I HOPED HER MOM would be gone once I showed up, but I can see her moving through the kitchen from where I stand on the sidewalk. She answers my knock on the side door, and gives me a thin smile.

"Hi. Could I speak with Olivia?" I ask.

It's freezing out, but still, part of me is thinking she won't invite me in. But she pulls the door open and tells me to come inside.

"Olivia," she shouts up the stairs. "Your friend is here."

When Olivia appears, she smiles at me but her face is full of awkwardness. After a stiff hello, she waves for me to follow her to the basement.

"When I get back with the groceries, I expect you to meet

me at the door to carry things in," Olivia's mom says when we're halfway down. "And no going up to your room."

She heads back upstairs while Olivia does this silent laugh.

"What?" I ask.

"She's acting like you're a boy," she whispers, "and I'm not allowed boys in my room."

"Wow. Guess I should be glad Blake's parents aren't like that."

Downstairs, we take the same seats we had last time I was here. Olivia looks around the room like she's never been here before.

"Okay, I guess it's up to me to start," I say, and she focuses on me now. "I didn't mean to freak out on you that day."

She says nothing.

"I just wanted you to finally tell him off, you know? It was your chance."

"It was *your* chance," she says. "I didn't want to scream at him."

"But you want to put up an embarrassing picture of him for the whole school and the mayor to see?"

"Maybe." She shrugs. "Blake thinks I should quote his photo with *I'm a psycho stalker who treats girls like crap because my perfect face makes up for it.*"

"Is that what you want to say to him?"

"I don't know what I want to say to him."

In my mind, Colby's photo is up for the town to see, Blake's quote plastered all over it. If he's not there to see it, then he finds out about it online. And it's me who gets retaliated on. Because I'm not going to sit by and watch Olivia get in trouble again.

348

Johnny pops into my head—Johnny sticking up for me and getting in trouble all the time—and I think maybe I get it now. Loyalty.

"Okay," I tell her. "If you need to do this, then I'm in. I'll send you the photo. You do what you have to with it."

She smiles, clasping her hands together against her chest.

"But, Olivia," I say. "I won't be there that night—you know that, right? I'm not allowed to be on school property."

"I know."

"Blake will be there, though. She'll have your back."

"You know—I haven't spoken to my Toronto friends in weeks. I was best friends with these two girls, but ever since I met you guys . . ." Olivia tucks her hair behind her ears and places her hands on her knees. "Living with my mom is not so good, but when my dad comes back, I don't think I'll be moving back in with him."

"Castlehill is a pretty cool place, actually. I don't know why I'd spend so much time talking crap about it and going off about Toronto being so great," I say. "People get murdered all the time in Toronto."

"It is *not* that bad."

"It's pretty bad." I do this exaggerated shrug. "In my opinion, I think staying here would be safer for you."

We smile at each other, and soon it starts to feel a little too cheesy, so I clear my throat and put my regular chill face on.

"I'm so glad we're all okay now," Olivia says. "Because I have been so worried about what happened to you after the fight. Your face looks better. Blake says you live with your

349

brother now. I'm so glad for you. You must be so happy."

She gets it. She's the only person who hasn't frowned and acted all sad about my not living at home anymore. She gets that home doesn't always have to mean the place where your parents are at.

So I fill her in on what's been going on, and I even show her my tiny pipes.

"Um, Pen—there's nothing there. It's squishy," she says.

"What are you talking about? It's firm," I say. "I've only been lifting weights a couple days. Give me time."

When her mom comes home with the groceries, I help bring a couple bags up and then I take off. On the bus ride home, I think about Colby's picture and how now I better find a way to be at that anniversary celebration, just in case anything were to go down.

FIFTY-ONE

A WEEK LATER, ON THE THURSDAY OF THE ST. Peter's anniversary, Blake calls at lunch.

"So, what time are you guys going to the celebration tonight?" I ask.

"It starts at seven. My dad's driving me there at six because Olivia wants to be there super early to make sure everything goes smoothly," she says. "But I don't want to go without you."

"You have to," I say.

"Has Olivia told you what she's up to?"

"No," I say. "And that's why you have to make sure to be there."

Olivia can't be alone for that. I'll be there, but I'll be hiding outside, keeping an eye out for trouble. I doubt Colby and Garrett will show up tonight—this so isn't their scene—but guaranteed that crap will end up online so fast.

"I know, I know. I wouldn't miss this for anything," Blake says. "Plus, my parents are coming to see our work."

"I'm going to need you to describe the look on everyone's faces when they see the photos. Especially Mr. Middleton."

"I will," she says. "We're still on for tomorrow night?"

"For sure. You're coming over, we're making tacos, then we're playing video games. And Johnny's going out, so . . . you know."

There's a knock at the door, which is weird. Johnny's at work, and I haven't had to answer the door here yet. I tell Blake I'll text her in a bit. The knock comes again, so I go answer it.

My mom's in her going-out clothes, and her cheeks and nose are red the way they usually are when she's out in the cold for more than two minutes. My dad's not with her. She's holding one of my old backpacks.

"I talk to school lady today," she says.

"Oh."

"The lady said you can go to party-time at school today. The lady tell me Mr. Middle say good things, so you go and say thank you to the man."

351

"Really? I can go tonight?"

Mom nods while she stands there in the hallway, the bulky bag held tight against her waist. Relief washes over me, knowing I'll be right there for Olivia's photo revenge.

"You like the girls?" Mom asks, and as if she thinks I might not have understood what she meant, she goes, "You kiss the girls? That's okay. That's okay. You don't need the boy clothes. You don't need cut you beautiful hair. You can kiss the girl and be a nice girl. It's okay."

"That's not why I'm not a *princesa*," I tell her. "It's not about that. They don't go together." I liked boy stuff before I knew I was into girls, so I don't think one caused the other. I'm pretty sure that's not how it works. "I'm the way I am because that's how I am. That's it."

"It's okay if you want to be . . . *lésbica*," she says. *"Seu prima é uma."*

"You're not listening, Ma. I dress like this because I like it. It's how I'm supposed to look, even if I'm not kissing anybody," I say, but then it's like my brain's only now processing the last thing she said. "Wait—which cousin is a lesbian? Melissa?"

She shrugs like that wasn't the point, but I so know it's gotta be Melissa. She's thirty and she lives with a girl she calls her "roommate." I barely know her because she's from my mom's side, and a lot of that side's still in Portugal.

I take a few steps back so Mom can step forward and take this whole scene out of the hallway where the neighbors can hear. She makes it as far as the welcome mat, and the door closes behind her.

"I try my best, Penelope," Mom says. "When you small one, small baby, you always want you *irmão*. Always *Johnny this, Johnny that*."

"He's a good guy," I say. "He's the best guy."

She sighs, and it takes her a moment to finally nod along, like she's not totally sure she wants to agree with me.

"You can tell people you kicked me out," I say. Eventually my parents will have to explain to the rest of the family that Johnny and I are gone; them having kicked their bad kids out to teach them a lesson is going to come off a whole lot better than admitting both of your kids decided to walk out.

We look at each other for a minute. She hands me the bag before nodding and turning around to open the door. In the bag are some pants, some shirts, a pair of skater shoes, my cologne, and other products. Lots of underwear and socks. I think that maybe, if she came here with this bag, she must've expected to be leaving it with me and going home empty-handed.

I'm full of bad feelings.

Not because I feel guilty, or because I regret what I've done, though. It's like I keep telling Olivia when she thinks about the abortion: it's okay to feel bad about how things went down, but it's not okay to drown in guilt and regret every day for having made decisions other people don't agree with. At some point, we all have to man up and decide to do what we have to do, despite the people around us who try to get in the way.

THE LECTURE HALL HAS been completely pimped out for this twenty-fifth-anniversary thing: streamers, big

353

confetti-looking things hanging from the ceiling, and fancy lighting that makes this place look nothing like St. Peter's. The only people in the hall this early are teachers and the other photo reps working on their displays. There are four stations set up in different areas of the hall, one for each grade. I look around, waiting for my group to arrive. I sort of didn't tell them I was coming, just in case my mom misunderstood and I end up getting kicked out by a teacher. I spot Mr. Middleton fiddling with an extension cord, so I make my way over.

"I'm glad to see you, Pen," he says, giving me this knowing smile.

"Yeah, thanks for whatever you said. I didn't really want to miss tonight."

"No problem. And you're looking very sharp this evening."

"You too, sir."

"That looks painful," he says, pointing to my chin.

"It is. Been taking a lot of Tylenol."

"Better get to work. Good luck tonight," he says.

My phone vibrates against my butt so I drift away. It's a text from Blake telling me to get over to the grade-twelve hallway bathrooms. Guess she must've spotted me. I cut through the back exit and head over.

She jumps me when I push the door open.

"You did not tell me you were coming! What's wrong with you?" she says.

We eat each other's faces until I whine in pain.

"Can you maybe try to stay toward the right side of my mouth?" I say, and she palms my chin. "And do you think you could maybe lend me some of that skin-colored stuff? Do you think it would hide the red?"

"You're going to let me put makeup on you?" she says, wagging her eyebrows.

"Only to cover this up."

I give her a once-over: She's wearing these tight black pants that really look like another layer of shiny skin, and her shirt is super flowy and silky and goes all the way down past her butt. And her shoes—

"Babe, your heels are seriously hot."

"These are pumps." She extends her foot to show me the side. "Rockabilly-style, platform Mary Jane pumps encrusted with rhinestones."

"I don't even know what that means," I say. "Your parents buy you this stuff?"

She laughs. "As if. My parents think I dress like a freak. I buy my own clothes, or else I'd be stuck wearing . . ."

"Wearing what?"

"What Olivia's wearing." She clenches her teeth in a wince. "Not that there's anything wrong with it. It's just so not me."

"Yeah, I totally feel you," I say.

"So? How are you here tonight? What happened?"

I tell her about my mom working tonight out with the school, and Mr. Middleton having something to do with it. Blake thinks my mom's all of a sudden chilled out, and I let her think that.

"No more talking." I hook my finger in hers and lead her to the accessible stall, which I lock. She doesn't even try to stop me when I pull her shirt off, so I don't stop her when she slides her hands under the back of mine.

"Let's ditch tonight," I whisper. "Let's go somewhere."

"Don't be a horny jerk. Tonight is important," she says, but then she undoes my belt, so I slide her tight pants down a couple inches. "We have about ten minutes until we absolutely have to get to the lecture hall. Olivia will be freaking out if she's by herself."

I pull away with a thought. "You know this isn't all I like doing with you, right?"

"Huh?"

"I mean, I don't want you to think all I'm into is this stuff. I want to do everything with you. I think you're smart, and so fun, and—" She covers my mouth, but I manage to push out the word "gaming."

"Me too, Pen, but," she says, "this stuff is really good, and we only have ten minutes and I'm not even wearing a shirt right now so—"

"Oh totally. I'm shutting up now."

This is so wrong, because there's a toilet right next to us, but damn.

THE COVER-UP IS A tad orange for my skin tone, but it's better than blotchy red. We head for our station. Olivia tries to get all girly-excited when she sees me, as though she thinks I'll start hopping in place and clapping my hands right along with her. Instead, I try to fist-bump her, which makes Blake laugh.

"We have work to do, Team Three," Olivia says.

"So?" Blake says to Olivia, totally the opposite of subtle. "Anything . . . *unexpected* we should be, you know, expecting?"

"No," Olivia says. "Nothing you need to be concerned with."

Now Blake and I are staring at each other wide-eyed, but Olivia turns her back to us.

We've uploaded our pics onto Mr. Middleton's main flash drive, and the slide show will play on a loop on the TV-sized monitor at each station. We also have a portfolio with our series of photos printed out. Blake made a sign with the description of the concept for our photo diary, and a shorter version of it shows up at the start of our slide show. When I glance around the hall at the other stations, it's pretty obvious ours is the best. Lots of pics are cool, but ours say something with each shot. It really does win everything.

As soon as we're done double-checking that everything works fine, Olivia starts obsessing. "But what if the slide show glitches? Or what if someone steals the portfolio!" she says, keeping a hand on the album. "It's so good that you're here, Pen. We can take shifts to guard this with our lives. I'll go first."

Blake pulls out her phone and holds it up to take a picture of her. Olivia makes a face and puts her hands on her hips. "I'm putting this little maniac on Instagram," Blake says.

With less than ten minutes until everything officially begins, the place is getting packed. There's a registration table manned by a group of grade-nine kids who tick people off the list and hand out name tags. One of them must be "Team Pen" because she can't look at me without blushing, and she giggles. I wink at her, just for fun.

There are slide shows projected on the wall with all kinds of photos from the last twenty-five years at St. Peter's. I linger there for a bit because it seems like the students from years ago look way older than we do. And they have really weird hairstyles. I keep hoping to see some pics of Johnny come up, but the most I get is a shot of Dom in the background. Blake pulls me along through the crowd, which is made up of a lot of people from school, but also a lot of older people I don't recognize, because anyone who ever attended St. Peter's was invited tonight. Everyone's so dressed up, which makes me glad I went for black cargo pants, my school shoes, and a black skater polo shirt with a designer zip skater hoodie. This is me, as cleaned up as I get.

Thirty minutes into the event, the principal hasn't even looked at me. That's good. Then finally, Johnny walks in with Dom.

"Hey, dude," Tristan says from behind me.

"Hey," I say. Trent is next to him, so I give him a nod. "What are you doing here?"

Tristan laughs. "Well, duh. We came to see your project."

"Really?" I snap fingers with him.

"Pen's the one who introduced me to Masters of Crimson," Tristan says to Trent, who then nods all impressed. When I flash Tristan a confused expression, he smacks my arm. "You're the one who got me the first book in the series for my ninth birthday—you don't remember?"

"Not even a little bit." I try for a look of apology. "Johnny probably picked it out. I never know what to get people for their birthdays," I say. "Anyway, you guys should come stand by our booth."

"Cool," Tristan says.

I lead them through the crowd. When we get there, I lean my head close so only Tristan can hear. "Have you seen Colby here tonight?"

"Nah. They're not coming to this. They're in Toronto to meet some girls or something."

"All right, cool."

There's a silent auction going on along one of the walls, and there's a raffle for prizes. Each time Mr. Middleton goes to pick out winners for the raffle, he finishes by introducing one of the projects. That's when one of the series of photos gets displayed on the massive screen hanging above the podium. Most people in the crowd turn their heads toward the projection screen to, at least, watch the first few photos. Turns out some of the other reps are pretty decent photographers. One guy turned his photos into comic book panels; one of the girls distorted the images so that only one element is clear and focused.

But when ours comes up, though—people can't help but pay attention. Our words make it impossible to look away. I glance at Johnny, standing at the very back, and he gives me a thumbs-up.

"Wow," Blake says. "It's way more righteous on the big screen."

The three of us start making our way through the people, headed for Tristan and Trent, who stand closer to the front. Tristan's mouth is open, his eyes all wide with amazement, and he points at the screen while catching my gaze.

The very first slide has the title of our project, *The Truth Is*, with Blake's name and mine next to each other, and a mention of a silent partner below that.

Next is a text slide that says: *What's your truth? It probably sucks so let someone else tell it.* That was my idea. The next three photos go by and it gets pretty quiet, because people are seeing the students' faces in the photos first, then the truths appear on the signs they're holding.

Some of the truths are funny and we get some laughs. Like Jill, one of the volleyball girls who hits the tanning salons year-round and who all the guys drool over—her sign says, *I can go days without taking a shower. My mom forces me to wash every three days. Whatever.* Olivia thinks it was someone trying to mess with our project with dumb lies, but I wanted to include it because in this whole school, there are definitely more than a few greasy dirtbags. And we can't post just the emo truths.

Alek is this super-fat kid in grade ten, and he puts weight on sort of like my mom does, so he gets laughed at a lot. His sign says *I know my mom thinks she's prettier than me. I think she's right.* We're getting close to the end. I know because I've been keeping count of how many pictures have gone by. Finally, Blake's pic comes up. Her super amazing self is blown up huge for everyone to stare at. Her sign says *My dream girl? Mrs. Wexler. Definitely a total hottie.* There's a lot of laughing going on, and Mrs. Wexler looks shocked, hiding her red face like she thinks she'll get in trouble for some kid's weird truth.

That's my girlfriend right there.

Pictures slide along. And then there's this super-smart

kid Will from grade nine. He's in a wheelchair, so I can only imagine what people would think his truth is. His sign says, *I cheated on every test I've taken at this school.*

My heart starts beating, because the last photo is next. That means Colby's must be after that. Another sweeping glance of the crowd and there's no sign of Colby or any of his peons. Blake and I exchange looks, and I mouth *Here we go.*

I move to stand behind Olivia, but she doesn't seem nervous. She looks up at the big screen, her hands hanging loosely at her side.

And then he's up there, Colby in black and white. That I'm-better-than-you grin plastered on his face, his legs spread apart, head to the side.

The quote appears.

Olivia smiles to herself.

I walked my butt from North Castlehill to her place just to see her smile—and I'll keep doing it as long as she lets me.

I wait for the quote to change, to turn into something else.

But it's the end slide that comes up. *The truth is, being a student here can mean a lot of things, but we're pretty sure most of you can't handle our truth . . . right?*

People start clapping.

Olivia turns.

"Wait—was that it?" I ask her.

She leans in close. "Yes."

"Wow," Blake says, like she understands.

"But—I don't get it."

"I asked Elliott to give me his truth," she says. Her face

361

is red, and she can't look me in the eyes. "That's what he said about me."

"Elliott," Blake says. "He's such a righteous fellow."

"He seriously walked from his place to yours?" I ask Olivia. "What happened to his van?"

"It's his dad's business van, so he only gets it sometimes—anyway, that's not the point!"

"What *is* the point?" I ask.

Olivia shrugs. "The point is, that quote would never be Colby's—not in a million years—and that's pretty sad. For him."

"Well played. That wins everything." Blake holds her hand up for Olivia to give her a high five. "Oh my god, you guys, we totally rocked that! Did you see Mr. Middleton's face? He is so impressed."

"Our idea was genius," I tell her, before her parents show up. They look so proud of her, Blake's dad with his thumbs-up and his mouth all wide. We wave at each other, and I leave Blake with them.

Olivia starts moving toward our station, so I rush through the crowd to catch up. Everyone goes back to mingling, hitting the refreshments table, going up to meet the mayor, and checking out the anniversary stuff that's on display. People keep swarming our station to flip through our portfolio, especially the ones who missed some of the slide show.

I tap her shoulder and lean in. "Colby's picture—I thought—"

"I realized that it doesn't matter what I say to him—he

doesn't care," she says. "And humiliating someone like that is not really my style."

"Yeah, true."

"I don't care about him getting the message. I don't even care if he ever sees the photo. I have nothing to say to him." She pulls her phone out and gets lost texting for a while. My eyes find Blake and her parents talking with Mr. Middleton, and I wonder where Johnny is.

When Olivia's attention comes back to me, I say, "I can't believe that guy walked all that way—in the freezing cold—just to see you."

"You wouldn't walk across town to see Blake?"

I shrug. "Good point. I totally would."

That's when I spot Johnny standing with a group of older dudes, and Mayor Amit Chandra's got his hand on Johnny's shoulder. Johnny reaches into his back pocket, and next thing I know he's handing his business card to people the mayor points at. My smile is aimed at the ground, and I think how awesome it would've been if our parents had been able to see that. But that's okay, because at least I was here to see it.

FIFTY-TWO

THE NEXT NIGHT, OLIVIA'S OVER TO HELP ME KEEP up with my suspension homework. After dinner, we relax on the balcony, sipping hot chocolate with our jackets zipped tight. The view from here is pretty decent, and it's quiet at night.

Olivia says, "Is Blake a good kisser? She looks it, with those pouty lips."

"She's amazing."

"Because—well, me and Elliott—he kissed me."

"Well, it's about time," I say.

She does her girly little smile that makes me roll my eyes every time. "He did this thing with his tongue—"

"No. Ew. No girl talk. I said no girl talk! Come on."

"Can I text it to you?"

"No! Come on."

"But he takes his tongue and—"

"Olivia! What's your deal, man? You want me to be picturing you two doing stuff with tongues? Stop it. I mean, good for Elliott that he's got some moves. But I don't need the details."

"But this is guy talk. I'm going to share some of Elliott's moves so you can make good use of them on your end. This is, like, bros helping each other out, is it not?"

"No. It's girl talk. And I got my own moves."

I push out of the chair and slide the balcony door to get back to the heat while Olivia offers to text Elliott's move to me again. So I lock her out there. Just for a minute.

"Are you guys arguing again?" Johnny asks as he passes through from the kitchen to his bedroom.

"She's trying to tell me all about the way Elliott kissed her so I can do it to Blake," I explain, while Olivia steps inside.

"Please tell Pen that's guy talk. The sharing of tips to help—"

"No, no. I'm outta here. I don't wanna hear this," Johnny says, covering his ears and heading for the front closet. "I'm gonna be home late. Clean up your damn mess in the kitchen!"

I meet him at the door to lock it behind him. Then Olivia meets me in the kitchen, where we begin to attack the mess we made earlier when we prepared a feast of hot dogs and nachos. Olivia fills the sink with soapy water, and I grab a butter knife to scrape all the crusty cheese bits off the stove.

"I really like this place," Olivia says. "I really hope you end up staying here for good."

"Why wouldn't I?"

"Well, you know how things can be with parents. It can be unbearable, and then just like that, it blows over. That," she says, "or they force you to come home no matter what you want."

"That's not really how it is for me. I didn't just take off because I had a fight with my parents."

Olivia nods, and before she can say anything else, the apartment phone goes off. I rush to the receiver to buzz Blake in.

"You need to leave," I tell Olivia.

She lets the nacho pan drip its excess water over the sink and flashes me her angry eyes. "You could be a little less rude about it, Pen!"

"Listen, it's Friday night and I have the place to myself. My girl's on her way up. Do you understand what that means?"

"I'm not stupid."

"I know you're not. So, uh, you need to go."

She puts the pan down on a dish towel laid out in front of the toaster, then she tiptoes to the living room to find her purse. "Okay, so the tongue thing. Just—"

"Oh my god. Stop!"

She flashes me an evil grin, because apparently she's got a bit of a mean streak. "Have fun."

When Olivia opens the door, Blake's standing there looking good. So, so damn good.

"I'm being kicked out now," Olivia says. "Bye."

Blake laughs and we both watch Olivia gliding down the hall like she's made some grand exit or something. After that it's Blake and me. I'm full of nerves.

She's not nervous, though. She never is about this.

I DON'T NEED RECYCLED kissing tips from Olivia, because I know my girl. I know what she likes. I'm okay with putting most of the focus on her. That's the best part.

"Can I touch you?" she asks, not for the first time this week.

"Yeah . . ." Because we've been at it for an hour and she

knows I'm weak right about now. "Maybe not. I don't know."

She's got almost no clothes on. I'm still in most of mine.

Usually I can get her to stop trying to turn the focus on me by ramping up my game.

"Stop!" she says, pushing herself up on her elbows and pushing my hand away. "What's wrong? Is it me?"

"Ha!" I sit up next to her, trying not to let myself die of shame at being rejected. "As if it could ever be you. You're . . . everything."

"You're everything, too. So, what gives? Are you shy or something?"

I close my eyes even though it's total darkness in here. "That makes me sound like the biggest douche in the world."

She pushes me down and then lies up against me. There's a topless girl against me. I almost wish I wasn't wearing a shirt.

"You know that I know you're a girl, right?" she says. "I'm okay with that. I like that."

"I know."

"So . . ."

We lie there in the dark, and after a while I stop thinking about this naked topless girl against me and start thinking about what she's actually saying.

"Say I was okay with you touching me, but I wanted you to touch me the way you touch a guy—would that make sense?"

"Totally," she says.

And then she's on top of me, and the breath rushes out of my lungs. She grabs my collar, then runs her fingernails down my neck and—okay, yeah, this I'm into. This is—

367

"Damn," I say.

When she holds me—her arms are wrapped around my neck, around my waist—and when her voice is in my ear—it's all just . . . righteous.

FIFTY-THREE

THREE WEEKS LATER, I'M BACK AT MY PARENTS' to help Mom with the Christmas decorations. School's breaking soon for the holidays. Johnny drops me off on the way to Dom's, and he tells me to call if I need to. This is the first time I've been back here without him.

It's been snowing lightly all day, and the air smells clean. The street is quiet and dark. I look up at the window of my room, but there's nothing inside me that makes me feel homesick for it, like I'm glad to be home. Except I do want to see my mom and my dad.

"What's up?" Colby says.

I look over at his house, and now I see him on the porch, the tip of his cigarette glowing red. He's sitting on the railing, his feet threaded through the iron bars to keep from tipping forward into the bushes. He must be waiting for a girl, so he can take her down to his place through the back so his parents don't know.

"Hey," I say.

"So you don't live here anymore."

He's two doors down, and it's like our voices are disturbing the night. Like I've done a million times since I was nine years old, I cross the neighbor's lawn over to Colby's house, except I don't go up the path to the porch.

"Nah. I live with Johnny now," I say.

He nods. "That's cool."

"Yeah."

We stare at each other. I know he's waiting for me to say something, but it's not going to happen.

When his cigarette is done, two drags later, he finally says, "It's kind of crazy how everything played out."

"I guess."

"You guys put my picture up in your project," he says. "Without asking. Isn't that a copyright thing?"

"Maybe. You could try suing us to see what happens."

He gives me this look like he wasn't expecting me to answer that way.

"She made me crazy," he says. "Olivia."

"You could've just been nice to her. You could've just stopped with your crap and tried being decent to her," I say, and he stops in the middle of shaking a fresh cigarette out of his pack to look up at me. "She was already loyal to you. You could've been the same to her. I mean—she had you by the balls, but she let you go."

He gives me an unblinking stare. I lift my head higher. Then he's pulling out a cigarette and slipping it between his lips.

369

"Maybe," he says. "Or maybe I should've just never talked to her in the first place. Because then none of this would've happened."

"Some of it would've still happened," I say.

"Yeah. I guess so."

"You don't get to pretend it never happened, though. She doesn't get to do that. I don't get to do that."

"I forget nothing, okay?" he says. "I might walk away, but I forget nothing."

Maybe to him, that means a lot. But in real life, that means shit. "It's what you do that matters, dude."

He untangles his feet from the railing and climbs off. "Punching you—that wasn't cool. A lot of things weren't . . . cool, you know?"

"Yeah. A lot."

Footsteps echo somewhere to my right, and when I take a look, a girl is coming down the sidewalk. So I take a couple steps back. Colby hitches his chin up at me, and smoke pours out of his mouth. So I take a breath and shrug before turning back the way I came.

I think—if I wanted—it could've been worked out. I could've asked him if he got *Rusted* on Xbox yet. Then we would've talked about that for a while. He would've asked what it's like at Johnny's. And it would've felt regular, just talking.

Instead, I'm walking away.

I wonder what kind of guy he'll end up being once he realizes his rules and his code are total bull. It's not my problem anymore. I got my own code.

JOHNNY PICKS ME UP just after ten. I load a couple bags of my stuff into the cab of the truck, then head back to the house, where my mom's waiting with a stack of plastic containers filled with leftovers.

"You wanna come home, I won't say nothing no more," she says when I'm about to head off. "This is you *casa.*"

Oh, man. It's too much to keep my eyes level with hers. "I'm all right with Johnny, Ma. I'm gonna come visit and hang out more, but I want to stay where I am."

"Okay, okay. You go with you *irmão*, leave *Mãe e Pai*." She rolls her eyes and waves me away with a flick of her hand, and I think she just can't help herself. Because the family will be up next week for Christmas, and my parents will have to keep up this lie about having kicked Johnny and me out for being disrespectful kids. My mom's like me and she doesn't want to look weak in front of other people. And she's like Colby in the way that she has to take hits at other people whenever she feels threatened. That used to make me want to cave and do what she wants. But it doesn't anymore.

I walk away from her. At the truck, Johnny leans over to grab some of the food containers so I can hop into the passenger seat.

"Always with the food, that woman," he says, then he lifts plastic lids to peek at the food and smiles when he sees the fish. "Your girl coming over tonight?"

"Nah. She's rehearsing. And she's freaking out because the Battle of the Bands in less than two weeks," I say. "What are you gonna be doing New Year's Eve?"

"Me and my buddies have tickets to this show," he says. "We're gonna see Drowning in Shadows."

It makes me grin like a douche. "They're really good. I swear."

"They better be." His face changes and he goes, "So how'd it go in there?"

"I was thinking," I say, buckling in. "I'm gonna start paying for the electricity bill."

"The electricity bill?"

"Yeah. You're paying for everything yourself. That makes me a pretty crappy roommate."

"You're not my roommate," he says, putting the food back in my lap. "If I wanted a roommate, I would've let Naveed move in with me."

"Say I pay the electricity bill, though, then it'll make this more worth it for you."

He reverses the truck into the street, then we're off, back to the apartment.

"You just pay your phone bill and do your homework. And clean up after yourself," he says. "And buy your own body wash and all that. That's all you gotta do. And maybe . . . sweep. Those damn dust bunnies. Wooden floors, man."

"What if I give you, like . . . a hundred a month for rent? It's not a lot but—"

"Stop that, man. For real. Where's this coming from?" He pulls out a cigarette and rolls down his window. When I don't respond, he exhales out the window and snaps his fingers in front of my face. "Huh? What's up?"

"Ma wants me to come home. She says she'll stop bothering me if I do," I say. "But I don't want to go back."

"So don't."

"I want to stay at the apartment."

"So stay."

"You won't try to send me back? Say you try to bring a girl to your place or something, and I'm sitting there eating chips on the couch—you're not gonna try to send me back?"

Johnny slows the truck and pulls over to the curb. "I got that second room for you, all right? Listen up, Pen—I swear to god you can relax and stop worrying, because I'm not gonna send you back. Even if you act like a little douche, I won't send you back. Got it?"

"Even if I don't sweep?"

"Unless you start stealing from me, or you do heroin, or hurt animals, you're good."

I nod, and Johnny puts the truck in drive.

While we head home, I think about how when I grow up, I want to be just like my brother. That's the kind of girl I want to be.

ACKNOWLEDGMENTS

THANKS TO . . .

I shall begin my thanks with Linda Epstein, my agent. Linda—you picked Pen and me out of the pile, whipped us into shape, and guided us through the whole book publishing thing. I owe you many, many thanks for being a badass agent. To my editor, Jill Davis—I am so thankful for the awesome experience of working with you. You knew exactly where this story needed to go. It would not have grown into what it is without your expert input and guidance. Mega-thanks to the folks at Harper. First, the Katherine Tegen Books people, including Katherine Tegen and Katie Bignell. Then to the HarperTeen group, including Ro Romanello, Stephanie Hoover in publicity, and Nellie Kurtzman's marketing team, including Bess Braswell, Elizabeth Ward, Julie Yeater, and Sabrina Aballe. I'm insanely proud to be sending this book out into the world through Harper and its badass team of professionals. I am so grateful for HarperCollins Canada and the stellar opportunity to be co-pubbed in my kickass country. Melissa Zilberberg, Cory Beatty, Shamin Alli, Suzanne Sutherland, and Hadley Dyer—plus all the people I met during my visits at the offices: You guys are so welcoming, professional, and enthusiastic, it blew me away. Special thank you to my Canadian editor, Suzanne. I'm so glad the timing of all this brought us together! Thank you to Alexei Esikoff, Mark Rifkin, and Veronica Ambrose: Your thorough copyediting and proofreading skills left me feeling like you've got some kind of superhero powers. Jacket artist Adams Carvalho and designer Katie Fitch: You guys made my book cover kick some serious ass, and I thank you both a million times for that. Malinda Lo, you chose me to be one of your Lambda workshop participants, and then you went above and beyond. I am beyond grateful for all the support you've given me. Thank you for all of your advice and many discussions about Pen and her story. I didn't have to explain—you just got who she is! To Michael Cart, I. W. Gregorio, Lauren Myracle, Sarah Ryan, and Ariel Schrag: It is an honor—and a mind-blowing fangirl experience—to count you amongst my first readers. Thanks for the words! I must thank Julie Anne Peters for writing the book that sparked my love of contemporary queer YA. It's no coincidence that Pen's high school is named St. Peter's. Thanks to my friend Laura Chandra—who I met at the 2013 Lambda retreat—for being the fastest and most thorough beta reader ever. Your feedback was invaluable when it came to rewriting the crap out of this story. I want to thank Lambda Literary and the YA/Genre workshop crew for giving me the opportunity to live amongst queer people for a week (twice!), for the many friends I've made, and for opening my eyes in a million different ways. Thank you to all the writers I've met along the way for the support, the tips, the opportunities to rant, and the many examples of what being a writer can look like. I also have to mention the stellar coffeehouses that allowed me to sit for hours while I wrote, revised, and rewrote—Coffee Culture, Williams Coffee, Starbucks, and the few indie spots I tried out in between. Combined, you were the best office this working writer could ask for. To my family for not laughing at me when I started going around saying I was suddenly a writer, and thanks in advance for buying multiple copies of my book. For real, though, I have the kind of parents who brought me up to believe I literally could go as far as I felt like taking myself—no limits. Maman et Papa, je le sais que vous êtes fiers de moi pour cette idée folle de devenir écrivaine, pis c'est pas mal encourageant, donc . . . merci! And finally, thank you to Melissa Silva for the inspiration, the insider look at all the Portuguese goodness, for reading almost every draft of this story, and for dragging me deeper into gaming, toys, and horror. I <3 you. There would be no Pen if it wasn't for you.

APR 0 3 2017